18889

Albuquerque Academy

D0045865

HUMAN DEVELOPMENT BOOKS:

A SERIES IN APPLIED BEHAVIORAL SCIENCE

Joseph and Laurie Braga, *general editors*

HUMAN DEVELOPMENT BOOKS is a series designed to bridge the gap between research and theory in the behavioral sciences and practical application by readers. Each book in the series deals with an issue important to the growth and development of human beings, as individuals and in interaction with one another. At a time when the pressures and complexities of the world are making increased demands on people's ability to cope, there is a need for tools that can help individuals take a more active role in solving their own problems and in living life more fully. Such information is not easily found or read by those without previous experience or familiarity with the vocabulary of a particular behavioral field. The books in this series were designed and executed to meet that purpose.

DRS. JOSEPH and LAURIE BRAGA, both developmental psychologists, are on the faculty of the Department of Psychiatry at the University of Miami School of Medicine. The Bragas are authors of *Child Development and Early Childhood Education: a Guide for Parents and Teachers* (City of Chicago, 1973), *Growing with Children* (Prentice-Hall, 1974), and *Learning and Growing* (Prentice-Hall, 1975).

HUMAN DEVELOPMENT BOOKS

*Growing with Children,* by Joseph and Laurie Braga
*Growing Older,* by Margaret Hellie Huyck
*Learning and Growing: A Guide to Child Development,* by Laurie and Joseph Braga
*Death: The Final Stage of Growth,* by Elisabeth Kübler-Ross
*Culture and Human Development,* by Ashley Montagu
*Children and Adults: Activities for Growing Together,* by Joseph and Laurie Braga

# CHILDREN
# AND
# ADULTS

# CHILDREN AND ADULTS

Activities
for
Growing Together

**JOSEPH and LAURIE BRAGA**

A SPECTRUM BOOK

PRENTICE-HALL, INC., ENGLEWOOD CLIFFS, NEW JERSEY

*Library of Congress Cataloging in Publication Data*

Braga, Joseph.
  Children and adults.
  (Human development books)    (A Spectrum Book)

  Bibliography: p.
  Includes index.
  I.   Parent and child.      I.   Braga, Laurie, joint author.      II.   Title.
BF 723.    P25    B685         649'.1'019         75-33538
ISBN: 0-13-130351-1

**A Spectrum Book**

Printed in the United States of America

10   9   8   7   6   5   4   3   2   1

*Illustrations by Skip Williamson.*

Prentice-Hall International, Inc., *London*
Prentice-Hall of Australia Pty. Ltd., *Sydney*
Prentice-Hall of Canada, Ltd., *Toronto*
Prentice-Hall of India Private Limited, *New Delhi*
Prentice-Hall of Japan, Inc., *Tokyo*
Prentice-Hall of Southeast Asia (Pte.) Ltd., *Singapore*

WE DEDICATE THIS BOOK TO

*each other,*
*our son Tommy,*
*and*
*all kindred spirits*
*who are friends of children*

To MARGARET GIBSON, this book is devoted to the hope you treasured, for a world in which children could aspire, above all, to grow to be good and loving human beings.

Special thanks to SHIRLEY COVINGTON and MARJORIE STREETER for the high degree of competence and quality you consistently contribute to the production of each Human Development book.

# CONTENTS

# CHILDREN
# AND
# ADULTS

# 1

# Learning and Growing with Children

*We need to feel more with the reason and think more with the heart.*

Ashley Montagu

We have been inadequately prepared and educated for the present we are now experiencing or for the future we face. How shall we prepare our children to cope with the demands of a future we can feel no security in predicting? How can we learn to cope better ourselves?

*Children and Adults* offers some tools to help you help your children[1] learn and grow while you learn and grow yourself. The activities offer an opportunity for you and your children to gain practice in human skills which you need in order to cope successfully with the challenges of the present and the uncertainties of the future.

This book emphasizes the development of human skills to help you and your children each understand yourself and the other better and improve your human relationships. Many of the activities focus on these goals. Some activities in the book are more conventional. They will help you give your children opportunities to learn such culturally expected skills as feeding themselves neatly, using their bodies skillfully, reading, and writing. But,

[1] We will often address the reader as "you," realizing that you may be a parent, other relative, teacher, or simply friend of young children. When we say *your children*, we mean just that. We all, as adults who are concerned about children, take a personal responsibility for every child whose life we touch in these important early years.

1

even these more traditional learning games stress the socio-emotional aspects of the human interactions that are part of each activity.

The activities were designed as (1) guides to how children develop and what you can do to help, (2) catalysts for you to get more in touch with your own growth potential and needs,[2] and (3) illustrations of ways you can make growing with your children an integral part of your day-to-day life.

The purpose of this book is to give you insights and tools to help you and your children grow together. It is obvious that your children need you in order to grow, because they cannot satisfy their own needs or take responsibility for their own survival. You need your children, too, though in a different way.

You give your children nurturance and guidance which makes their healthy and happy growth possible. They provide you the opportunity to grow to be more truly who you are and more fully human.[3] Through serving the needs of another growing human being (observing and responding to them in an unselfish, loving, and unconditional manner), you can fulfill one of your own adult needs. Through investment in your own and another's growth, you contribute to the further development of the human race.

Your children will learn through shared activities with you from (1) the opportunities you give them to practice emerging skills; (2) the model your behavior provides them of ideas, behaviors, skills, and so on to try out for themselves; (3) your responses to their behaviors (reinforcing some through your attention to them and extinguishing others through your lack of reponse or negative reactions); and (4) the pleasure of the interaction with you.

You, in turn, can learn more about children through interactions with them and, from that, about your own essential self. Try to act in ways that you will be pleased to see your children copy. Become involved in the activities enough that you can relax and experience them from your children's point of view rather than from an adult perspective. Through these efforts, you can reawaken the neglected child within yourself, relearn how to be childlike and spontaneous in your approach to living, and rediscover how it feels to be a human being.

[2] We have tried to intersperse discussions of your children's developmental needs with references to your own needs, now and in your own childhood. In addition, we would like to ask you, also, when you're reading, mentally to substitute yourself for your child, to see how those needs we discuss in terms of your child apply to your own development. In particular, think about the internalized "parent" you carry around inside your head as a monitor to your behavior. Ask yourself, as you read, whether that part of you is restricting or enabling your growth (e.g., Are you as understanding of your own mood swings when you're going through a stressful transition in your growth as we've asked you to be of your child's? See page 37 for further explanation). At the same time that you're concentrating on being a loving, supportive caregiver to your child, pay attention to whether you're doing the same for yourself. Be kind to yourself.

[3] Ashley Montagu, *The Natural Superiority of Women*, rev. ed. (New York: Collier Books, 1974), pp. 189, 224.

## UNDERSTANDING AND ENABLING GROWTH

On the following pages are some principles of human growth and development which will help guide you in the activities and in other interactions with your children.

### FIRST, DO NO HARM

Let this be a guiding rule for all your behavior toward your children. Carry it inside your head as a monitoring device, reminding you always to assess before you act whether what you're about to say or do might hurt your children's feelings, interfere with their human rights and needs, impede their growth, or in any other way reflect an absence of concern and respect for them.

One of the most important factors in a good human relationship is trust, trust that your partner will be there when you need him and will not let you down or do you harm, either intentionally or through negligence. The foundations of trust are built in childhood; the capacity to trust in others enough to form meaningful relationships grows from a child's earliest experiences with his primary caregivers. From their treatment of him, he generalizes to the rest of the world and decides whether or not it's a safe and rewarding place to be.

If you internalize the rule "First, do no harm," and use it as a guide, you can insure that your behavior will reflect the loving concern essential for your child to develop a basic sense of trust in human relationships.

### IF I WERE YOU, AND YOU WERE ME

The ultimate test to which you should put all your behavior is whether it conforms to that age-old human rule "Do unto others as you would have them do unto you." Before you say or do something which will affect your child (directly or indirectly), stop to ask yourself "How would I feel if our situation were reversed, if I were she and she were me?" "How would I want to be treated? How did I feel when I was a child and someone treated me this way?" Apply these questions, also, to your past behavior toward your child.

Think back to when you were a child. Can you remember the things you swore you'd never do to *your* children? Do you remember the way you wished adults would treat you, things you wished they'd do or not do? Think about when you listened and when you tuned out, about what made you really mad or hurt your feelings, about the times when you were most happy. Try to keep these things in mind when you're with children.

Sometimes this is very hard. When we are children, we learn patterns of behavior, not just our parts in those behavioral interactions. Then, when we are adults and find ourselves in relationships which resemble those we experienced as children, we automatically "replay" those learned interactional patterns, but this time we play the adult role. In interactions with other adults, we may play any part of the interaction, depending on our partners' role.

None of this is inevitable. We can choose to change our interactional patterns and to behave in ways that are consistent with our own convictions rather than reflecting blind portrayals of roles we didn't choose. It's hard to change, to break out of learned patterns, especially when it means trying out new ways of behaving with which we have no practice and, often, no model. But it's important to try, to examine our behaviors toward children (and adults), identify those which reflect learned habits rather than conscious choice, and change those which are inconsistent with our human values. The Golden Rule is the best guide we have for doing this. By practicing putting yourself in your children's shoes, viewing the world through their eyes, and treating them as you would wish them to treat you, you will grow as you enable them to grow.

## EXPECTATIONS

Examine the reasonableness of your expectations of your children in relation to the Golden Rule. Can you pass your own rules? Can you meet the expectations you have of your children? If not, you should consider modifying your expectations and rules until you can. It really isn't fair for you to demand of your children (or anyone else, for that matter) what you cannot or do not do yourself.

For example, do you insist your children eat all their vegetables? Then you should eat all of yours too. Do you make them always give something new a try before rejecting it? If so, then you have a responsibility to try all the activities you ask them to get involved in. Do you expect them to be polite to people they don't like? Then, you'd better show them through your model that you do the same. In class, do you require total silence and obedience? How would you feel if that were asked of you? Do you talk to your children about being honest, never lying to you or anyone else? Examine your behavior—are you everything you insist they be? It won't work to ask your children to be better than you. You will teach them, through your behavior, what their behavior should be.

After you have examined your expectations of your children in relation to your own behavior, evaluate what is left. Write down the expectations that remain, and look at them. Are they (1) reasonable, (2) fair, (3) sensible, and (4) important? If they pass all these tests, then let your children know what they are.[4] At the same time, talk with them about what their expectations are of you. Be sure to include in your discussion any unreasonable expectations you have of one another. Just deciding they're not important won't automatically make them go away, and it helps for you and your children to know what things may upset either of you if the other does or does not do them.

Putting your expectations of one another into words can help your relationship with your children. You can begin to reduce the hidden feelings of resentment that can build up when one of you does or does not do something that was inconsistent with the other's unexplained expectations. Children typically love their caregivers and want to please them, and adults usually care deeply for the children in their care. Understanding, *clearly*, what the other expects of you can help you and your children meet one another's human needs and express your love for one another more successfully as you both would like to do.

## BEHAVIOR SPEAKS LOUDER THAN WORDS

It is important that your own behavior be consistent with your expectations of your children not only because it is fair; it is also practical. Children do *not* "Do as I say, not as I do." If you want to see a behavior in your children, one of the most reliable ways of insuring that you will is to act that way yourself. If you don't want your child to act in a particular way, don't act that way yourself. The model your behavior provides to your children is one of the most powerful influences that exists on their learning.

You "teach" your children far more by your model than through deliberate instruction. An example of this is language learning. Your children will learn to speak at their own pace, following their own inner developmental "instructions," and you cannot "teach" them to speak any better or faster than is consistent with that developmental timetable. If you try, for example, to get a small child to imitate your way of talking, to substitute it for her own, it won't work; she'll simply "translate" your verbalization into a form consistent with her own level of language production at the time.

---

[4] Clearly, you can only communicate your expectations *verbally* to children who can understand and use spoken language. With your younger children, just try to make sure you are consistent in your expectations and that your expectations are not beyond your children's developmental capacity to meet them. In addition, try to be alert to your young child's unspoken expectations of you. Learn to be an interpreter for him, translating his nonverbal messages so that you and others in his life will be able to be more effectively responsive to him.

However, your *model* is absolutely essential to your child's language learning; if you never spoke to her and around her, your child would never learn to speak herself. And when she does develop language, it will closely resemble your own—in accent, vocabulary, and even in terms of many of the uses to which she puts it in dealing with her own thoughts, the world, and other people.

This same principle applies in all other areas of learning including, especially, the socio-emotional realm. Your children will learn to approach and respond to other people in many of the same ways that you do.[5] Even their emotional "tone" will be strongly influenced by your model—whether they are generally happy or generally somber will tend to reflect your own characteristic emotional tone as well as your treatment of them.[6] Your children's self-concept—how they see and feel about themselves in relation to others—will be a product of their own experiences with the world of people and things as well as the model with which you present them. If you're a person with a strong belief-in-self, your children probably will be too (for other reasons in addition to modeling, but that will be an important contributing factor); if you are filled with self-doubt, you'll teach your children through your model and through your responses to them that reflect your lack of positive feelings about yourself, to feel the same about themselves.

Your role as a model to your children is important to consider in terms of activities also. The best possible approach you can take in many of the activities is to use your influence as a model consciously and deliberately, exhibiting through your behavior actions you want the children to imitate and avoiding behaving in ways you would not want them to copy. For example, when participating in a small group activity, be sure you are equally attentive and positively responsive to all the children, and they will learn from your model to be fair; make sure you never ridicule or belittle any child's response, and the children will learn from your model not to be unkind.

You lead the way in the content of activities, also, by your example. You

---

[5] Clearly, the number of important people a child has in her life who serve as models to her will influence the range of behavioral interactions she will include in her repertoire. She won't act *just like* you or *just like* her mother (although given our present style of childrearing, she will be more likely to resemble her mother behaviorally than anyone else because they spend so much time together in her formative early years). She'll extract behaviors from each parent, from grandparents, siblings, teachers—any important people she admires and wants to become more like—and she will combine them in her own idiosyncratic manner so that she behaves like herself alone.

[6] The effects of modeling on babies' development of personality characteristics within the context of the mother-infant relationship is dramatically illustrated on film in the "Maternal Behavior and Infant Development" film series produced by the Child Development Research Project, City University of New York, New York City, Sylvia Brody, Director, and Sidney Axelrad, Co-director.

give the children a model that they can use as a reference point and goal to keep in mind while they gain increasing skill through practicing. For example, in "Feed the Bear," Two to Three Years, page 140, you show the child how to throw a beanbag or ball into a box: you provide the model. Then, she must practice on her own in order to achieve any competence in the skill. Deliberately and incidentally, in formal activities and in day-to-day occurrences, you continuously serve this function for your children—they see, from your example, something they would like to learn to do; then they pursue that skill in the context of their play until they've mastered it. It's one of the most effective modes of learning that exists. Learn to use it more, purposefully, as a substitute for any less productive and unenjoyable "training" procedures you may be using now.

## ACTION ←→ REACTION

The interaction between you and your children is an important aspect of the learning process. You are not a passive model, and your children are not passive receivers. Each of you is continuously modifying the other's behavior through your reactions to their actions. How you behave toward your children—which behaviors of theirs you pay attention to and which ones you ignore—is a major influence on their behavior toward you and others. At the same time, how they react to different behaviors you exhibit influences the particular behaviors you'll continue to display toward them.

For example, if you smile back at your baby each time he smiles at you and get very excited over his having smiled, it's very likely he will increase the frequency with which he smiles. If your baby quiets his crying and becomes apparently quite content when you pick him up and rock him, you'll be likely to use that technique again in the future when he cries.

You do not create your children's behavior any more than they create yours. What you both do is selectively reinforce some behaviors over others, increasing the possibility of their continued occurrence. You each are capable of a large range of behaviors; which ones will become relatively permanent fixtures in your repertoire of behaviors in interaction with one another depends on your reactions to each other's actions.[7]

It's important to keep in mind the impact your reactions to your children's behavior can have in encouraging them to repeat or discontinue different behaviors. For example, if your little boy brings home a picture he drew in school, and you don't pay attention to him when he enthusiastically asks for

---

[7] This "rule" of human behavior applies at any stage of life in any interaction. Watch yourself, for example, next time you're talking with someone. If the person nods or smiles, you probably will continue what you're saying; if he looks distracted, tells you that your idea is stupid, or in some other way indicates he's not interested, chances are you'll discontinue the conversation.

your approval, or you make some negative comment about it, he may be less enthusiastic about drawing activities in the future; he certainly will be reluctant to show you any more drawings. If, on the other hand, you respond to his enthusiasm with some of your own, he will be more likely to engage in that activity again.

Much "molding" of children's behavior occurs through reinforcement and punishment[8] by you and others. For example, little girls and boys are given nonverbal messages, from birth, about who they can be and what they can do by the way they're dressed, the kinds of toys they are given to play with, and which of their behaviors are encouraged or ignored. Be conscious of your reactions to your children's actions. Be an encourager, not a discourager. Be responsive rather than reactive. Take the time to think about the consequences of your behavior on your children's behavior before you respond. Help your children realize their full human potential by not unthinkingly cutting off their options of what they can do and be.

## THE LONGEST JOURNEY BEGINS WITH ONE STEP

Patience is an essential part of guiding children in growth. Try to remember that children always will grow more surely at their own pace than if you push them to grow at a pace you define. In your concern for what your child will become, don't forget that she's somebody very important right now, and she, unlike many adults, lives in the present, not in the future. So, don't worry about bad habits your child might develop, for example, if you give her the attention she demands as a tiny infant. Needs lose their urgency when they're fulfilled; they don't go away when they're ignored.[9]

Children grow; they need less training for the future and more supportive guidance now. Help your children to grow one step at a time, at a pace that's comfortable enough that each new step can be approached with eagerness rather than with reluctance or fear. Let your children help you learn to live for now, experiencing each new day as a wonderful adventure in being, and thus becoming yourself—not through striving toward some far-off goal of

---

[8] If a person does something, and something pleasant happens to him, he is likely to repeat that behavior. His behavior has been "reinforced." If he does something, and he is ignored or he gets a negative reaction, he probably won't do it again. His behavior has been "punished." (Ignoring is a punishment in the sense that it is a lack of attention; attention is a universal reinforcer, so much so that if the only way a child can get attention is through negative behavior that provokes a negative response, he'll do it; negative attention is preferable to no attention at all.)

[9] You should ignore your child's inappropriate, negative, and nonproductive behaviors; you should not ignore her needs. If she's learned to get attention through negative means, then help her (through showing her and reinforcing positive behaviors) to learn more acceptable means of gaining the attention she needs. But you should not ignore the need that is causing her to behave in a negative fashion.

growth, but rather through making each day a single step on the continuous journey of growth.

## TRUST; YOU CAN IF YOU WILL

Children have a sort of built-in "self-starter" for growing. They need an atmosphere to grow in that supports and facilitates that growth; they do not require a "trainer." You can trust children's capacity to grow in the right direction without your pushing or pulling them. In fact, your intrusion on their natural course of growth, in order to teach or demand of them things *you* deem important at the time, can only interfere with their optimal development.

For example, parents who are content to wait for toilet training until their child essentially is ready to "train" himself generally will have no problem with this developmental step: the child needs a model of what to do,[10] the physiological capacity to control the muscles responsible for holding in and letting go purposefully, the cognitive capacity to recognize when he has to go, and the motivation to assume control of his own body functions. When all these elements are present, he will learn fairly quickly to assume control of his own body functions; until they are present, parents are only training themselves to catch their child at the right time, and they might be creating emotional roadblocks to the child's learning on his own when he's ready.

Enough is known now about how children develop to state with confidence that they do not need to be "trained." They are not uncontrolled, disorganized little savages whose natural impulses must be brought into check in order for them to be fit to enter human society. Children need your guidance and the benefit of your wisdom as a human being who has lived more years than they, but your wisdom and guidance always should be tempered by an understanding of their developmental needs. Your approach should be one of a helpful let-be, knowing when to suggest, when to restrain, and when to simply step back and let go.

For example, in a dramatic play activity, if you have suggested to a child that he be a bird, and he says he'd rather be a butterfly, then you should let him be a butterfly. He'll be a better butterfly than a bird simply *because he chose it.* On the other hand, if your child wants to stay up every night until midnight, but you observe that he starts rubbing his eyes, gets cranky, or shows some other signs of tiredness by eight o'clock, you should apply your own informed judgment of your child's needs (versus his desires) to the

---

[10] Your level of modesty with a two- to three-year-old child should be consistent with what is comfortable for you. You shouldn't make a big deal of being seen in the bathroom one way or the other; it's just a normal part of your daily routine. But if you need complete privacy, then ask an older child to show the younger one how to use the toilet, and you help with the cleanup.

situation. The point is that if you have a basic trust in your children's capacity to "know," from within, what they need in order to grow, and you become adept at "reading" their behavioral cues, then they are your best guide to how to guide them best.

It's very important, also, that you trust children to do things for themselves before they are capable of doing so competently. Becoming competent and responsible for oneself takes practice. The time for your child to get the practice he needs is when he is eager to do so. If you don't allow him to assume any responsibility for feeding himself, cleaning up his room, and so on until you think he's skilled enough to do so competently, you create a conflict of interest. When he wants to do it, you don't want him to, and when you then want him to take responsibility for himself, he may no longer be motivated to do so. If you trust your child to begin doing things for himself when *he* shows an interest in doing so, there will be inevitable mistakes and accidents. But, he will gain skill with practice, and then the task will become a habit.

## "READING" YOUR CHILD

Children "tell" you, through their behavior, what their needs are. A vital element in being an effective caregiver to children is learning to recognize and interpret their messages. The first key to becoming adept at reading children's messages is trust that they do, in fact, have an inner sense of what is right for them. It is important for you to understand this in order to choose consistently to respond to your child's own behavioral feedback and other nonverbal communication of what she needs rather than relying only on some external standard of what you're supposed to do.

### Emotional Needs: Signs to Look For

**Crying.** Crying is a good example of babies' communicating their needs. Mothers have been advised for years to let their babies cry, because (they were told) responding to a crying baby would only spoil him and encourage him to use crying as a deliberate device to gain attention. Recent research[11] has confirmed what any mother knows in her gut—that you should pick up a crying baby. Tiny babies who are responded to consistently when they cry begin to cry less as they grow older and develop more varied means of communicating their needs. It is the baby whose cries are not responded to consistently who continues to use crying as a primary means of gaining

[11] Silvia M. Bell and Mary D. Salter Ainsworth, "Infant Crying and Maternal Responsiveness," *Child Development, 43* (1972), pp. 11–89.

attention; he has never learned to trust that his needs will be met (i.e., that his communications will be answered) *except* after a great deal of crying.[12]

An important finding of this study was that those mothers who responded quickly and consistently to their babies' cries also responded to their babies' other behavioral messages throughout the day. So, their babies (1) were less likely to cry simply out of loneliness and need for attention, (2) did not learn that crying was the only kind of communication that worked, and (3) developed ways other than crying to communicate their needs.

Crying is one avenue through which babies and young children communicate their needs. At different times and in different situations, the meaning of the message is different; but there always is a message that should be responded to. For babies, crying is the only means they have for long-distance communication of distress or some other need; it may serve the same purpose in an older child. In general, a child over a year who whines and cries routinely does so for one of two reasons:

(1) He has learned, through his interactions with others, that whining and crying works; in order to get him to stop, people often give him what he wants. Examine your behavior. Are you paying more attention to your child when he whines or cries than at other times? Do you refuse him things when he asks for them and then give in to him when he starts whining or crying?

(2) He is unhappy. If you have examined your behavior and that of others toward the child and cannot find a pattern of your reinforcing his crying and whining through your attention (positive or negative), then look at his life to see what factors in it might be causing his unhappiness. Are there too many demands on him? Is he expected to be too "grown-up" and responsible, beyond his age, too much of the time? Is he unable to compete successfully with siblings for attention? Does he lack areas in his life that give him feelings of competence and self-worth? Is he lonely?

**Characteristic Emotional Tone.**   Children tell you how they feel by the way they look and act. Happy children laugh and smile and sing and giggle and squeal with delight; they are generally alert and energetic, and they typically have an enthusiastic approach to life. Even generally happy children do go through difficult stages in which their mood tends to be more somber and when they are less in balance than is usual.

But, when a child's characteristic emotional tone can be described as solemn, listless, sad, unenthusiastic, joyless, and negative; and when she engages frequently, and over a long period of time, in "nervous habits" such as rocking, head-banging, facial tics, and nail-biting, that should be a signal to you that she's experiencing some difficulty coping; such behavior is a silent cry for help. Exactly what kind of help is needed depends on the particular

---

[12] No one can let a baby cry forever, so the baby learns that if, and only if, he cries hard enough and long enough, someone will come to his rescue. Children in institutions whose cries are never responded to do stop crying, but then, they stop growing also.

situation, but in general, a relationship with a loving, supportive, attentive adult who is consistent and dependable is helpful to any child who is in psychological distress.

### Learning Needs: Signs to Look For

**Attention.** Children "tell" you through their behavior what they're ready to learn. When you present an activity to your child and get a response of rapt attention, then the task matches her interests and abilities. On the other hand, if her response is one of boredom or frustration—if she's fidgety, her attention wanders, she seems tired and easily exasperated—then the activity and the child are not well-matched. Watch children engaged in self-chosen, self-directed activities for clues to what their learning needs are.

**Time.** Watch how long your children spend at different kinds of activities for further clues both to what's interesting to them and to how long you can expect to sustain their attention with a similar activity. Those activities they spend most time on and return to often should form the top of your list to choose from as source material for your shared activities together.

You should not expect your child to spend as long in a game with you, however, as he spends either on his own or when he's playing with other preschool age children. This will depend, somewhat, on the nature of the game as well as on how good you are at really getting into the spirit of the game as if you were your child's age rather than "teaching" like an adult. When your child's attention begins to wander, leave the game and either go onto something else, or let your child pursue his own interests while you pursue yours.

**Enjoyment and Repetition.** When you see your children engaged in some activity, laughing and squealing with joy, you can be assured they're learning something. If it were nothing more than practice at being happy and involved, that would be sufficient; but you should look at the content of the activity, also, for clues about their learning interests and needs.

If you observe your children playing at the same activity, over and over, you can feel confident that they're learning. Whenever children engage in highly repetitive activities, you can know with certainty that it's satisfying some developmental need. Repetition enables children to practice and consolidate present skills while expanding, extending, and combining these skills to develop more complex skills, thus increasing their level of competency.

Use these growth opportunities your children communicate to you so clearly to join them as a model and partner in development. See, for instance, "Give and Take," Birth to One Year, page 87. This activity is an extension of a game many babies try to recruit partners for on their own toward the end of their first year. It is a good example of using children's own self-initiated activities as a source from which to develop learning and growing activities for you to share.

Try to be alert to your children's communications of their interests and skills. By participating in their self-chosen activities or expanding on them to create new games, you not only help them extend their learning. You also contribute to their feelings of competence and self-worth when you choose to join them in the activities they have invented.

**Questions.** Once children's language skills are sufficiently developed, they "tell" you what their learning needs and interests are by asking questions. The kinds of questions your child asks should give you a good idea of how he thinks and what interests him; the kinds of answers he is happy with should inform you further.[13]

Supply short, simple answers to your child's questions rather than lengthy, complex explanations. In addition, use your child's questions as source material for shared activities. For example, when your child asks about such natural phenomena as the sun and rain and moon, he might enjoy hearing Indian folk tales about how things got to be the way they are;[14] the stories are very animistic in nature and are particularly satisfying to children's ways of thinking about the world.

Children tell you what their learning needs and interests are through the questions they ask, the activities they choose for themselves, and their responses to different approaches you use with them. Children *know*—from within—what they need, and their self-chosen preferences should guide your selection of activities. Choose ones which, though similar in content and process to those they choose for themselves, will take them on to some further learning they couldn't have achieved on their own. In this way, and through the model, companionship, and social interaction you provide when you join your child in play, you will be the best possible "teacher" to him you can be.


## FAMILIARITY BREEDS CONTENT

Children, like all of us, learn most easily when new material is similar to, but just a little different from what they already know and understand. This is best explained in terms of the basic mode of development which characterizes all living creatures: Development occurs through a process of active adaptation to the surrounding environment. This process consists of

---

[13] See "Why?" and "What If . . . ?," Four to Five Years, pages 233 and 235, for explanations of ways of responding to your children's questions.

[14] For examples of some of these kinds of Indian legends as well as sources of others, see Tom Hopkins and Mariana Jessen, *Kindergarten Curriculum Guide for American Indian Children*, Dallas, Texas: Jarvis Press, 1970. This excellent guide is filled with good ideas and humane guidance for providing meaningful educational experiences for any child, Indian or not.

two interrelated parts, *assimilation* and *accommodation*. As a child develops, input from the outside world is assimilated; it is taken in, filtered through, and made to fit with what she already knows. Learning occurs as the child accommodates (alters slightly) her way of thinking, talking, moving, and so on to account for the new input.[15] Thus, in order for the child to be able to learn something new, that new input (information, skill, or whatever) has to be close enough to what she already knows, understands, and can do that she has some internal structure to which she can relate it.

Think back to when you were a child about to enter first grade. If you'd been to nursery school or kindergarten before, then first grade probably was less awesome and scary to you than if you'd never been to any school at all. In the first case, you had something to which to relate this new experience: You'd been away from home part of the day, you'd had a teacher, you'd been with a large group of children, perhaps you'd played with some of the same kinds of materials. But, in the second case, if first grade were your very first school experience of any kind, then everything was new. You had very little to which to relate it, and thus it was hard both to assimilate all the new input and to accommodate yourself to fit this new structure.[16]

This illustrates, on a broad scale, the process that occurs in relation to each and every new bit of learning that is required of children. To the extent that new information is familiar or related to what they know already, it will be easily learned. Learning to use a fork, for example, is much easier for a child who already knows how to use a spoon than it is for a child who has never before used an eating utensil. And to the extent that new information is unfamiliar and unrelated to what children know already, it will be difficult to learn or will not be learned at all. Suddenly being asked to cope with a whole new world of people and objects in a day-care center, for example, can be devastating if, at the same time, a Spanish-speaking child is also required to process all this new input in terms of standard English.

Thus, "Familiarity Breeds Content" is a double message: If the content of activities and materials presented to children is similar to what they already are familiar with, (1) they will be better able to learn, and (2) they will be happier, more comfortable, and more content.

## A BRIDGE FROM HERE TO THERE

Understanding the concept of assimilation and accommodation can help you assess your child's readiness to learn new skills and information.

---

[15] For further explanation, see Jean Piaget and Barbel Inhelder, *The Psychology of the Child* (New York: Basic Books, Inc., 1969), pp. 5–6.

[16] Your adjustment to school, of course, was related also to other factors such as positive or negative associations you had with previous school or school-related experiences.

This is true for both special learning activities and events in his day-to-day life.

For example, you should not expect your child to be able to understand something, follow a direction, or perform a skill that is substantially different from what he knows and can do now. Rather, you should base your expectations of what your child should be able to do now and what his next step of development will be on careful observation and recording of his present level of information and skill in that particular area.

When new information is very different from anything in a child's experience, you need to find an "accommodating mechanism" to help him get from "here" to "there." You can help your child learn something which he cannot assimilate easily on his own by providing a bridge between what he knows already and the new information.

You go through the same process in your own learning. If, in school or on your own, you're confronted with information that is very different from anything you know already, then it's hard to find something in your experience to which to relate it, and it's difficult to learn. If the material is similar to something you know already, then it's much easier to learn. Actively and consciously, or without conscious thought, your mind searches for past experiences and knowledge that you can apply to understanding this new material; you look for bridges from what you know to the new information.

Notice while you're reading this book, for example, which parts interest you and make the most sense. Probably, they are parts which are slightly familiar, that are similar to what you already know, and that have some importance or personal meaning to you. Or, if they're not in themselves familiar, then probably they're examples in which we've tried to provide bridges from what we thought you might have experienced to the information we're presenting. This is what you need to do for children.

You should provide bridges from what your children know and have experienced already to new information and skills. At the same time, you should help them learn to look for their own accommodating mechanisms. In solving problems (whether mundane, routine, or complex), children need to learn to apply search techniques to locate information and strategies from their past experience which they can use as bridges from those previous experiences to the problem situation. For example, a child can be helped to learn to use his own personal experiences of having been bullied or hurt by another person as a bridge to understand how other children feel when he does something similar to them.

## A DIFFERENT WORLD VIEW

Young children don't simply know less than adults and older children; they think differently. As they grow, children add more information and experience to their memory storehouse. New input always is filtered through this backlog, and it is added to it when there's a proper match between the two. By this process, children continuously alter the structure as well as the content of their thinking. For example, in their first year or two, children deal with the world in terms of here and now, concrete reality. They *know* the world only through directly experiencing it. Gradually, as they grow, children learn ways to represent, symbolize, interpret, and store experience (e.g., through words, internalized images of things, and make-believe).

The change in the kinds of new input children can assimilate at different stages of their development reflects this change in their internal mental structure. They most readily assimilate input that is similar in both content and form to their own internalized way of viewing the world at the time. For example, young children's thinking is different from adults' and from older children's in its flexibility; this, in turn, influences what kinds of things they can understand.

Can you remember, for example, being very confused, when you were preschool age, by someone's using a word differently from the way you used it? Can you remember how funny puns became as you grew older and your thinking began to become flexible enough that you could understand the same word simultaneously with two different meanings? The two-year-old's need to have all things stay the same reflects, in part, her lack of understanding that some things that are changed can be changed back again the way they were; to her, when you change the property of a thing, it becomes a different thing.

Be observant of the way your child views the world at different stages in her development, and try to keep your demands of her, your input to her, and your responses to her requests for information or your help consistent with her own structure of thinking at the time.

## IT'S NOT WHAT YOU WANT, IT'S WHAT YOU NEED

There are an unlimited number of things children, and adults as well, may want. But there are a limited number of things human beings actually need, even though they may convince themselves that many of the things they want are necessary in order to satisfy their needs.

An understanding of what human beings'—children's and adults'—needs really are can help you (1) meet your own and your children's needs more effectively and (2) learn to tell the difference between what you want and what you need and help your children do the same. Having what you want does not necessarily get you what you need; and in order to live a happy and productive life, you have to have what you need.

Your needs and your children's are both based in and influenced by your interpersonal relationships, with each other and with other people. They are predictive of the kinds of relationships of which you will be capable in your role as a caregiver to children as well as in other roles. Therefore, it is very important that you examine your own needs in relation to your children's needs so that you can meet one another's needs reciprocally without either of your needs becoming sacrificed for the other's.

Each individual's specific growth needs (i.e., needs that must be fulfilled in order for growth to be possible) are personally distinctive of him, but they nevertheless can be located, in a general sense, within the following theoretical construct which is applicable to any human being, child or adult.[17]

## Physiological Needs[18]

First, and prepotent over all other needs, are physiological needs—sleep, hunger, thirst, and so on. These are the primary motivators for tiny infants and for anyone else who is deprived of them. If the satisfaction of any of these needs is threatened, it will interfere with a person's ability to function on any other level. In caring for a baby, it is not sufficient to satisfy her physiological needs alone. But no other needs will become motivators of her behavior until the physiological needs have been met. A hungry baby, for example, will not be very interested in playing learning games.

## Safety Needs

Safety needs include not only freedom from danger and physical harm but also existence in a secure, stable, and consistently responsive environment, one in which you can predict events because they are routine and familiar and in which you can have some feeling of control. Young babies' safety needs must be met in order for them to figure out how their world works and to develop a sense of trust and belief that they will be cared for and that they have some capacity to make their world respond to them.

Safety needs tend to reemerge in children and adults during periods of significant growth involving major change in responsibilities and demands, and at any time when they feel out of control of their own life. A high level of safety needs is characteristic of children around two and a half years

[17] This "hierarchy of needs" is part of an entire, comprehensive theory of human motivation and personality. If you find the ideas in this section thought-provoking, we would encourage you to look at Abraham Maslow, *Motivation and Personality*, 2nd ed. (New York: Harper & Row, Publishers, Inc., 1970) or any of Dr. Maslow's other work, and at Frank Goble, *The Third Force: the Psychology of Abraham Maslow* (New York: Pocket Books, 1970).

[18] For an explanation of the hierarchy of needs, related specifically to the various stages of young children's growth, see Joseph and Laurie Braga, *Growing with Children* (Englewood Cliffs, N.J.: Prentice-Hall, Inc., 1974), pp. 12–19.

and many adults, too, whose typical stance toward the world is "Do it my way!" [19]

## Love and Belonging Needs

For children and adults whose safety needs are relatively well satisfied, love and belonging needs emerge; these relate to your need to love and be loved by others, to engage in affectionate relationships, and to feel yourself a member of a group. Love and belonging needs should be able to be satisfied, to a great extent, within the context of family relationships, but often they are not. Real love must be given in order to be received; it requires honesty, trust, unselfishness, and commitment; and it must be unconditional (i.e., not contingent on the specific behaviors of the other person). Few adults have the courage to open themselves enough to experience this kind of love with one another.

Your child can be a model and an opportunity for you to practice a truly loving relationship with another human being. Because you are less likely to feel psychologically threatened by a child than by an adult, you can be more yourself, more relaxed, and more spontaneous in your expression of feelings with them. You don't have to worry about children being judgmental or rejecting; they'll just be delighted at your loving efforts.

Loving behavior toward children can be characterized by the dictum: "Ask not what your children can do for you. Ask what you can do for your children." [20] The paradox about satisfying your own needs is that you are most likely to do so through meeting another's needs. If you direct all your efforts toward obtaining satisfaction of your own needs, often neither your own nor others' needs are met. But if you take a "you first" rather than a "me first" attitude, directing your efforts toward meeting others' needs, often your own needs get met too.

For example, if your love for your children is given unconditionally, because you care deeply about them as human beings without regard for their specific behaviors, then your children will love you back and fulfill your needs for love as well. That doesn't mean you don't care how they behave; it just means that your caring for them is not dependent on their behaving a

---

[19] Although a high level of safety needs is expected in young babies and again in children and adults during periods of stress caused by "change overload," an adult whose safety needs were relatively well-satisfied in childhood should be able to adapt to change in most routine situations without major difficulty. When an adult habitually needs to control all aspects of his world and can't cope with variations from his expectations, his behavior reflects that his safety needs never were met sufficiently in his childhood to enable him to grow beyond this point. Unfortunately, this failure to grow is not unusual; the extent to which it is considered by others to be pathological depends on how much control the individual is able to exert over his own life and others. For example, a man who totally controls his wife and children may be considered by some to be perfectly normal. But, although it may be "normal," it certainly is not healthy.

[20] After John F. Kennedy and George St. John.

certain way. If your love for your children depends on their fulfilling your expectations—acting in a certain way that you have defined inside your head as representing love—then you'll satisfy neither your own nor their love needs. They'll feel rejected because they'll feel you don't really love *them*, but that you love merely some idea you have of how they should be. And you'll feel rejected, because your children will never be able to fulfill perfectly your expectations of the way they'd be if they really loved you.

Children need to be loved, completely, consistently, and for themselves, in order to grow and to be able to care about themselves and others. Be sure you communicate to your children how much you really care about *them*, always, no matter what.

## Esteem Needs

Having been able to love and be loved by another, unselfishly and unconditionally, enables a human being to proceed to the next level of need [21]—the need for esteem. Esteem needs can be divided into the need for respect from others and the need for self-respect—to consider oneself worthy and competent.

Parents who are overly concerned that their children "show them some respect" often work against their own needs for esteem from their children by denying their children's needs for esteem from them. In order to be able to show respect for the needs and rights of others, you have to have satisfied your own esteem needs. And in order to develop a feeling of competence and confidence in your own worth as a human being, you first have to have felt, at some time in your life, that others have some respect for you. If you show your children a model of a person who respects the rights and needs of others, starting with them and your mate, then they will learn that model from you. They will not only be able to respect themselves, but they also will show you the respect you need and deserve.

You can observe this in operation with your friends and associates. Those people whom you respect probably are the same ones who respect you, and they're probably better friends than are those people whom you do not respect and who probably also don't have much respect for you. The reason for this has to do with your own "defense of self."

Everything you do can, in some way, be seen in terms of your need to enhance or defend your self-concept. If you think someone has no respect for you, then you automatically rush to your own defense. In doing so, you

---

[21] Even those who have not experienced such "perfect love" will move onto this next level of need if they have been able to experience some kind of love relationship with another human being. But, they will go onto this next stage with some unresolved love needs which they will continue to carry with them and which will continue to affect their behavior until those needs are sufficiently resolved.

necessarily must lessen your respect for that person's judgment, because if she had good judgment, then she'd be able to see your value. (This may be, but usually is not, thought out consciously.) On the other hand, if you feel someone thinks highly of you, then your self-concept is enhanced by her judgment of you. You, in turn, can think highly of her because she fulfills, rather than threatens, your need for esteem.

You can break this cycle by transferring your need for esteem from an outer to an inner focus. If your self-respect depends on other people responding to you in certain ways, it always will be unstable. In contrast, when your feelings about yourself are contingent only on your own carefully considered standards, you can like and respect yourself regardless of others' opinions. As a result, you can then value and respect others for themselves rather than for what they think of, or do for, you. And through your doing this, others will, in turn, value and respect you since you'll no longer be threatening their self-concept.

It's important that your behavior toward your children reflect respect for them as well as for yourself that is not contingent on their respecting you. Because you respect them, your children will respect you; and because your self-respect is based on your own internal valuing system rather than on external standards, including theirs, you can continue to show concern for your children regardless of their behavior toward you. Through the model you provide for them, you will enable them to become, like you, increasingly more intrinsically motivated as they grow older, and more able to go on to the highest level of human need—the one that transcends all other kinds of needs and permits a person's growth to full humanhood—the need for self-actualization.

## Self-actualization Needs

Self-actualization is a lifelong process of becoming increasingly more and more consistently everything that you have the capacity to be. Self-actualizing people, according to Maslow, are a prototype of highly evolved human beings. They are the tip of the iceberg of what can be if factors in developing human beings' personal and social culture permit and support their growth.

At the present time in human history, it is very difficult for people to become self-actualizing. Most people in the world, like most species of animals, operate almost entirely on the basis of physiological and safety needs; they have to put nearly all their energy into just staying alive. For those whose physical environment frees them from such concerns, self-actualization is still difficult because it requires a very strong belief-in-self.

One of the essential characteristics of self-actualizing human beings is their intrinsic motivation. They act as they do because of their own "inner supreme court" that serves as the final judge of all their behaviors. They tend to reject stereotyped role definitions of who they "should" be and what they "should" do, in preference for their own inner definitions of themselves. Most human societies define what is "normal," and thus acceptable, in terms of a fairly narrow range of behavior. Hence, they tend to discourage the development of self-actualizing human beings whose behavior, by definition, differs from the norm.

Self-actualizing persons are characterized by a generalized belief-in-self which, though not invulnerable to outer circumstances that don't support such a feeling, is able to be sustained even through periods of little or no positive feedback from others. They are relatively immune to the need for approval of others and are able to accept praise as well as criticism without its affecting their self-concept. This is in distinct contrast to most other people, whose substantial needs for approval from others results in their self-concept being dependent on external feedback. The "extrinsic motivation" fostered by society directs people to look outside themselves for self-definition.

A self-actualizing human being is freed to be concerned about others in terms of *their* needs, since she is not concerned about them in terms of what they can do for her, what they think of her, or how they feel about her. She can "rise above herself" and put herself in someone else's shoes to see things from his perspective. Because she is not afraid of others' response to her, she can direct her energies into doing for others what will make them more comfortable rather than trying to act in ways that will make them approve of her. Her general life-orientation is characterized by continuous growth toward increased self-actualization and increased humanity toward others. She is cooperative and concerned with others' needs rather than competitive with them to meet her own needs.

If this all sounds familiar, it is because this "ideal" of adult growth closely resembles the exemplary caregiver to children we have urged you to try to be. In order for children to be able to begin their life-long journey toward self-actualization, they need a caregiver who will permit and support their growth at the same time she presents them, through her behavioral example, with a humane and loving model of a human being who, herself, is continuing to grow to become all that she can be.

## Now I Know Who I Will Be When I Am Truly Me

Only a small proportion of the total population of human beings alive today can be characterized as self-actualizing in the sense that their generalized approach to living reflects a transcendence of the lower needs, an overall strong belief-in-self, a clear understanding of who they are in contrast to the outside world's definition of who they should be, and a continuing commitment to their own and others' growth to self-actualization and full humanhood. However, every human being has the capacity to become self-actualizing; and many people have experienced periods—what Maslow has termed "peak experiences"—in which they have felt what they could be like were they really to become themselves.

Peak experiences offer you a glimpse of what *can* be. They should serve as a beacon to you in your growth. They are those rare and wonderful moments when everything about yourself and your life seems very clear; when you feel as if you're standing one step back and viewing yourself in realistic perspective unclouded by your ordinary concerns; when you feel at peace with the world and understanding of others as having the same kinds of needs and hopes and fears as you; when you feel a great surge of energy and capacity to do whatever you set your energies to; when you feel a sense of joyfulness and exuberance at the opportunity to be alive; when you are able to focus on and rejoice at all the things you have (e.g., a functioning body, people who care about you, food to eat) rather than bemoan the things you lack; in sum, when you understand your purpose on this earth.

Unfortunately when people do not understand the meaning of these peak experiences, they may become very disappointed and discouraged that they can't sustain them. They may expend their energies attempting to recapture the experience. But, it's very difficult to make that kind of dramatic jump from where you ordinarily are in your day-to-day life and where you were during a peak experience. The learnings gained from such an experience must be integrated into your daily life, and that ordinarily takes time.[22] Your growth, just like your children's, proceeds step by step by step. Use your peak experiences as a shining light along the path of growth to show you the way and where you're headed. Then commit yourself to the long and sometimes difficult journey there.

## The Desire to Know and Understand

There are a few more needs which Maslow has identified as being important to human beings' development, though he was not able to establish them as being basic needs in the same sense as the ones we've already discussed.

First, there is the desire to know and to understand. This lies at the basis of human beings' quest to figure out how the world around them works and what their place in it is. Babies and young children are the best illustration of this human need. Without any pushing or prodding, a healthy baby will

[22] With help and support from caring individuals, people who are dying sometimes are able to grow dramatically in very short periods of time, simply *because* they understand the finiteness of their time left, and they use it all productively. Elisabeth K. Ross's volume, *Death: The Final Stage of Growth* (Prentice-Hall, 1975) explains this and offers insights and tools to help all of us, no matter how much time we have to live, learn to grow through acceptance of the finiteness and unpredictability of our existence on this earth, urging us not to postpone really living until our time is nearly up.

spend endless amounts of time exploring the world around her, testing herself against it. Young children continue, if their other needs are met sufficiently that they feel safe enough to do so, to experiment on and investigate the world of things and people, looking for meaning and the system underlying all of it and finding out where they fit.

## Aesthetic Needs

The other category of human need comprises the aesthetic needs—the need for beauty, symmetry, harmony, and order. This is related both to a need to experience such beauty in nature and the need to reproduce it in our surroundings. The lack of beauty in one's life can lead to sickness—a feeling of isolation and alienation—just as can the lack of safety, love, esteem, and opportunity for self-actualization. We can see the expression of this need more clearly in children than in adults, who may have learned to deny and submerge it. Children find beauty and wonder in the world, and they seek it out as well as try to reproduce it themselves through their own creative self-expression.

## Needs and Growth

There are several interrelated principles that will clarify further the relationship between your own and your children's needs and the growth of you both: (1) The path of growth may be viewed as parallel to movement to increasingly higher need states; (2) a person will advance to higher levels of need through the satisfaction of preceding needs; (3) needs are urgent, insistent, and growth-prohibiting to the extent that they are not met; but, (4) a need loses its potency and importance as a motivating factor of a person's behavior once it has been sufficiently satisfied; and (5) human beings are inherently growth-oriented; they will continue throughout their life span to move steadily in the direction of growth as long as their environment and experiences permit and support their growth, i.e., enable their needs to be fulfilled.

In the ideal circumstance, human development is characterized by a steady, regular, and natural progression through these levels of need while still in early childhood, thus beginning at an early age the lifelong process of self-actualizing. Though different needs might reemerge at different stages to be dealt with again on a higher level, with a greater degree of consciousness, once having been relatively well satisfied in early childhood, they will lose their sense of urgency, and the individual's energy can be directed primarily toward continuous growth.

In reality, however, many people—even those who appear to be "well-adjusted" and successful by extrinsic standards—still have many enduring needs left over from their childhood which interfere with their growth as human beings.[23] To the extent that this is true, the individual will be inhibited in his ability to relate to others in terms of their needs instead of his own. He will feel a need to be "in control," of himself, his environment, and other people, and he will be motivated more strongly by a desire for others' concern and respect for him than out of his own concern for and commitment to them. His own unmet needs will diminish his capacity to open himself to, trust, and care for another human being.

It is clear, therefore, that in order for you to be able to meet your children's needs successfully—so that they can grow to be all that they have the capacity to become—you will at the same time have to make a commitment to your own growth. For, to the extent that you have unmet physiological, safety, love, and esteem needs that motivate your behavior, you will be that much less able to respond to your children, freely and without resentment, in order to meet their needs.

But, *you can grow with your children*, growing as they grow. You can gain insights about your own unmet needs through observing your children in different stages. You also can begin to satisfy some of those unmet needs through finding ways in which your needs and your children's are congruent rather than conflicting. For example, through giving your children unconditional love, you enable them to love you back, thus fulfilling some of your own love needs. Through taking pride in the value—above all other roles in life you may assume—of giving love, nurturance, support, and guidance to another growing human being, you can satisfy some of your esteem needs; this is true whether you are male or female, despite the fact that the culture does not value child caregiving as highly as many much less important life-roles. Most of all, through the very practice of trying to be a loving, supportive caregiver to your children, you will grow, to be ever more consistently all those things and more of what is truly you.

## UP IS DOWN

There are many things in life that really are upside down from what we've been taught to believe; in order to enable our children and ourselves to grow,

---

[23] Typically, most people's needs are met to some extent in their childhood; if they were not, they would not grow at all. But, usually, their needs at each level are incompletely satisfied, so that they continue into adulthood to be plagued by partially unresolved physiological, safety, love, and esteem needs. Most behaviors that most people exhibit, therefore, are multimotivated, i.e., motivated by several needs simultaneously. For example, a person may strive to make a lot of money (1) to ensure his physiological needs will be met, (2) to give himself feelings of security (safety needs), (3) to gain friendships and membership in a certain group (love and belonging needs), and (4) to earn the respect of others and feel that he is a worthy person (esteem needs). Only the behavior of the self-actualizing person (who, by definition, has sufficiently satisfied his lower needs to grow beyond them) is more or less singly motivated, by the need to grow to become more aware of and consistent with his own inner standards.

it's important that we begin seeing things in more accurate perspective. Most important of these has to do with our basic beliefs about ourselves as human beings. There is a generalized belief that human beings are inherently destructive, evil, competitive, disorganized creatures who require the rigorous training of civilized society to turn them into respectable, responsible citizens. The opposite is true.

Human beings are, in reality, basically good, cooperative creatures whose species' characteristics include educability, plasticity, and the capacity for continual growth and transcendence. They are highly organized organisms who will, if their environment and experience supports their growth, grow in a positive direction toward increased cooperation with their fellow beings at the same time they develop as unique individuals.[24]

Unfortunately, however, the very same characteristics which make human beings capable of such development toward full humanhood also make them vulnerable to distortions of their personalities to become, at best, only a small proportion of what they could be, and at worst, the self-fulfilling prophecy of all the dire predictions that have been made about them.

It is the upside-down thinking of human cultures and the actions such thinking has produced that are responsible for human beings having become the destructive, selfish, competitive, distrustful, frightened, and insecure creatures that too many of them are. By not recognizing human beings' inherent tendency toward growth and acting in opposition rather than in harmony with their natural inclinations, human cultures have served, nearly universally, to suppress rather than enhance the development of human beings.

This has happened more often through blind acceptance by well meaning people of what was passed down to them through the models of their elders than through deliberate action or malicious intent. Human cultures are made up of individual human beings. And just as people have created cultures which do not support the growth of human beings, so we can create a culture which will be consistent with and supportive of the best in human beings.

Such an enormous undertaking never will come about as a result of a mass movement. It can be done only by individuals who each make a personal commitment to their own growth and the growth of their children and the other human beings with whom they interact. And, it will take an act of faith and commitment to what will be beyond your own life span, because such change will take many generations to be extended significantly beyond the confines of individual families. But, it is possible. And it is essential if human beings are to survive.

[24] For a fully documented explanation of this fact, see the works of Dr. Ashley Montagu. *The Humanization of Man* (Cleveland, Ohio: The World Publishing Company, 1962), *The Direction of Human Development* (New York: Hawthorn Books, Inc. Publishers, 1970), and *Culture and Human Development* (Englewood Cliffs, New Jersey: Prentice-Hall, 1974) are just three of Dr. Montagu's many outstanding volumes which deal with this subject from a multitude of perspectives.

Much of what is required has been discussed already. Primary is the understanding of developing human beings' need for love in order to grow. It is the inability to receive and express love—to experience that essential human bond of committed caring—that causes the distortions of human personalities we see too much of today. Lack of love causes fear of others and anger toward them; it creates an approach toward others as objects rather than as human beings like oneself. In fact, people who have never been loved are essentially self-less. Without love, the self cannot develop; and a counterfeit, loveless self can have no compassion for others since no one had it for her; having never had a model and the experience of being loved, such a person cannot love herself or others.

In *Culture and Human Development*, Dr. Montagu explains the devastating effects of a cold, unloving, and unresponsive environment on children; in extreme cases, they may become physically and intellectually as well as socially and emotionally retarded. These are dramatic illustrations of what can happen to human beings when they are denied the loving care they require to grow. We must take the message communicated so persuasively by these children's example as a clue to the perhaps more subtle and less obvious impact unloving and inadequately supportive environments are having on a much larger population of children. And, we must, as individuals, do what we can to help the children in our care—to give them love so they can learn to love themselves and others now and in their own adulthood.


## BEHAVIOR MANAGEMENT: HANDLE WITH KINDNESS [25]

A further illustration of "up is down" can be found in relation to traditional disciplinary practices with children. Many genuinely well-meaning and caring adults, either through blindly acting out the behavior toward their own children that they learned through the model of their parents' behavior toward them or by following misguided advice about how to "train" children, end up reinforcing and even creating the very behaviors they are trying to get rid of.

For example, when you hit a child in order to punish her for hitting another child, you teach her instead that physical aggression is an acceptable behavior. In getting angry at a child for anything, you call attention to the behavior you are intending to eliminate by your punishment. Any time you pay attention to a behavior, whether you consider the attention positive or negative, you reinforce that behavior and increase the likelihood you'll see it again. This is especially true if you pay more attention to a child when she's doing something wrong than when she's behaving acceptably; she probably

[25] A more extensive discussion of behavior management principles and techniques can be found in J. and L. Braga, *Growing with Children* (Prentice-Hall, Inc., 1974), Ch. 6.

will increase the negative behaviors in order to increase your attention to her.

Strong negative reactions to your child's behavior—yelling, spanking, slapping, hitting, and other forms of physical or verbal punishment—*may* be effective in temporarily stopping her from what she's doing. But, they have other drawbacks that, in the long run, are far more serious than whatever her offense was. When you administer a harsh punishment to a child (or adult), you cause her to become angry and afraid of you. When people experience these unpleasant emotional reactions, they will seek to escape from or avoid the source of those feelings—in this case, you, as well as the situation.

This is obviously an undesirable consequence because you don't want your child to come to associate unpleasant feelings with you and thus seek to avoid you. In addition, to the extent that you provoke these kinds of negative feelings in your child, you will be that much less able to be effective as a teacher to her. And, in the long run, you would be far better at helping your child to learn to behave appropriately through your model and through calm and kind forms of teaching than through aversive punishment.

Behavior management should *not* be punishment for misbehavior. Rather, its focus should be to help children assume increasing control of and responsibility for their own behavior as they are capable of doing so. Thus, with very young children, you should use a combination of (1) preparation of the environment to remove potential sources of problems, (2) distraction of the child from the problem, and (3) removal of the child from the problem-causing situation. It's not necessary or productive to punish a small child.

As children get older and can understand language, you should use problem situations as opportunities for learning. We all make mistakes and we often repeat them, but with help, your children will repeat their mistakes no more than the couple of times necessary for them to remember, before they do something, not to do it. There's no better time to teach somebody something than when they've just done something wrong.

Remember when you were a child and you got caught doing something you shouldn't have been doing? You never were more willing to pay attention to your parents or teacher than when they confronted you with some wrongdoing, *if* they did not put you on the defensive. If they were compassionate and forgiving and simply explanatory of what the problem was and why it happened, you were so grateful that they didn't get angry, you'd do anything they said. Remember this with your children.

You remove the possibility for learning of *internal* controls when you punish; in fact, you interfere with the child's learning, because when you get angry at her, she *must* defend herself internally. So, while you're trying to teach her some lesson through spanking her or telling her how terrible her behavior was, she's very busy inside her head, excusing herself and erecting her defense, telling herself she's not really *such* a bad person, and what she did wasn't really *so* awful. Can you remember doing that when you were a child—blocking out the wave of abuse by psychologically "escaping" inside yourself? Next time you start to punish your child, think first about how you used to feel when you were punished and what it really taught you.

As a general rule, *pay more attention to the things your children do right than to the things they do wrong.* Reinforce, through your attention and by your model, the behaviors you'd like to see more of, and ignore (as long as they're not hurting anyone) the behaviors that are negative and disruptive ways of getting attention. Don't ignore your child if her behavior is clearly "a cry for help," as misbehaviors often are. Find out what the problem is, and try to help her find more productive ways to get your attention in the future.

Let your "punishments" simply be the natural consequences of your child's actions. If she breaks a toy, it's punishment enough to lose the toy without your adding to it.[26] If she does something to upset you, your being upset is enough without your doubling the effect by getting angry over her having upset you. If your child spills something, the natural consequence is that she has to clean it up; there is no place for anger or making her feel bad because she was careless or clumsy. Through experiencing the natural consequences of mistakes, children will learn faster not to repeat them than if they also have to deal with the emotional overlay of your having gotten upset at them for whatever they did.

If your child does something to hurt someone else, remove her from the situation and give her a "time-out" to consider the reason for her behavior. Talk with her after her time-out to find out what her reason was, and try to help her develop better ways of getting what she wants or to express herself than striking out. Remember, when you're dealing with an aggressive act, that aggression breeds aggression. Only through your model of calm, acceptance, kindness, and reason will you teach your child to substitute those behaviors for her aggressive ones.

Quite a few of children's "misbehaviors" are nothing more than bad habits they have developed in interaction with others who reinforce their continuing to act in those ways. Therefore, in order to change your children's behaviors, you have to change your own toward them. For example, if your child whines every time she wants something and cries if she's refused, you probably are reinforcing these behaviors by not giving her what she wants when she asks and then giving in to her when she starts whining or crying.

In this case, or in any other like it in which your behavior is clearly reinforcing your child's, you can change hers by ignoring the behaviors you want to get rid of and paying attention, instead, to behaviors which are acceptable and incompatible with the undesirable ones. For example, when your child asks you for something, if it's a reasonable request, give her what

[26] If you're sympathetic about your child's loss, she's far more likely to really hear you when you explain, calmly and with kindness, that this is why you asked her to be careful than if you yell at her or in some other way make her feel bad for having broken her toy.

she asked for. Consistently refrain from responding to her when she tries to gain what she wants by whining or crying. If she understands language, explain to her that you're tired of the two of you causing problems for each other as you have been, and that you are going to try to do things differently and you would like for her to try also. Explain that when she wants something, she should ask for it. If you say no, you mean it. If the answer is yes, then you'll give her what she wants *if* she asks for it in a reasonable way. Then, do what you say, and do it *consistently*.

Avoid "win-lose" situations in which a problem is easily predictable. Try to anticipate the problem, and change your behavior before it happens in order to avoid it. If you can't, and you do end up with your child whining or crying to get something she wants (not something she needs), then just ignore her and do not give in to this kind of communication. Remember, in this situation, as in any other, however, to be kind and understanding. This problem is not just your child's; the two of you created this kind of interaction together, and you must end it together also so you can begin to relate to one another in a more human and mutually responsive way.

This same principle applies to any other behaviors your children have which you find annoying or which are, in some way, interfering with your relationship. Dawdling, playing with food, not responding to you until you tell them something ten times, even hitting a sibling or taking his toys, are all examples of behaviors which can develop and continue because you pay attention to them. Start paying attention to your children's good behaviors more than to their "bad" ones. Teach them more acceptable behaviors to replace their unacceptable ones, and ignore those that are just annoying, but which don't hurt anyone.

## SELF-CONCEPT: THE SCRIPT FOR THE PLAY

The early years of a child's life form the foundation upon which all the rest of his experiences will be built. He learns the fundamentals of the basic human skills from which all future skills will be derived. For example, he learns to move on two legs, use his hands as tools and in the use of tools, use language for communication with others and as a tool for thinking, think symbolically, and become aware of himself in relation to others.

Growth of the child's self-concept is the most important of all the areas of his development in this period, because it underlies and pervades all the rest. It influences and is influenced by every other of the child's growth. As a child becomes increasingly more conscious of himself in relation to the rest of the world of people, things, and events, it's imperative that his concept of who he is reflect a generalized belief in himself and in his capacity to be effective and successful. The set of feelings he develops about himself in his early years, as he learns who he is and what he can do, will become a filter for the rest of his life experiences. This "filter" will greatly influence the child's approach to situations as well as his interpretation of them.

The following pages summarize the major developmental changes children go through in developing a sense of who they are in relation to the rest of the world. Notes are made of the kinds of care and attention children need at different stages in order to enable them to develop a strong and healthy self-concept.

## Who Am I?

When a baby first enters the world, she has no self-concept. She doesn't even know there's a "me" that's separate from other people and things; she experiences herself as a part of all that surrounds her. Gradually, the baby learns to distinguish between "what is me" and "what is not me." She learns to make this distinction through such experiences as: feeling the difference between biting her own toes or fingers and biting her mother's breast or a toy; watching her own hands as she moves them in front of her face, slowly learning that she can control their movements herself, and comparing that visual "event" with those not in her control such as the people who come and go in front of her and the things around her that never change; finding out that *she* can make things happen (move her own body, reach out for and grab a toy, make a bell ring by kicking a hanging toy with a bell inside it, get people to come when she "calls," get someone to smile by smiling at them, and so on).

A baby's finding out that she can have an effect on the world is an important part of her developing a strong self-concept as someone who can have some control over events in her life. You can foster your baby's development of such a feeling of mastery and self-confidence through (1) being personally responsive to her. Develop an effective system of communication with her from earliest infancy. Let her have control and direction in as many areas as possible. For example, when her nonverbal signals tell you she's had enough to eat, don't force her to eat more. Go to her when she cries. Smile back at her when she smiles at you. Talk back to her when she babbles at you; and (2) providing her with opportunities to test out her competencies. For example, give her interesting things, in her bed and other places she spends time, to practice looking and reaching. Give her room to move around on her own when she's ready. Provide her with materials to investigate and manipulate, to practice her developing skills with her hands.

Further, it's important that you be aware of the feelings you communicate. Babies experience all that happens around them at first as if it were a part of them. Your baby will absorb your anger as well as your joy and "make it a part of herself." Try to make her feel that the world around her is a good place to be and that she is loved.

The most important thing when your baby begins to discover that she is not a part of the world around her—that she is a separate individual—is that she does not find at the same time that she is alone. As the baby's consciousness increases, and she begins to develop enough memory about the surrounding world that she can tell the difference between what is familiar and what is not (usually in the second half of the first year), it becomes increasingly important that she feel secure and loved so that the transition from connected to separate being is a comfortable one.

## Shifting Gears

When babies begin to be able to get around on their own, and they develop the ability to assert themselves in word and deed, they present a new challenge to their caregivers (who usually are just beginning to become comfortable and competent caring for a dependent infant when they suddenly are required to shift gears). Now babies begin to need (and demand!) "room to grow in," socially and emotionally as well as in other areas. The baby's very natural attempts to conquer his new-found world are often in conflict with his caregivers' very understandable sense of concern for their baby's safety as well as for the order of their lives that is suddenly disrupted by this adventuresome little human being.

The period between about ten and eighteen months is truly a test of caregivers' flexibility, understanding, patience, and good humor. There simply is no way to make a baby this age conform to the needs and desires of one or more adults without a substantial sacrifice of his capacity for happy and healthy growth. You cannot keep a baby in this stage continually barricaded by fences, a playpen, or a continuous barrage of NO!s and still enable him to develop the skills he will be able to develop if he has the opportunity to practice exploring and investigating, within *reasonable* limits, the world around him. Competence and responsibility, two qualities babies this age are short on in comparison with their enthusiasm for exploration, require practice (like any other skill) in order to be learned.

Therefore, as an investment in your baby's happy and healthy growth now and in the future, you will need to make a few sacrifices in your life style until he's learned more responsible behavior. For this period of time, it will be necessary to "baby-proof" your environment, removing anything that he could hurt himself with or which he could damage. In addition, you should try to be accepting when, in spite of all your precautions, problems do occur. Be understanding that your baby's behavior is not malicious; it's only a bit overzealous. Be flexible about the condition of your living environment during this period, because it's very hard to keep a home neat and clean with a baby this age. Finally, prepare yourself for some "mock-battles" as your baby tries out his growing capacity to assert himself. If you don't take it too seriously, he'll soon establish his place in the world without so much need for negativism.

## From Babyhood to Childhood

In the period from eighteen months to three years, children become increasingly self-conscious. They gradually begin to recognize that they are not the center of the universe, that the world does not revolve around them, and that they do not have the power to command the attention and services of all who surround them. This end to their reign as monarch of the family can be comfortably counterbalanced by a gain in competence and independent action that enables a child to feel good about her ability to do things for herself rather than being dependent on others to do them.

The problems arise in this period, however, when the loss of pseudo-power (i.e., the ability to command others to do their bidding) that typically accompanies the end of babyhood is compounded, as it too often is, by increased demands and restrictions upon the child (e.g., to be toilet trained, to feed herself neatly, to share with others, not to destroy other people's possessions).

By three years, most children are aware enough of themselves in relation to others that they can learn to act with consideration for the property and personal rights of another. But before that, you'll save yourself and your child a great deal of aggravation and hurt feelings if you don't expect her to be too considerate of the rights and needs of others. Try to arrange the environment (e.g., see "A Space of My Own," Two to Three Years, page 144) so that your child is allowed to have some things *her* way, and limit your demands of her to those which are reasonable and necessary. She's still as much baby as she is child, and too many demands will interfere with rather than encourage her growing more responsible.

This can be a stressful period of time for children, characterized by swings from high to low, reasonable to unreasonable, assertive to dependent, and "mature" to infantile. Understanding this, you can guide your children comfortably through the transition from babyhood to childhood so they emerge feeling good about themselves and the world around them.

Unless you pay too much attention to negative behaviors, your child is in no danger of staying habitually the way she is in her low moods (e.g., whiny, tantrum-prone, overly clingy and demanding). Nor is she yet capable of sustaining her behavior as it is when she's in her high moods (e.g., responsible, helpful, "grown-up," reasonable). With your patient, loving support, your child will gradually decrease her negativistic outbursts and infantile behaviors and increase her positive acts of self-assertion and mature, autonomous behaviors. Thus, she can emerge from this period with feelings of self-respect and the assumption that others respect her too.

This period is very important in children's lives because the basic structure of the "script" of each child's life takes shape during this time. ". . . the self-picture is fairly well integrated by the third year of life. Once it has developed, it becomes the evaluator, selector, judger, and organizer of future experience, and the child's behavior may be seen as organized to enhance and maintain his view." [27] Help your child enter into consciousness with a positive view of herself and the world.

## Enter into Consciousness

Dr. Maria Montessori[28] speaks of age three as the dawning of consciousness. It is the boundary between the unconscious creation of basic functions that occurs in the child's first three years and the conscious development of skills (through the integration, extension, and expansion of those basic functions) for acting deliberately on the world that occupies the next three years.

"Only with the advent of consciousness do we have unity of the personality, and therefore the power to remember. . . . At first, [the child] was guided by an impersonal force seeming to be hidden within him; now he is guided by his conscious "I," by his own personal self. . . ." [29] If you think back to the earliest clear memory you have, it probably is not before three years. Until you have a consciousness of your self, there is nothing to which to relate memories. You cannot remember what happened to "me" until you are conscious that there is a "me." All memories after this point, like all actions, are in terms of the self. The child's (or adult's) self-concept has become a filter through which his experiences are filtered and interpreted so that they reflect and reinforce what the person feels and believes himself to be.

For example, children who enter consciousness with generally positive feelings about themselves will tend to be confident, competent, happy, and friendly toward others. These qualities are likely to make them successful with the world of people and things which, in turn, will feed back positive feelings to them about themselves.

In contrast, children who enter consciousness with negative feelings about themselves—who do not respect themselves or feel that others respect and care about them—will tend to act in ways that reinforce these feelings. Their self-doubt will interfere with their effectiveness with people and things. Their lack of security about their capacity to be successful will block their efforts and contribute to their failure to succeed. These negative experiences, in turn, will feed back further negative feelings to them about themselves.

[27] Ira J. Gordon, "The Beginnings of the Self: The Problem of the Nurturing Environment," in Braga, *Growing with Children*, pp. 97–104.

[28] Maria Montessori, *The Absorbent Mind* (New York: Dell Publishing Co., Inc., 1967), Chapter 16.

[29] Ibid., pp. 166–67.

It doesn't have to be this way, but changing it takes the special, loving efforts of another human being. That person will have to work hard to insure that such a child is able to be successful at what he tries and that he receives caring and respect from others despite the behaviors he exhibits which cause people to respond negatively to him.

Please take the time to give some positive attention to these children who need it so desperately—children who were not fortunate enough to make it through their first years of life with good feelings about themselves as worthy human beings. You can help salvage them, whatever age they are, if you care enough. If you don't, then maybe nobody ever will. And unhappy children grow up to be unhappy adults who not only are unable to contribute constructively to their world, but who may be quite destructive in "payment" to all those who didn't care enough or weren't willing to take the time to show them some loving, human concern when they were children.

From three to four years, if their experiences up to this point *have* supported their growth, most children are becoming aware that other people have needs and feelings as they do. They are becoming able to empathize with others who experience something similar to their own experiences. They are learning to share objects and attention with others, to cooperate, and to take turns. In other words, they are becoming able to take their places in the human social order. Give children positive reinforcement when you observe them behave in ways that reflect awareness, concern, and thoughtfulness for other people's feelings, rights and needs. In this way, and by providing a model for such behaviors by your own example, you can help children continue to grow increasingly more human.

Children in this age group who seem to have problems playing cooperatively with others may have unmet needs that prohibit them from growing to this point as well as learned habits of doing things their own way. They may never have had any practice sharing time, attention, and possessions with another child. For whatever reason, they will need your help and patience to be led from whatever level they are at, one step at a time, to a point that they can begin to become more responsible for their own behavior. It doesn't matter how old a child (or an adult) is who is functioning on an "unconscious" level socially and emotionally. Whatever age they are, you have to begin where they are and help them, slowly, to grow at a pace that's comfortable enough that it can be pursued with delight instead of fear.

## I Can Be Anything You Can Be

From four to five years, children are continuing to try to define their place in the world around them. They're full of questions about the world and other people, usually both in relation to themselves. They wonder what it would be like to be different people. They spend time in dramatic play pretending to be people they know and have seen, as if trying on different roles to see how they fit. All of this is part of children's finding out what is consistent with their own self-concept and what is not. They try out different behaviors, preferences, ideas, mannerisms, and so on, and they assess which ones feel right for them to adopt and adapt to themselves. As the year goes on, children are becoming increasingly more conventional in their behavior, adapting their behavior more and more to fit with their cultural norms.

Children this age take modeling an additional step into consciousness. They further define their own self-concept through *identification* with others whom they admire and resemble in some way. They align themselves with their identification figure and try to act in ways that will make them more like her. An identification figure may be a parent, teacher, older sibling or other child, or just a friend. At this age, the person probably is not an age peer, but she could be.

Children borrow behaviors from their identification figures and are strongly influenced by them. Therefore it's very important that the children have people to identify with who offer a range of alternatives representing many different ways of behaving, thus giving the children flexible models to copy rather than stereotyped roles. This is important in relation to sex roles, culturally-defined stereotypes, and socio-economic class stereotypes—self-imposed and other-imposed.

In our discussion of human needs, we explained that to the extent a person is a captive of extrinsic definitions of who she is and should be, she will sacrifice her own intrinsic definition of self. Further, a person who is dependent on others to define who she is and whether she successfully meets *their* role expectations of her is not able to be relaxed and comfortable enough with them to be concerned about their feelings and needs.

Through working on releasing yourself from confining stereotypes which dictate what behaviors are permissible and acceptable, you will grow. Thus, you will be better able to care for others—children and adults—in terms of *their* needs rather than your own. You also will be presenting your children with an open, flexible identification model which will help guide them to become themselves rather than carbon copies of others who, themselves, are carbon copies of others.

For example, by having both men and women participate in the care of children, at home and in preschool and day-care situations, you show children that child care is not just "women's work." Make a conscious effort to share various responsibilities rather than always having women involved in "feminine" activities such as meal preparation and housekeeping while men participate in "masculine" activities such as woodworking and ball playing. Your models will encourage children to develop skills on the basis of their own interests rather than because of what sexual equipment they possess.

As damaging as are the arbitrary activity choices which are made for children solely on the basis of their belonging to one group and being excluded from another are the behavioral requirements and attributes these stereotypes impose. Racial, cultural, sexual, and socio-economic stereotypes are destructive from the outside in and from the inside out. For people who are members of the group, there are expectations from within which communicate to the developing child (and to adults) that "You are only acceptable and will only belong and be cared about *if* you behave in the way *we* prescribe." Those who are not members of the racial, cultural, sexual, or socio-economic group are rejected because, due to some superficial characteristic, they automatically are disqualified from membership. This is particularly damaging to the self-concept of the developing child who belongs to an "out" group of any kind—female, poor, or nonwhite.

Please remember that we all are human, and our similarities are greater than our differences. Don't teach your children, directly or through your model, to think more or less of themselves or anyone else because of some "group" identity. And don't dictate to them, deliberately or through your own uncritical acceptance and enactment of the stereotyped behaviors that have been imposed on you, who and what they must be. Help your children, through your model and through your thoughtful and loving guidance, to become as fully human as they can be.

## Help Me Not to Be Afraid

Between five and six-and-a-half years, children go through another transition period similar to that they experienced from eighteen months to three years. The demands and expectations of our society are "pushing them upstairs" to school and other responsibilities. They are growing and changing physiologically as well as psychologically from preschool children to school age children.

Children between eighteen months and three years are pulled between babyhood and childhood. In a similar way, children between five and six and a half years are pulled between wanting to retain their dependent status as "young" children and needing to move on to a new, more demanding and responsible life-role as a school-age child. The same sort of pros and cons on each side exist at this stage as existed for their younger selves. On the one hand, assuming more responsibility for one's own life has the promise of many rewards. On the other hand, however, the advantages to giving up all the benefits of being a young child who can depend on someone else to take care of most of his needs and desires may seem questionable in comparison with the dubious advantages of growing up.

Most children—even those whose parents and teachers have been, and continue to be, very supportive—have some misgivings about this stage of growth. They show it through temporary regressions to younger behaviors including baby-talk, wetting their pants or their bed at night, "nervous habits," whining, clumsiness (falling and knocking into things), and increased demands for attention. Also, as in the stage between eighteen months and three years, they tend to show a temporary resurgence of safety needs. This leads them, at once, both to need more structure in their lives (e.g., established, predictable routines; understood expectations) and to try to exert more control on situations.

Like their younger selves, children in this stage can become unpredictably disturbed by changes in routines or other expected occurrences. They are subject to abrupt mood swings, moving quickly and often unpredictably from states of elation to states of depression. Their self-concept is similarly labile, exhibiting swings from extreme self-aggrandizement to extreme self-doubt and self-depreciation. The most difficult thing for a child this age to do, it seems, is to make a decision.

This is an exaggeration of some characteristics of children in this stage. Some children may suffer none of these bouts with insecurity deriving from the combination of their increased self-consciousness and the societal demands on them to leave old ways behind and go on to a new stage in life. Nevertheless, it's very important that you understand why these behaviors occur in those children who do exhibit them so that you can help make their life less stressful. In particular, you should try to relieve them of any unnecessary demands and expectations and, at the same time, make explicit what expectations of them you do have and why. This will help provide them with the structure they need in order to cope with all the other changes in their life.

Try to be patient and understanding of their occasionally unreasonable behavior. It won't last forever, and it should not be viewed as a bad reflection on your effectiveness as a caregiver. It is simply an expected consequence of the combination of too many changes at once. Think about yourself when you have to cope with too many changes and disruptions in your normal routine (e.g., if you move, change jobs, lose a mate); your behavior, too, reflects the stress of too much change. How it comes out depends on your personal style. How well you are able to cope with "change-overload" depends on the support system you have (e.g., people who care about you and are there to give you whatever kind of help and support you need) as well as on your own childhood experiences with change in periods such as this one.

Try to be the kind of support system for your child during this time that you would like to have and need when you're under similar kinds of stress. You'll not only permit him to continue growing instead of getting partially stuck at this point because of unmet needs. You'll also give him a model that he can internalize to help himself through similar times when he's older as well as to help his own children when they need it.

**In Sum**

All the different kinds of experiences your child has in her early childhood with the world of people and things—the developmental changes she goes through and others' responses to them—combine to contribute to the writing of her "life-script." This script, once written in these early, foundational years, forms the basis of the scenario of your child's life. Human beings are characterized by the capacity for continual growth, change, and transcendence. Nevertheless, it is more difficult to alter an entire life-pattern once it has been formed.

With this in mind, try to help your child make happy and productive use of her early childhood years. Be alert to her developmental signals of what she needs at different times. Help her meet those needs so none of them remains an unresolved part of her life-script, subjecting her to continual "reruns" of the same scene and blocking her growth. Try to reinforce good, loving, human, and self-assertive behaviors when they appear. Capitalize on your child's strengths, helping her to find areas of competence in her life that will make her feel she's a person of worth.

Be patient and understanding in difficult times. Try to guide your child through them rather than drawing so much attention to them that they become a habitual part of her behavioral repertoire. Above all, show her a good, kind, loving model through all the stages of her growth, and you will enable her to emerge from her early childhood still growing and firmly established on her life-long journey toward self-actualization.

# A GUIDE TO THE ACTIVITIES

## *BEGIN AT THE BEGINNING*

The remainder of the book, after this section, contains activities for children from birth to six years. We recognize that although some of you may have small babies, many of you are parents or teachers with older preschool children. Whatever the age of the children in your care, we hope that you will look at all the activities rather than simply turning to the ones that pertain to your children's age level. To explain further:

1. You may have incomplete views and perspectives of principles of development explained throughout in relation to the activities if you look only at those of one age level.

2. There is a developmental sequence to the activities that reflects the characteristic skills of children within each age level. Your awareness of

this sequence will provide a context for the activities at your children's age level.

3. Since every child and his interests differ from any other, some of the activities at other age levels may be more enjoyable and appropriate to your children than some of the activities contained in their age level.

In general, it's a good idea to try some easier activities first. This will give your children the guarantee of success as well as practice in foundational skills needed for activities at their age level. At the same time, it will give you some baseline information on what skills your children have in their repertoire and which ones they need practice with.

## ONE CHILD'S CEILING IS ANOTHER CHILD'S FLOOR

Children's capacity for different kinds of learning changes as they grow. A great activity for a three-month-old usually is quite boring to a three-year-old, and a challenging activity for a five-year-old would likely prove frustrating to a two-year-old.

Children are different from one another. Just because an activity is designed for four- to five-year-olds doesn't mean every child in that age range will like it or that some three-year-olds or six-year-olds might not enjoy it. In fact, many of the activities in the three- to six-year range may be applicable to or adapted for children at any age within that range. Such activities can be particularly useful in situations in which children in this entire age range are allowed (as they should be) to participate together in group activities rather than being separated into same-age groupings.

The age ranges in which activities are located and those cited under "Participants" are approximations, averages based on observations of many children at each age level. But each child has her own particular backlog of experience which will guide her response to an activity. Always, the child herself should be the final judge of what's a good activity for her. Try out different activities with your children, based on your knowledge of their interests and abilities. Let their responses guide the amount of time you spend on an activity as well as your future selection of activities.

## SPECIAL CHILDREN [30]

For children with special learning problems, it's even more important to select activities which will provide stimulation at their present level of skills

[30] See the Resource section at the end of the book for resources with activities for teaching children with special learning problems. See, also, the section on Learning Problems (pp. 170–172) in the Resource Chapter in Laurie and Joseph Braga, *Learning and Growing* (Englewood Cliffs, N.J.: Prentice-Hall, Inc., 1975) for a more extensive list of resources to help you understand and deal with children's special learning problems.

development in an area regardless of the age level for which those activities are specified.

The activities in this book are as appropriate for children with special learning problems as they are for children who are able to learn normally. The differences between teaching the two groups are that children with special learning problems may (1) be ready for an activity at a different time, (2) require more repetition and a slower pace, and, in some cases, (3) need to have material transformed to a different modality in order to be able to process it. For example, a child who is blind will need to have visual events, to the extent possible, translated into forms that he can feel and hear. For instance, rather than just hang different items from a blind baby's crib for him to touch, you'll have to spend time helping him discover how each item feels and responds to his actions.

The most important point in helping children with special learning problems to learn is to concentrate on the things they *can* do more than on the things they can't do. This is important both as it affects their feelings about themselves and as a guide to effective teaching. As with any child, you should use the skills and interests a child with a learning problem has as a bridge to other, related, skills he does not possess.

Furthermore, through paying particular attention to capitalizing on a special child's available skills rather than to all the things he needs to learn, you can keep his human options open. Just because a child has problems with spoken language, for example, does not mean there is no area in which he can excel. An example frequently cited is the story of Yoshihiko Yamamoto, a renowned Japanese artist who is mentally retarded and severely limited in his ability to communicate verbally. Through the sensitive guidance of a very observant and skillful teacher, a natural skill was enabled to develop through which this individual is able to communicate articulately with others in his art and live a fulfilled and productive life rather than being "handicapped" by the verbal skills he lacks.

There are resources listed in the resource section which contain activities for helping children with special learning problems learn many of the skills expected by society. In addition to engaging in these kinds of activities, however, it's essential that you continually reassess the priorities you are setting for your child to insure they really are in his best interests as a human being. Always put your child's comfort and happiness above all else. Increased anxiety and feelings of insecurity due to excessive pressures to achieve can only interfere with learning.

The most important thing is for a child to grow to be a good human being. He needs to learn to get along with others, be attuned and responsive to his own and others' needs, make decisions which are neither at his own or someone else's expense, and—to the extent that he can—take responsibility for his own behavior. Keep these and other human skills in mind when setting priorities for your special child. Don't let the cultural expectations of what skills a person should possess in order to be acceptable and effectively competitive in an achievement-oriented society take precedence over any child's *human* development.

## PARENTS AND TEACHERS

The activities for children from birth to age three are, to a large extent, worded and oriented for children at home and in a one-to-one play experience. Our reasons for this are that (1) There are more children in this age range at home than in group care situations, and (2) Whatever the setting, younger children and babies tend to function better in a one-to-one interaction with an adult than when they have to share the adult's attention with other children.

Many of the activities for children three years and older, on the other hand, are worded and oriented for small groups of children in a preschool setting. Our reasons for this are that (1) Children from three to six years typically enjoy group activities and function well as participants in them. (Some younger children enjoy being together or with older children, too, but they're not usually interested in more restricting sit-down, organized group activities); (2) A growing number of children in this age group are engaged in some sort of group care and educational experience; and (3) We anticipate that a large number of our readers will be teachers in such settings.

Any of the activities oriented to home environments can easily be adapted for children in group day-care or play groups. Parents whose children are at home should translate the group activities into one-to-one activities for themselves and their children, or small group activities for several family members. If you have more than one child, many of the activities are highly appropriate for older and younger children to play together. If you have only one child, you should try to arrange with some other parents to have your children participate together in some kind of small group play on a regular basis.

## JUST US

In their first couple of years, children usually are much more interested in adults than in other children. As they get older, children begin to notice and approach each other more, though at first not to play cooperatively. The older children get, the more interested they become in being with friends their own age and older.

It's important for children to have a chance to be together when they become interested in each other. For very little ones, if you have only one child, a trip to a park where there will be other children is usually enough. But, as your child grows older and you notice him spending more time with other children at the park (or another meeting place), see if you can arrange for him to be with other children some of the time. After about three years for most, though younger for some, children enjoy spending time together for part of each day.

Parents can become weary of being with their children twenty-four hours a day, seven days a week. Children also can get tired of being constantly with their parents. They enjoy the opportunity to get away from an adult-oriented world. They need a place where they can be more relaxed, communicate on their own level, be with people whose view of the world and orientation toward life is similar to their own, and work out relationships with those other children, all on their own level, at their pace, in terms of their needs.

Children learn their role models initially from adults, but they need the social interaction with their peers in order to learn interpersonal competence. They need to be with other children in order to safely play out some of the various roles and social interactions they observe in the adult world. Only in play with other children can a child work out social interactions on a level where he has enough status to risk trying out certain social strategies. In the adult-child interaction, the child typically is limited to certain role behaviors that are appropriate because he is a child. With other children, his options usually are more open.

Children learn from other children the same age and other ages. They admire and imitate others' skills and help each other out. They are not competitive with or jealous of each other unless these feelings are reinforced by others. You and other important adults in children's lives can put them in the position of having to compete for attention and of feeling jealous or resentful of one another. You create these feelings through such actions as consistently giving one child more positive attention than others; not giving enough attention to any of your children; and comparing them, e.g., setting one up as an example to the others: "Why can't you be like . . . ?" On the other hand, if you are kind, attentive, sensitive, and fair to all your children, they will learn from your example and from your responses to their behavior also to be kind, fair, and cooperative.

## SOME TIME FOR MYSELF

There should be a balance of activities which are adult-initiated and in which you play a major part and ones which are initiated and carried out by a child or group of children on their own. There should be activities in which you participate and ones in which you leave the children to their own devices, to direct themselves.

Don't remove children from productive activities in which they're involved on their own to get them to join a group activity you're leading. *When children are involved, they're learning.* By diverting children's attention from an enjoyed self-directed activity to a compulsory group activity, you discourage and work against their development of persistence, a skill that is essential to successful problem-solving.

When you do play with children, take care that you are not so directive that you take away from them all feeling of initiative and personal accomplishment. Be a companion in their play when you join them. Teach them more by your model than through direct, specific instruction. Be a guide and a facilitator to their learning, not a dictator of what they can and should do.

Give your children time and space to be alone. Just as children need to be alone together away from adults, each child also needs the opportunity to be by herself. She needs time and space to rest, be quiet, gather her thoughts, and "recharge her batteries" away from the obligations and responsibilities of relating to others (and you need this too).

Children need time by themselves to do things *they* want to do without anybody telling them what to do, how to do it, when to do it, and whether they did it well enough. They need the time to get away from the "busyness" of their day-to-day lives and back in touch with that quiet place inside themselves. Enjoying being alone, by oneself, is an important aspect of your children's development which, if nurtured now, will continue to serve them well throughout their lives.

## THE MEANS SHAPE THE END

The way you go about doing an activity, the process, is as important as, perhaps even more so than, the content of the activity in determining what and how well children will learn. The end result you seek will be achieved more surely through concentration on the means than through focusing on the end goal to be reached. The same activity may be a valuable learning experience or a complete disaster, depending on the way you conduct it.

If you don't feel like participating in an activity—because you're tired or in a low mood, or because you just wouldn't enjoy it or feel comfortable doing it—you shouldn't force yourself any more than you should push your child to engage in an activity he won't enjoy. If your relationship with your children is characterized by fairness and concern for each others' needs and feelings, then they will understand when you explain to them that the activity wouldn't be fun for you, and that you wouldn't want to spoil their fun by being a grouch. But, encourage them to do it without you. In some cases, you can act as a "special consultant," on call if needed.

## FUN AND GAMES

When you do choose to participate with the children in an activity, both you and they should have a good time. Everyone learns more when they enjoy what they're doing. And you teach the children, through such experiences, to think of learning as an enjoyable activity.

Activities should be conducted in a spirit of fun; they should be approached as games, not as tasks. You can take the most potentially exciting activity and make it into drudgery by conducting it as a stiff, adult-directed training procedure. In contrast, you can take a very ordinary, routine task and make it into a fun game through an enthusastic and relaxed approach.

Children are fun to play with. They're often less inhibited than adults in their range of responses, and they are able to find joy in small things. Let their example be a model to encourage you to do the same. Follow the children's lead (1) in selecting activities that relate to their spontaneous interests and (2) in capitalizing on their enthusiasm and capacity for un-self-conscious involvement.

If you find that an activity just isn't interesting to the children, despite all your efforts to make it fun and engaging, don't continue it. Excuse any child in a group activity who isn't attending and enjoying himself. Try working with him later on a one-to-one basis. For now, suggest he find something else he'd prefer to do.

## LET YOUR HEART LEAD YOUR MIND

When you're involved in an activity with children, your first concern always should be for their thoughts and feelings, rather than for the content of the activity. Thus, you can help them learn effective social interaction. This is, after all, the most important form of learning children engage in. It forms the basis for everything else they do now and in the future.

Be flexible enough to sense a child's need to digress from the subject matter of an activity to share something that's on her mind. Learn to respond to your "gut" reactions to the children's needs as you participate with them in activities. Always be sure your interactions with the children in the context of an activity reflect a concern for them as whole human beings, not just as minds. Don't let the content of an activity take precedence over the children involved in it. Teach children, not activities.

## ME, MYSELF, AND I

When you're engaging in activities, keep in mind that everything you do together is filtered through each child's self-concept, and, at the same time, contributes to it. Every success and failure, every new skill acquired, each new challenge posed both reflects each child's set of beliefs and feelings about who he is and what he can do and provides feedback to him which helps to further define his "self-picture."

It's important, therefore, that you "step outside yourself and into each child's shoes" long enough to evaluate how to gear your questions and comments to him. Your approach should take into account his past experience, interests, and skills in a way that insures his success in the activity. With this kind of orientation, each time you participate in an activity, it should be different. It should reflect the particular interests, skills, and background of the children who are involved.

## COOPERATION, NOT COMPETITION

Your choice of children to participate together in a group activity should reflect your knowledge of each child's interests and level of skills development. There should be a good blend in a small group of (1) children who are just learning the skill, (2) children who need practice in the skill, and (3) children who are competent enough already in the skill to serve as models to the other children.

As long as you don't make group activities competitive, you needn't worry that the children with greater strength in the area will monopolize the games. In fact, the more skilled children can be of help to the less skilled ones because they are not many steps of growth removed from them. Just make sure you praise each child equally, according to her *own* level of performance relative to what you know about her level of skill in the area. Be careful not to give more praise and attention to the more skilled children.

Through your model, show what the behavior of a teacher should be toward her students: Give each child encouragement and helpful guidance so she can take herself just one small step beyond where she was before. Do *not* concentrate on getting each child to give one particular correct response, the same for all. And be careful not to correct a child in a way that makes her reluctant to try again. Emphasize cooperation, helping each other, and showing respect and concern for each child's thoughts and feelings. Then, once the more skilled children have learned the game, they can be helpers to the other children. If you've been a good teacher, so will they be.

## IF YOU CAN'T EXPLAIN IT TO A THREE-YEAR-OLD . . .

You should always know *why* you're doing an activity. If you can't give the children a simple and reasonable explanation of an activity's value, then perhaps you shouldn't be doing it. By explaining to children why you're doing something, you contribute to their learning about learning. You help them understand the different ways they can use their mind and body and what kinds of activities are appropriate for those different purposes. Further, through having to explain the reason for doing an activity, you will think more about what the different skills are that children need to learn. And you will avoid wasting the children's time on meaningless activities.

Teaching and learning should contribute to development; it should not consist of unrelated bits of information. It should be related to everyday life. You should ask yourself why you're teaching something. Why is this important for children to learn? How will it help them? You should not, for example, teach isolated words. Words are only meaningful in the context of some concrete experience or concept that children already understand; then words can serve as a short-cut and to communicate with others.

## DO-IT-YOURSELF ACTIVITIES

This book contains a number of activity ideas at each age level. Based on what we've included, you probably will be able to think of many more. The statement of purpose and developmental explanation of each activity should provide a springboard from which you can improvise others that accomplish a similar purpose. Your knowledge of your receiver—your children—is far more precise than ours could possibly be. Using the ideas contained in the book's activities as bridges (accommodating mechanisms), you can invent your own activities which are specifically oriented to the growth of the individual children in your care.

When you're developing your own activities, keep in mind that it's important to give children a multiple of alternatives of different types of activities to engage in that will enable them to develop the fullest possible range of their potential human skills. Try to think of activities that will help your children function better and be successful in all the various areas of their lives. And concentrate, particularly, on providing them with opportunities to develop generalizable and adaptive skills for solving problems and dealing with different kinds of people and situations they may never have encountered before. These kinds of skills are both useful and help give children a sense of confidence to deal with the constantly changing world they live in.

## YOU, YOUR CHILDREN'S GREATEST RESOURCE

You are your own best source of material for creating activities. Think of the games you enjoyed in your own childhood, and try them out with your children. Also, use yourself as a resource in evaluating skills you have that are very useful to you, or ones that, if you had them, would make your life easier and more productive. Examine these to see if any of them can be translated into simple games to play with your children, or just incorporated more consciously in your own behavior toward the children to teach them through your model.

Keep in mind that your children's own developmental needs, interests, and skills must always be the final determinant of what is a good activity for them. Keeping that as a check of the appropriateness of your ideas, explore your own personal experience—now and in the past—for interests, skills, and insights to share with your children.

## IT TAKES NO MORE TIME

In the activities section of the book, there are a number of ideas for using daily routines as learning games. On the basis of the examples we've offered, you probably can think of many more specifically related to your own day-to-day existence. The point is to make use of activities such as going shopping, cleaning house, and the like—routines that tend, at best, to get dull and, at worst, to create sources of conflict between you and your children—as times for learning and growing. Make them opportunities for sharing time together, learning about new things, increasing vocabulary, developing new skills, and so on.

These tasks can become enjoyable for you, too, and they present the most fruitful opportunity for learning you could find or create. Being a "good" parent, when you incorporate your daily experiences as an important part of your learning and growing activities, doesn't have to take much more time, if any, than just being any kind of parent at all.

Observations from cross-cultural studies of children's learning and thinking confirm what we know from common sense: "People are good at doing the things that are important to them and that they have the occasion to do often." [31] Within this statement lies some clues to teaching and learning related to what we've been discussing: For children to learn any skill or

[31] Michael Cole, J. Gay, J. Glick, and D. Sharp, *The Cultural Context of Learning and Thinking* (New York: Basic Books, Inc., 1971), p. xi.

information, they must have practice at it, and it should be important to them personally and to the life they lead (so that it will have carry-over, and thus use, in their day-to-day lives). This is best assured through actually translating children's routine life experiences into learning and growing activities.

You and your children wouldn't need special activities for learning and growing together if you could just naturally live a life with that kind of orientation. But, unfortunately, most of our lives these days are taken up with activities that have nothing at all to do with learning or growing. Thus, it becomes necessary to set aside special times to do just that.

What you learn from participating in these activities with your children should have some carry-over into the rest of your lives together. We hope it will help you learn to make good use of the time you have with your children, so you spend increasing amounts of it engaged in growth-oriented interactions.

## RULES OF THE GAME

The following principles of teaching and learning should help guide your approach to the activities. They'll also be useful in constructing your own activities that capitalize on your children's particular interests and skills.

1. Children learn best when the new material is similar to, but slightly different from what they already know. Observe their spontaneous choices of activities for clues to what they're ready to learn. See "Familiarity Breeds Content," pages 13–14, for further explanation of this.

2. You should prepare children for new experiences by relating what they can expect to see, do, and so on to things they have experienced in the past. Provide them with bridges (accommodating mechanisms) from familiar material to the new material. See "A Bridge from Here to There," pages 14–15, for further explanation.

3. You will be most effective in facilitating children's learning through (1) providing them with opportunities (including materials, space, and freedom) to practice emerging skills; (2) introducing them, through your model, to behaviors, skills, and ideas they may want to try out for themselves; (3) permitting them, at their own pace, to "make these behaviors their own" through repetitive playing; (4) joining them in some activities, extending and expanding their learning while still retaining the spirit and pace of their own self-initiated play; and (5) being conscious of your behavioral responses to them so that you encourage their learning and reinforce their productive behaviors.

4. Preschool children need direct, practical experience with real things before they can deal with those things as verbal ideas. You should continually ask yourself: "How could I present this so that it will be (1) personally interesting and motivating to my children, (2) close enough to what they already know that they can relate it to their repertoire of experience, and (3) a practical, concrete experience?"

5. In general, real objects are easier for children to deal with than any kind of representation (e.g., words, pictures) of the objects. If a child is having trouble understanding an activity in which you're using some form of representation of an object, see if she does better with the real thing.

6. Words alone are not enough for most preschool children to be able to follow an unfamiliar instruction to perform some action. They need the combination of actual demonstration and the words. This is important to keep in mind for activities as well as for asking children to do things around the house or classroom.

7. Realistic looking pictures—drawings and photographs—are easier for children to decipher than abstract ones. Both color and details should be clear, uncomplicated, and realistic. This is particularly important when selecting books for children or pictures to use in making their homemade books.

8. Identifying an object named by someone else (e.g., "Show me the orange.") is an easier task for young children than naming it (e.g., "What is this?"), and naming it is easier than defining the same object (e.g., "What is an orange?"). If a child can't tell you what an object is or give its name, see if he can identify it when you supply the name before you assume he doesn't know what the object is.[32]

9. Matching [e.g., "Find the one that's the same as this (the first) one." □ △ ○ □ ] is an easier task than identifying the same thing (e.g., "Point to the square." □ ○ ) and both are easier than naming the thing (i.e., asking "What is this?"). Whenever a child can't do one of these tasks, see if she can do the simpler one.

10. Matching (i.e., identifying two things as the same) is an easier task than differentiating (e.g., identifying one object in a group that's different from the rest; identifying two sounds as being different from

---

[32] Even if a child can't identify an object when you name it, he may still know something about it. If you gave a child an orange and he peeled and ate it, he knows what an orange is even though he doesn't know its name.

each other). For example, the first of the following tasks would be easier for young children than the second.

a. Show me the one that's just like this (the first) one.

b. Show me the one that's not the same as the others.

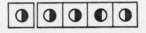

11. On matching or differentiating tasks, the difficulty level is increased as the similarity among the choices is increased, and the task is made easier by increasing the differences among the choices. For example, the second of the preceding tasks is harder because of the similarities among the pictures than it would be if the one that was different were a totally black or totally white circle. In a sound game, it would be easier for a child to tell the difference between a bell and hands clapping than between a doorbell and a table bell.

This is a rule you should find very useful for activities that you've repeated so many times with the same children that you need to make the game harder, or in adapting activities for use with younger or less skilled children than they were designed for.

12. The number of choices you give children in a task also affects the difficulty level. The simplest task gives a child a choice of two things, e.g., "Is this an orange or an apple?" As you increase the number of choices, you make the task harder, e.g., having a child find a picture the same as one she saw earlier among a choice of twelve is much more difficult than finding it among a choice of four.

13. Recognition, i.e., identifying something familiar, is easier than recalling, i.e., calling to mind something from the memory store. For example, if you ask a child to listen to a tune and then identify it later as being the same one, that's much easier than asking him to reproduce that tune for you later. This also has something to do with the next rule.

14. Reception precedes expression. Children learn to understand language before they learn to use it. They learn to read before they learn to write. They learn to process visual images before they learn to draw. They are able to process music before they are able to sing, and so on. Expressive abilities are more difficult because they require motor

activity which takes a while to bring under control so that the child's actions can match her intentions (i.e., her inner "image").[33]

15. Fine motor tasks—those requiring the control of many small muscles in coordination with one another for fine, precise movements—are generally more difficult and take longer to learn than gross motor tasks—those requiring control of the larger muscles in coordination with each other for grosser movements of the whole body or the arms and legs.

    The rule for the development of motor skills is that control proceeds from the head down and from the midline of the body outward to the extremities. So, for example, control of the arms for reaching precedes control of the legs for standing, and control of the fingers for skilled grasping of very small objects follows control of the hand for crude grasping of larger objects. This rule is useful to keep in mind when observing a child to make sure you're not expecting him to accomplish a task that's way beyond his present level of motor development.

16. If you want to see a behavior again, pay attention to it. Children (and adults) tend to repeat behaviors which are associated with positive consequences. Some sorts of attention (e.g., yelling, spanking) may not seem to you to qualify as positive consequences, and for many children they do not. But, children will take it any way they can get it, and if that's the only brand of attention they can get, they'll repeat behaviors which receive that kind of attention. In contrast, if you want to see a behavior disappear, ignore it or, if necessary, give the child some sort of mild negative consequence (e.g., removing him from the situation, frowning).

17. As a general rule, a good number of children for a "small group activity" is no more than five. Some more energetic activities which do not necessitate sustaining individual children's attention can be accomplished successfully with a larger group. But a small group of five or less is preferable for activities in which you're concerned with obtaining and observing the participation of each child individually.

18. Activities generally should be challenging enough to interest the children involved in them, but not so far beyond their capacity to respond positively to them that they are forced to withdraw psychologically from the activity out of fear of failing.

19. "Feelings provide the 'go/no go' switch for all behavior." [34] Children

---

[33] This is true for adults too. For example, think about all the songs that sound absolutely perfect inside your head, but when you try to sing them, your voice doesn't match your inner melody.

[34] Robert B. Livingston, quoted in Muriel Beadle, *A Child's Mind* (Garden City, New York: Doubleday & Company, Inc., 1971), p. 107.

will learn most easily when they enjoy what they are doing. The activities they choose to engage in and become joyfully involved in on their own are your best clue to their learning needs and interests at any point in time.

# 2

# Birth to One Year: Off to a Good Start[1]

In the first year of their lives, infants grow more and at a more rapid rate than at any other time of their lives. When they enter the world they are helpless. They cannot care for themselves; they have no voluntary control over their bodies; they cannot move around; they can't even roll over. They may have some difficulty at first with eating and digesting food, breathing, and maintaining an even body temperature.

By the end of the year, most infants move around quite effectively. They can reach smoothly and accurately for and grasp things, pick things up deftly between their thumb and forefinger, drink from a cup and hold it themselves with two hands, and eat from a spoon (but not efficiently by themselves for another year). They can chew and digest semi-solid or chopped foods. They can understand some words and may even say a few themselves. They recognize familiar people and things and know that even when things are not in sight, they still exist. And they begin to learn about themselves—that they are persons separate from the world of people and things around them.

[1] Each of the following chapters begins with a brief overview of developmental characteristics of children within the age range covered by the chapter. For a much more extensive and detailed description of children's behavior at each age level, combined with suggestions of activities to stimulate development, see L. and J. Braga, *Learning and Growing* (Englewood Cliffs, N.J.: Prentice-Hall, Inc., 1975).

In the first six months of life, most infants develop muscular control over the upper portion of their bodies—eyes, head, neck, shoulders, arms, and upper torso. They learn to follow moving objects with their eyes, then eyes and head, and to reach for and grasp stable objects (leading with the shoulders now more than with the hand). They also learn to sit with support. But it is in the second half of their first year that infants usually accomplish the most dramatic motor achievements, the ones which make them mobile. From six to twelve months, most infants master unsupported sitting, rolling completely from stomach to back and back to stomach, standing with help, pulling up to standing, creeping on all fours, and even walking with a little help. Even though they are not achieved until the latter part of the first year, the motor achievements just listed have their origins in muscular control and coordination developed previously.

Communication between infants and their caregivers begins with the baby's first cries for food, comfort, or company. But those early cries aren't conscious and deliberate, and they're not very efficient. Over the period of their first year, most infants develop more varied, efficient, and deliberate means of communicating. They learn early to smile back to a smiling face and look into the person's eyes. They develop a repertoire of noises and speech-like sounds with the rhythm and tonal qualities of real speech, and with facial expressions and gestures to accompany their sound-making. By a year, a few "real" words may be included in many infants' vocalizing.

The first year of infants' lives is marked by growth in their ability to make some sense out of the world around them—to apply some organization to all the information coming into their sensory channels (eyes, ears, skin, mouth, and nose). When babies are born, all their sensory receivers are in good working order. But they need experience before any of the information coming into these receiving stations makes any sense. Through their first year, building on their initial wired-in reflex responses to the world, infants learn increasingly more varied and integrated actions on their world.

Through their own action schemes, children selectively react to, act on, and organize sensory input. For example, in the first month as their eye muscles strengthen, most infants look at anything that happens to be around, without any real regard; then by three to four months, they look to see—they look at what interests them. What interests infants, and, therefore, what they attend to visually, changes through the first year with growth in their memory and in their motor skills. At first it's the familiar—infants' own hands and other people's faces. Then it's something similar to the familiar.

By the end of the first year, children respond to things slightly different from what they are familiar with by reacting to the new thing in the way they would react to the familiar thing. They are learning to organize sensory input into "chunks" based on how it relates to what they have already experienced. Gradually those chunks become integrated and internalized so that infants consolidate their knowing. They learn that things stay the same from day to day and that they can be known in various ways; they begin to construct a consistent reality for themselves.

When they're born babies don't even know that there's a "me" that's separate from the rest of the world of people and things. Slowly, through experience, infants begin to define themselves as persons in relation to other persons (a process that will continue through their lives). Infants develop feelings about themselves based on the feedback they receive from others. If the world around them is positively responsive to them, children will feel good about themselves. If the world is unresponsive or unreliable, they will feel incompetent and fearful. And they will carry those feelings into their future; they will learn to anticipate the kind of responses they have become used to receiving and will adapt their behavior accordingly.

## HOW DO YOU TELL A BABY YOU LOVE HIM?

**Participants:**   Babies in the first year of life, before they can understand verbal language, and members of their family.

**Explanation:**   Adults sometimes have a hard time communicating with babies since babies can't talk and adults often have lost the ability, in their own childhood, to communicate nonverbally. But there's no better opportunity than when you have a baby to relearn this skill. Following are a few tips on how to communicate nonverbally with a baby.

1. Touch is the most important avenue of communication with a baby. You tell a baby you love him through gentle, secure holding, tender caresses, and affectionate stroking. You tell a baby you love him through letting your body express all the love you feel for him.[2] Tense, jerky, abrupt handling gives the opposite message; it tells the baby this is not a comforting, secure place to be.

2. You communicate to babies through your eyes and general facial expression. When you look at your baby eye to eye and smile at him with your whole face, he feels the love you're expressing. In contrast, if you fail to look him in the eye, if your face is tense and unsmiling, you communicate these feelings to him too.

3. Your voice communicates to your baby how you feel about him. If your voice is gentle, soothing, and full of love and joy, your baby will feel it

[2] See Ashley Montagu, *Touching* (New York: Perennial Library, 1971), for an explanation of the significance of touching for human development.

too. On the other hand, if your voice is filled with anxiety and frustration or thinly masked anger and annoyance, if you speak to your baby in sarcastic tones, or if you hardly speak to him at all, your baby will sense the negative feelings your voice is carrying.

4. The point is that very young babies, because it is the only mode of communication they have, sense the feelings underlying any action in relation to them even when these feelings are not directed at them. Your baby has no way of knowing that you're angry because you had to wait in line too long at the grocery store or that you're tense when you feed him because you had a hard day at the office and your boss yelled at you. He knows only what he feels, and he takes each feeling delivered as a direct message to him. It's very important, therefore, that you be aware of your own nonverbal behavior when you're interacting with your baby.

5. This doesn't mean that you'll do irreparable harm if you handle your baby roughly, speak to him impatiently, or look at him impassively once in a while. But, if this kind of behavior is the norm of your interactions, it will do harm.[3] And it's a lot harder to undo feelings of insecurity than it is to implant them. So try to be careful when you're interacting with your baby that you let him know how much you really do love him—that your behavior reflects well the feelings you really have for him.

**Purpose:**   The purpose of the activity is obvious: to make your baby feel loved and secure and safe through all your various means of communicating nonverbally with him. Experience of all kinds with the world of sights and sounds and smells and tastes and feelings is necessary for the baby to learn to make order out of his world. Touch is particularly important because the skin is the largest "organ" of the body, and through it the baby experiences his first communications with other people. Further, there is more than just a verbal connection between the word feeling as a label for touch and the word feeling as another word for emotion. Good early experiences with touching and feeling can help the child develop the capacity for being "in touch" with his own emotional reactions to life experiences.

[3] Consistency of negative behavior has the same effect as consistency of positive behavior. Children learn best and most fundamentally from consistencies—things that are usually true—in their environment. The feelings you communicate consistently to your child will have a dramatic and significant effect on your child's perceptions of his environment and on the patterns of behavior he learns and displays not only now, but in his own adulthood and in his role as a parent himself.

## A PICTURE FOR BABY[4]

**Participants:**    Babies, birth to three months.

**Materials:**    A photograph of the baby's family, blown up to a very large size (perhaps by the companies that advertise in many magazines that they will do this kind of enlarging from a snapshot). The picture can be of one face or the whole family. The expressions on the faces should be clearly visible, and they should be happy and comforting, as if actually looking lovingly at the baby.

**Explanation:**    There are many commercially available pictures and decorations to adorn babies' environments. But since the first thing a human infant is interested in looking at is the human face, why not put a picture of one or even several of those who surround her in a spot that would otherwise be just a blank space?

1. Choose a snapshot of the family that portrays a loving feeling, or take such a picture. Send it off to be blown up (to about two feet by three feet). If you can't find a place that does enlarging through magazine advertising, check with a camera store.

2. Tape the picture to the ceiling above your baby's head so that when she is lying on her back, she can look up and see it. Point out to her, on different occasions when she's lying in her bed, who is in the picture: "Look, Tania, there's Mommy and Daddy." As you do so, point also to yourselves to help her, slowly, begin to make the connection.

**Purpose:**    To provide an interesting visual experience for your baby from which she can (1) practice using her eye muscles to focus on a stable, two-dimensional visual event, (2) learn to apply meaning to what she sees through beginning to decipher the visual details and gestalt of the picture and associate it with familiar objects in her environment, i.e., her family, and (3) derive pleasure from seeing a pictorial representation of the human beings who love and care for her. This idea is especially good for the first months of

---

[4] Many of the activities at this age level, like this one, do not deal in any direct way with your growth as an adult. But as you participate in these and other activities with your baby, you will grow. By viewing and experiencing life through the eyes of your baby, you can rediscover—now on a conscious, adult level—the kinds of complex learnings required to be able to do all the now simple, seemingly automatic, tasks you do daily. And, through learning to read your baby's nonverbal messages more and more effectively, you will become increasingly more successfully responsive to her. You also will be gaining an invaluable human skill which can be translated into many uses in your adult human interactions.

the baby's life when she's developing strength in her eye muscles, learning to derive meaning from the people and things around her, and beginning to develop into a social being. Some babies may continue to enjoy it, also, after this time.

**Variation:** When the baby seems to be losing interest in the picture (i.e., when she stops looking at it attentively for any period of time during her day), take it down and substitute another—of her, a favorite toy, or just a pretty design. If your baby doesn't seem to like the picture (if she cries and frets when she looks at it, or if she looks away from it), remove it.

## A VARIETY SHOW FOR BABY

**Participants:** Babies, birth to six months, and adults.

**Materials:** A frequently changing assortment of objects from the baby's environment, such as:
> empty cans and boxes
> metal and wooden spoons
> swatches of bright, colorful material
> interesting looking hats, scarves, men's ties, ribbons, and the like
> a glove or mitten
> plastic measuring cups and spoons
> pieces of foil made into interesting shapes
> costume jewelry
> pictures from magazines mounted on cardboard
> photographs of people and things in the baby's life
> old Christmas cards
> balls made from old socks
> plastic and wooden bracelets
> clothespins
> a metal mirror
> rattles
> stuffed toys
> aluminum pie tins

empty match books or boxes with interesting pictures or designs on the covers

Christmas bulb lights

sound toys—with their bells, squeaks, or animal "voices" safely within the toy so the sound-maker can't be gotten at by the baby

heavy, clear plastic bags filled with different materials, e.g., flowers, sand, marbles, pieces of shiny colored paper, leaves, even a caterpillar on a plant

anything from the baby's environment that would attract his visual regard and invite his participation with it through reaching, grasping, and touching

strong heavy rope or elastic to stretch across the baby's crib

string or monofilament with which to hang individual items

a homemade or commercially produced "sensory stand"

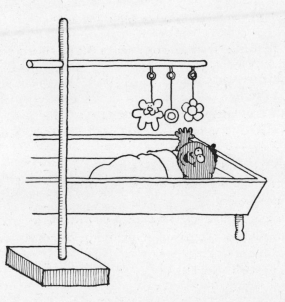

**Explanation:**  Babies in this age period are busy developing control of the muscles that enable them to: focus on their visual environment; move, lift, and support their head; use their arms and hands for reaching, grasping, and touching; and combine all these skills in order to reach with accuracy for things they see near them. Following are some ways you can help your baby develop these basic visual-motor skills:

1. Hang a few items from a sensory stand (see illustration), from a piece of elastic or rope strung across your baby's crib, or from a coathanger suspended from the ceiling. Change the items and location at frequent intervals in response to your baby's skills at the time and the duration of his interest in your previous offerings. Don't overload him with too many things at one time; give him just enough (two to four different items) that he can really get involved with what he's got without becoming overwhelmed. Then, when his interest begins to wane, change his environment with some different items.

2. What you hang at any time and where you hang it should reflect an awareness of the level of your baby's skills development at the time. For example, in their first couple of months, babies do more looking than anything else, so you should provide a variety of interesting forms of visual entertainment. At this time, since the baby's not yet able to reach out and grab things, it's safe to put little things such as strings of colored beads or stars and other shapes made from foil on your baby's visual display. But as your baby starts to grasp things and put them in his mouth, be sure to take off anything that could be swallowed.

3. Be careful, also, when hanging things like ribbons, scarves, and ties that you attach them so there's no danger of your baby getting himself entangled in them. When your baby is beginning to reach for and grasp things, a few wooden or plastic bracelets and a stuffed animal with "handles" for grabbing hold of could be hung by elastic from the side of his crib or from the sensory stand.

4. What particular items your baby likes at any time will depend both on his level of skills development and on what he's had experience with in the past. New objects should be chosen which resemble but are slightly different from ones he's enjoyed before. Watch your baby to see which of the things you give him he pays most attention to—looks at intently, tries to grab, "talks" to, smiles at, and so on. When those particular items no longer spark his interest, try ones that are similar to them but somewhat more complex in their characteristics, e.g., a rubber ball with a bell inside to replace a plain rubber ball; a foil pie tin with different-sized holes punched in it to replace a plain one.

5. Any number of things can be done with these kinds of materials to provide interesting stimulation to your baby. You can make mobiles with pictures or objects. You can hang things at various places in his crib to give him opportunities for looking, reaching, touching, manipulating, or batting with his hands and feet. You can make wind chimes by hanging stone, wooden, or metal objects so that they'll knock against

one another when a breeze strikes them. And you can move the sensory stand, with a changing assortment of goodies, to various positions over his bed.

6. Your baby will enjoy these various forms of entertainment when he's alone in his bed. In addition, you can increase his pleasure and his learning by participating in his play. In particular, when you're going to hang something new, take the time to "introduce" it to your baby first. "Dance" the object in front of him. Move it slowly from one side to the other, up and down, and in a circle. As he gains control of his eye and neck muscles, your baby will become more able to follow with his eyes and head the objects you move in front of him.

7. Dance the object to his hand while he watches. Depending on the level of development of his hand muscles, put the object in his hand or just give it to him to handle. Show him how it feels, rubbing his fingers lightly across the object. Shake it or squeeze it to make a noise if it's a sound-making toy. Talk to your baby about what you're doing with the object as you do it.

8. Then hang the new toy. Show your baby how to make it move. Hit the mattress with your hand to make all the toys hanging from elastic across his crib go into motion. Put him on his tummy sometimes so that he can get a different view of the toys and practice lifting his head to look at them. Hang a toy near his feet, and show him how to kick it and make it move. Attach a toy to a piece of elastic and hang it securely from the ceiling so that your baby can, with just a little effort, grab hold of it and pull it down to himself, then let go and let it swing away. Show him how to do it.

**Purpose:**   To stimulate your baby's development of visual, reaching, and grasping skills as well as to provide him with interesting material from his environment to nourish his developing concepts about the world. As your baby develops in his first year, he learns new skills and ways of responding to the environment. From the very beginning, he is an active participant in his own learning, and you can increase his learning through providing him with a changing assortment of objects that both respond to and stimulate his changing skills. The point is to watch your baby and give him interesting material for his developing skills, keeping the kind, number, and positioning of them consistent with his needs as communicated by his responses at the time.

Remember, however, that toys are no substitute for people. You are still your baby's most interesting plaything, and time with you is the best stimulation for his growth you can give him.

## THE BABY BOOK

**Participants:** Your child, from birth on, and you.

**Materials:** Large photograph album, the kind to which you can add pages and in which you can paste both pictures and other mementos; a small pad of note paper.

**Explanation:** Instead of (or in addition to) keeping a baby book for yourself and to show relatives and friends, keep a special one for your baby herself. Make it a record of her growth that she can look at as she grows—to see the changes she has gone through, in size, appearance, development of skills, interests, concerns, and so on. Following are some of the things you might include in your baby's book.

1. Photographs. If you don't have a camera, see if you can borrow one occasionally to make a record of your baby's appearance at different periods in her growth; you could even use one of those booths in which you take three or four pictures that develop while you wait.

2. Voice recordings. If you have or can borrow a cassette tape recorder, make a sound record of your child's voice as she grows—the sounds she makes in early infancy, beginning words, singing, telling stories, and so on.

3. Creations she makes in childhood—early scribbles, drawings, paintings, collages, and so on. If she's very prolific, you don't need to save everything she ever does; just pick a few that you and she like which are representative of different periods in her growth.

4. Stories that she makes up, poems, songs she composes, interesting or funny things she says, insights she has about life and people, and so on.

5. Most important, keep a written record to accompany the pictures, tape recordings, creative products, and other records of your baby's growth to give a context and gestalt to all these things. Make a few notes about what your baby is doing at the time—what new things she's learning, what she likes and doesn't like, interesting comments others have made about her, observations you have about her, experiences she has that mean a lot to her, and so on.

6. Make your comments anecdotal, as if you were telling your child a story about her younger self. For example, when she's learning to walk, you might write how she'd only walk when no one was looking at first or how surprised she looked when she took her first steps.

7. With these kinds of notes, you'll create a gift for your child more valuable than any kind of toy you ever could buy. You're collecting material for endless bedtime stories about "what you were like when you were little" (as even two-and-a-half-year-olds delight in such tales). You're keeping a record for her of a time that, without your help, she'd be unable to recall. You're helping her in the development of her self-concept by giving her a record of her growth—a word and picture story of who she was and who she is.

8. As she grows and becomes more self-conscious and more interested in hearing about herself when she was younger or in seeing her baby pictures, make the baby book available to your child. Look at it with her, and read to her about the way she was. If she ever reaches an age when she no longer finds it interesting, put the baby book away for when she's an adult. Because many of us are never more ourselves than when we're children, it might help her at a later time to rediscover who she really is.

**Purpose:** We've talked already of the purpose—to provide your child with a record of her own growth that can contribute to her development of a positive self-concept. Through your recording and sharing with her the record of her characteristics, delights, successes, as well as sadnesses, disappointments, frustrations, and so on, you can help your child keep in touch with her own roots at the same time as you are helping her to grow "wings." Having the opportunity to see what her concerns were at different times in her development will help her to gain a sense of perspective about the present in relation to the past and future that can enable her to cope better with current problems at any stage in her life. Keeping these records of your child's growth and sharing them with her can help you, also, gain perspective about your own life.

Another value of keeping this kind of record of your child's growth is that it will give you baseline data that will enable you to assess where she is in relation to various developmental milestones. This can be particularly helpful as she grows older and attempts or is confronted by complex activities and skills which require that she already has learned certain fundamentals underlying the more complex skills.

## CALMING BABY

**Participants:** A restless, cranky infant in the first months of life, and an adult.

**Materials:**   A cradle, a blanket for swaddling, music, light.

**Explanation:**   It has been found that continuous stimulation by light and sound and temperature and swaddling are effective in quieting babies who are restless and cranky; it can be used to help the baby sleep and stop crying and expending energy uselessly.[5] Following are suggestions of ways to apply these findings to calming your baby when he's upset:

1. Rock the baby rhythmically in a cradle.
2. Keep the room at a constant temperature, not too cold and not too warm.
3. Turn a light on in the room where he's sleeping.
4. Sing a gentle melody, play some soothing music, or have some other sort of constant monotonous sound going on. (Studies of the effects of continuous stimulation have used a high intensity of white noise.)
5. Wrap your baby snugly in a soft, light blanket or cloth to reduce his random movement.
6. These and other forms of steady, monotonous stimulation will soothe an upset baby and calm him down enough that he can sleep.

**Purpose:**   To calm a baby who is upset due to colic or some other sickness. Be sure to take a sick baby to the doctor; this technique won't take care of the illness, but it may enable your baby to get the sleep he needs in order to get well.

## EATING IS MORE THAN FILLING YOUR BELLY

**Participants:**   Babies, in the first year, and their mother (or other primary caregiver).

**Explanation:**   There is a relationship between a baby's experience in being fed and the development of such qualities as ability to (1) tolerate frustration and tension and postpone gratification, (2) invest energy in learning and in eventual rather than in immediate satisfactions, and (3) select action which

[5] Yvonne Brackbill and H. Fitzgerald, "Development of the sensory analyzers during infancy," in L. Lipsitt and H. Reese (eds.), *Advances in Child Development and Behavior*, Vol. 4 (New York: Academic Press, 1969).

can result in gaining appropriate pleasures from people and things.[6] Thus, it is essential that you pay attention to all aspects of your behavior in the feeding situation to insure that you are appropriately responsive to your baby's psychological as well as physiological needs. Following are some of the elements of your interaction which you should consider.

1. Feeding is the most important interaction you and your baby have together in her early life. You should be physically and emotionally relaxed enough that you can attend completely to the two of you sharing this experience. See "Attending Exercises," Five to Six Years, page 258 for some ideas that can help you learn to focus your attention and relax.

2. When you're feeding your baby, all your attention should be directed toward making the interaction as relaxing, pleasurable, and involving an experience as possible. You should not be distracted by unrelated concerns. For example, you shouldn't be preoccupied by thoughts of what happened earlier in the day or what you have to do when you're done feeding your baby. You shouldn't be overly concerned with doing "the job" quickly, efficiently, and without mess. Nor should you be nervous and afraid that you might not be "doing it right."

   You will do it right if you're responsive to your baby's nonverbal communications. To the extent that you make the feeding mechanical and overly-efficient, you are trading your time now for possible problems later, not only with feeding but also with your baby's capacity for learning, loving, and enjoying interchanges with people and things.

3. In the period before your baby begins to enjoy sitting at a baby-tender or low table to eat, hold her in your arms to feed her. Don't give her a bottle propped up in her bed, and don't feed her in an infant seat.[7] She needs the experience of being held and the skin-to-skin contact almost as much as she needs the food.

4. Hold your baby gently but firmly, enabling her freedom of movement while also providing her with comfortable support. Handle her with smooth and steady movements to give her a sense of security and relaxation.

5. Be aware of and responsive to your baby's behavioral reactions in the feeding situation. Pay attention to such signals as whether she's physically uncomfortable or relaxed, when she's had enough to eat, and

---

[6] Sylvia Brody and Sidney Axelrad, "Maternal Behavior and Infant Development, Mother-Infant Interaction," Discussion Guides to films produced by the Child Development Research Project, City University of New York, New York City, n.d.

[7] As with most things, we're talking about what you do habitually. In special cases, such as if you're absolutely exhausted from staying up all night taking care of another child who's sick, it won't hurt your baby occasionally to be given a bottle propped up in her crib; but this shouldn't be done routinely.

whether she's ready for semi-solid foods. For example, when she's physiologically mature enough, she'll be able to accept and swallow well-mashed foods with ease; before that (around three months), she'll choke and sputter. Her behavioral responses will "tell" you if she likes what she's eating, when she's had enough, whether she's comfortable, and so on.

6. Maintain a relationship with your baby during feeding that reflects mutual responsiveness and adaptation, a feeling of being "tuned-in" to one another. Provide direction that is based on your observation of her needs and that is neither overly controlling nor too tentative and apprehensive. As she grows older, let her assume increasing control in the feeding situation to the extent that she becomes able to do so.

7. Feeding should be physically and psychologically pleasurable for you and your baby. Stroke her gently. Look lovingly into her eyes. Talk to her in soothing, loving tones, and so on. Do these things in a way that is not intrusive or interruptive of her feeding, but is rather an integral, smooth, and natural part of it.

**Purpose:** To make the feeding situation mutually enjoyable and responsive to your baby's psychological and physical needs. Feeding is a large part of a young baby's waking life, and it is an area in which she is totally dependent on another for her very survival. Thus, the interaction between caregiver and infant during feeding sets the tone of their entire relationship and has an enormous impact on the child's total development.

Even if the only time a baby and her caregiver have together is during feeding, if it's a good interaction, it will contribute substantially to the baby's development in all areas. On the other hand, no amount of time devoted to special learning activities outside the feeding situation can make up for unpleasant experiences and neglect of a baby's psychological needs during feeding.

Positive experiences in the feeding interaction contribute to a child's developing a generalized sense of confidence and competence in dealing with people and objects in her environment. Negative experiences contribute to a child's developing apprehension and lack of confidence in her ability to obtain satisfaction from the world of people and things or to have any positive effect on it herself.

The feeding interaction is one of your best sources for practice in empathy with your baby, in "putting yourself in her shoes" and trying to feel what the world must be like from her point of view. It should be a very pleasurable experience for you, both physically and emotionally. It gives you an unparalleled opportunity to share an intensely personal relationship with another human being.

## A "WORKOUT" FOR BABY

**Participants:**   Babies from birth to three months and an adult. More complex and strenuous exercises may be enjoyed by older babies.

**Explanation:**   In the first months of life, your baby has little voluntary control of his own movement. You can help give his muscles tone and strength during this period by regular massage and exercise. After his bath, rub his body gently and smoothly, giving the muscles in his arms, legs, neck, and back a light massage. Then, do some simple "baby calisthenics."

1. One at a time, very gently extend, then flex, each of the baby's arms and legs. Fold his arms across his chest.
2. Supporting his head and neck carefully so his head won't flop backward or forward, bring him from his back to a sitting position and then to a head-to-knee position and back down.
3. When he's lying on his back, take hold of his head very gently at the forehead and turn his head slowly from one side to the other.
4. Turn him on his tummy and, supporting his head again, help him to push up on his hands and arch his back just slightly.
5. Be very careful to make your movements slow, gentle, and easy. Don't jerk your baby into any position or cause him to strain his muscles in any way. If he coos and smiles when you're doing these activities, you'll know you're doing them right. If, at any time, he frets or cries, stop right away.

**Purpose:**   To give the baby's muscles exercise and practice in the period before he can move them in a controlled fashion by himself; to help build muscle tone and strength.

**Variation:**   When the muscles of his neck are well enough developed that he holds his head steady by himself when he's seated in your lap, you can add to your exercises the following: when he is in a supine position (lying on his back), take hold of his hands and pull him slowly and gently to a seated position. Support him by his hands in the sitting position for a few seconds, and then slowly let him down to a supine position again.

## TAKE A WALK WITH BABY

**Participants:** Babies from birth until they can get about on their own, and an adult friend. Many babies will continue to enjoy this activity after they start crawling, because the view from someone's shoulder is different than the one from the ground.

**Explanation:** In the first half year or more of their lives, babies are completely dependent on others for entertainment because they have no way of getting around by themselves. And no matter how interesting you make your baby's personal surroundings, it's still only one view of the world. At fairly regular intervals, you should carry your baby about at your shoulder so that she can expand her world view.

1. Take her to places where there are other people doing things so that she can watch them.

2. Take her on a tour of your home, stopping regularly to observe the scenery, pointing out to her the most interesting visual events. (E.g., stop at the sink in the kitchen and let her feel the water splash over her hand. Stop to look out a window and talk about what you see.)

3. Go outside and talk to a bird, smell a flower, throw a peanut to a squirrel, or admire a tree. If it's winter, and there's snow, make a snowball and let your baby feel its cold and wetness; throw it at a bush or a wall and watch it break into pieces.

4. Wherever you walk, stop to take notice of the details as well as the big things, and talk to your baby about what you see and hear and smell and feel.

**Purpose:** To provide your baby with interesting experiences to broaden her horizons; to share in a mutually enjoyable experience with a favorite person; to help your baby develop an appreciation of language as a form of communication as you talk about the experiences you're having; and to help you regain an appreciation of the small things in life by sharing in your baby's wonder at the world.

## THE NAME GAME

**Participants:**   Babies from birth to six months, and one or more family members or friends.

**Explanation:**   Here's a game to help your baby learn to connect sounds to their sources and, in particular, voices to their owners.

1. With the baby in someone else's lap or in his bed, stand where he can see you, and call his name until he responds to you by looking toward you. Try whispering his name, and try singing it, too.

2. Then move to the side so your baby can see you if he turns his head slightly (how far to the side you stand should depend on how far to the side your baby is able to move his head). Call to him again.

3. If your baby turned his head toward your voice, make the game harder by moving further out of his line of vision (but still potentially within it if he turns toward you), and call out his name again.

4. Move behind your baby, and say his name. Does he look around for you?

5. If your baby can do the preceding activities with no problem, try this puzzle: Have another family member call out the baby's name while you stand in front of him and move your lips without actually making any sound.
   Did you fool him, or could he tell it wasn't your voice?
   Did he look at you with a puzzled expression on his face?
   Did he look around for the person who was really calling him?
   What happens if you both call his name at the same time? Does he look only at one of you, or does he look around for both of you?

**Purpose:**   This game gives the baby practice in hearing his name used, helping him establish a sense of self—that he is a person who has a name just as other people and things around him have names. In this sense, then, it is both a social learning and the learning of a language and thinking skill. Also, it gives the baby practice connecting people with their voices and tests his understanding of this concept through seeing if he picks up on the incongruity of hearing a strange voice come from someone whose voice he knows as part of that person. These are complex skills, and if your baby doesn't catch on now, try again later. (Obviously, the latter part of the game won't be appropriate until your baby associates your voice with you.)

## TOUCH AND FEEL

**Participants:**   Three- to six-month-old baby and an adult.

**Materials:**   Small swatches of variously textured material—velvet, cotton, leather, suede, burlap, silk, nylon, nappy wool, and so on.

**Explanation:**   Make your baby a toy that can be used to stimulate her sense of touch.

1. Go to a shop that sells materials and patterns, and ask if they will sell or give you small pieces of left-over odds and ends of different kinds of materials to make a toy for your baby. Most places will be willing to set aside small pieces for you. You might also look at rummage sales and thrift shops for material scraps.

2. When you've collected a good selection, sew them together into a large cloth. You can then use it as is or make it into a ball (stuffed loosely with worn-out stockings, socks, or other pieces of clothing), a star, an octopus, a doughnut, or some other kind of toy your baby can grab hold of with ease.

3. In short, fun playtimes with your baby, take her hand and rub it across one kind of material on the cloth or toy you made from the cloth. As you do so, talk to your baby about it: "Feel this. It's so soft." Then, touch her fingers to a different-texture material, and talk to her: "This one feels rough. Feel how rough it is."

4. You don't have to use those exact words. The point is to give your baby experience with different feelings and at the same time to accompany those feelings with words that describe those feelings. Even though your baby is too young to understand the words now, she'll enjoy hearing them, and children learn to understand and use language through repeated experiences associating words, objects, and actions.

5. Leave the cloth hanging on the side of your baby's crib where she can touch it when she wants to, or leave the toy you made with the cloth hanging from a piece of elastic from the top or side of her crib for her to play with and experience on her own too.

**Purpose:**   To give the baby experience using her sense of touch, to develop her capacity for discriminating among different kinds of feelings. This is helpful, also, in her learning to distinguish "what is me" from "what is not me"—learning, for example, the difference in the feeling of cloth from the feeling of another person from the feeling of touching or sucking her own fingers. In addition, it's an opportunity to give the baby experience connecting words and feelings and, most important, to participate in a mutually enjoyable activity with another human being.

You can grow from the experience, too, from the practice in resourcefulness you'll get from making the toy and from experiencing feeling the different textures as if you were doing so, as your baby, for the first time. We adults have learned to interpret and analyze everything; just experiencing can be both fun and educational.

**Variations:** When your child is older, you can use the same toy and some duplicate swatches of material to play a game in which she tries to match up two of the same kind. You can touch her body with a piece of material and ask her to touch the one on the toy that feels the same. Even later, when she's learned the words to describe the feelings, you can play a game in which you ask her to "Touch the soft ones," "Touch the smooth ones," and so on.

## TOUCH AND NAME

**Participants:**  Six- to twelve-month-old baby and adult.

**Explanation:**  Touch different parts of your baby's body and name them: "This is Tommy's nose." "Here's Tommy's foot." "Where's Tommy's arm? Here it is. Here's Tommy's arm!" Touch your own body parts too, and do the same thing: "Here's Mommy's nose." "Here's Daddy's nose." "Here's Tommy's nose."

**Purpose:**  To develop in the baby an awareness of himself and his body image and to help him understand the difference between himself and others. In addition, it teaches connections between words and objects and actions, including names and pronouns. Even though it will be a while before your baby uses these words himself, he is learning now, through this type of experience, to recognize the words and their connections to things in his environment.

**Variation:**  Once your child begins, through practice, to learn the names himself, try turning the game around and ask "Where's Tommy's arm?" "Where's Mommy's arm?" "Where's Daddy's arm?" "Where's your dolly's arm?"

## FUN IN THE BATHTUB

**Participants:** Six- to twelve-month-old baby and an adult. Bath time should be enjoyable for younger babies and older children too, but the activities will differ somewhat.

**Materials:** Soap, a sponge, a plastic cup, a rubber toy, a wooden toy or block of wood, a plastic container with a top, and other household items that can be taken in the water. Use only a couple at a time.

**Explanation:** Use the time you're bathing your baby to let her learn and play. For those of you who are thinking, "But I can't afford the time to play games in the bathtub," we suggest that you only need to do one special thing each time you bathe your baby. And, as long as you're going to spend the time doing the physical act, why not change it from a dull, even unpleasant, routine into a chance for learning as well as time for the two of you to enjoy together?

1. Rub some soap onto your baby's body, and instead of just rinsing it right off, talk to her about it: "Oh, it's so slippery." Show her how her rubber toy slides out of her hand because the soap is slippery. Rub the soap in your hands to make a lather. Put some on your baby's hand, and show her how to blow it off. Put some on the water, and point out to her how the bubbles float on top of the water.

2. Put some cold water on her hand, and say, "Feel the water. It's cold. Brrrr!" Then put some warm water on her hand, and say, "This water is warm. Ummm. Feel the warm water." Show her that the cold water comes out when you turn one knob, and the hot water comes out when you turn the other knob. Let her feel the hot water, but not so hot that it hurts.

3. Let your child play with the sponge, filling it with water and then squeezing the water out. At this age, many children like to suck on the sponge. It won't hurt them to get a little bath water in their mouth.

4. Show your child how the plastic bottle floats, and let her play with it. When she gets tired of it, fill it with a little water, and show her how it goes under the water a little. Fill it all the way, and show her how it sinks. Let her play filling and emptying it by dunking it under the water; you'll have to demonstrate and help with the top.

5. Give your baby, one at a time, some different materials to put in the water to see if they sink or float. Talk to her about it: "What's going to happen, Barbara?" "Oh, look, it's staying on top of the water. It's floating." "Look, Barbara, that one went down. It sank."

**Purpose:** To give the baby experience with different physical feelings (e.g., cold and warm, slippery, wet) and with the properties of objects in relation to water (some sink, some float, sponges soak up water, you can make bubbles with soap and water). As she gets older, your baby will be able to understand these things more intellectually, but for now she can *experience* warm and cold, sinking and floating, making bubbles, and so on. In addition, she'll develop strength and skill with her hands through handling the things in the water and through learning to fill and squeeze out the sponge.

You can grow, too, through your participation with your baby in this fun experience with water, through turning a chore into an interesting activity, and from your ingeniousness in thinking up other ways to make bathing fun and educational for your baby.

## INTRODUCING . . . BABY!

**Participants:** Seven- to twelve-month-old baby, a familiar loved one, and someone the baby doesn't know.

**Explanation:** "Stranger anxiety"—reacting to people they don't know with fear and apprehension—is a common response of many babies in this age range who have been raised among a small number of people, especially within a nuclear family (mother, father, and siblings). It is a sign of growth; the baby is beginning to distinguish between whom he knows and whom he doesn't know, and he is learning to establish meaningful human relationships with those who care for him. A fear reaction to strangers is not inevitable, however; it depends very much on the way the stranger approaches the baby. Introducing a baby within this age range to a stranger (even when that stranger happens to be the baby's grandmother) should be done with care. Following are a few tips on how to do it.

1. First, and most important, the baby should be (according to his own choice) either in the arms of, or in some other way physically near, his own mother or other primary caregiver. This will make him feel safe enough to allow the stranger to make friends with him.

2. The stranger should make some friendly overture to the baby's caregiver before attempting to approach the baby. If the baby sees that his caregiver is accepting of this strange person's attention, then he will be more open to accepting it also.

3. Next, the stranger can smile at the baby and talk to him, but she should not attempt to take him in her arms. Engaging the baby in some simple game such as "Give and Take," Birth to One Year, page 87, might warm the baby up.

4. From this point, once initial contact has been made, the stranger should proceed to make friends at a pace decided by the baby. Some babies already may be ready to go to the stranger as long as their mother is within eye's view. Others will continue to be reticent or will be friendly only as long as their caregiver is holding them.

**Purpose:**   To help the baby who is at the stage of "stranger anxiety" to get to know someone who is unfamiliar, at a pace that is responsive to his own needs and style. The apprehensive response babies in this age range may have to strange people is paralleled by a generalized growth in their thinking skills which indicates they are beginning to know the difference between the familiar and the unfamiliar in all areas of their life.

Because it is embarrassing to parents to have their baby cry when some friendly stranger approaches (especially if that person is a relative), sometimes parents do not respond appropriately. Understanding that this is a normal developmental reaction, and that it will go away with sensitive handling, can help you respond in a way that reassures your baby of his safety and your love at the same time that it helps him learn to make new friends.

Think about how you feel when you walk into a room full of strangers. If you have a friend with you, you'll feel much more comfortable about approaching or being approached by these unfamiliar people. The purpose of this activity is for you to provide that kind of a safe "home base" for your child when he's in a situation that feels that way to him.

## MIRROR GAMES

**Participants:**   Six- to twelve-month-old baby and one or two others. Older children will continue to enjoy this kind and more complex kinds of mirror play. See "More Mirror Games," Three to Four Years, page 184, for some ideas for using the mirror with preschool children.

**Materials:**   A ball, a doll or stuffed animal, a hat for the baby, a full-length mirror, and a box.

**Explanation:**    Sit with the baby in front of the mirror. Put the toys and hat in a box beside you. First, just let her respond to her image in the mirror in any way she chooses. She may smile at herself, pat her image, and so on. When her interest begins to wane, you can rekindle it with some mirror games:

1. Put the hat on the baby's head, and let her play with that. Try out different views and positions. Talk to her as she plays. Ask her "Who's that in the mirror? Is that Amanda?"

2. Sit behind her and make a motion. Does she look around at you?

3. Copy her movements; do whatever she does. Does she increase or change her actions to stimulate your copying further?

4. Make silly faces in the mirror and see if she tries to make some too. Wave bye-bye to her in the mirror and walk away. What does she do? Play pat-a-cake with your mirror image. Can you get her to copy you?

5. Play the "Touch and Name" (page 71) game with her, yourself, and her stuffed toy while she looks in the mirror.

6. Hand her the ball, and see if she notices its image in the mirror. Roll the ball away from the mirror while she watches, then roll it back toward the mirror. Give the ball back to her to see what she does with it.

7. If there are two of you playing in addition to the baby, both of you do some simple actions at the same time, and see if the baby will try to join in. Clap your hands; open and close your eyes; put your hands on your head; stand up and sit down; and so on.

**Purpose:**    To help develop the baby's self-awareness and body image through experiences in seeing herself and playing with her mirror image. In addition, this sort of game is a foundation upon which the child will eventually develop a concept of left and right. Now it helps with other spatial concepts such as up and down, in front and behind, near and far, and so on. It will be a while before the baby understands these concepts in terms of language, but this kind of game begins to give her a feeling of them in relation to her own body.

## WALK WITH ME AND I'LL CREEP WITH YOU

**Participants:**    Babies between six and twelve months who are beginning to crawl and who can stand with help, and an adult.

**Explanation:** The most important thing to do for your baby when he's beginning to try to get about on his own is to give him room in which to do so. Even if you have to leave him in a playpen sometimes in order to get your work done, don't keep him captive any longer than is absolutely necessary. He needs the freedom to try out his newly developing skills in large spaces.

1. Put a pad on the floor if you don't have a rug or carpet, and clear the room of anything your baby could knock over or hurt himself on. Then, put him on his tummy and let him practice. Sometimes a push on the backs of his feet will help when he's having trouble moving from the spot he's on. Sometimes you can get down on the floor and crawl or creep with him. (Crawling, which is belly on the floor, comes before creeping which is belly parallel to the floor.)

2. Lift your baby to his feet by pulling gently on his hands, and hold him up under his arms so he can get the feel of being on his feet. Bounce him up and down lightly just a little, and see if he can take a step with you holding him under the arms.

3. As time goes on and his muscles strengthen and his skill improves, give your baby help at whatever level he's reached. Lead him by both hands in taking a few steps when he's able. Later, lead him by one hand only. Let him walk around holding onto furniture, and make sure it's sturdy enough to support him without toppling. Don't push him, but be there to give help and support that is responsive to his developmental needs and skills at the time.

**Purpose:** To provide the baby with the opportunity, space, and support to practice his developing capacity for moving about under his own steam.

## BABY'S FIRST BOOK

**Participants:** Babies, nine to twelve months and older, and an adult.

**Materials:** Pieces of sturdy white or off-white fabric, enough to cut into about ten $8 \times 12$ inch pieces; scraps of different materials in bright colors to make "pictures" with, including small pieces of different-textured materials to represent different feelings (e.g., leather or naugahyde for a ball, a cotton puff for a bunny's tail, a piece of sandpaper for a Daddy's beard); a small, round unbreakable mirror; cake flavoring, perfume, or other odor-producing materials to make the pictures smell; yarn or thread to sew with; a pen with permanent ink to write or draw on the cloth.

**Explanation:** You can introduce your baby to books by making her one from cloth that you can play with together. It should provide her with stimulation for her developing fine motor hand skills as well as for all her senses.

1. Cut the material for pages into ten pieces, and sew together five sets of two pieces each to make five pages of double thickness. Then bind the five pages together like a book, using thread or yarn to sew the binding. You may want to wait to bind the pages together until you've completed all the individual pages, but if you do, remember to leave enough room on the sides of the pages so that, when you sew them together, you don't cut off parts of any pictures.

2. Next, decide what you're going to put into your baby's book. Each side of every page should have a large, colorful picture of a single object that is familiar to your baby and a single word or phrase written below the picture in large capital letters describing the picture.[8] Following are some examples of the kinds of pictures you could include:
   a. A picture of a shoe made from leather; you could even punch holes and string a lace through them for a shoe that ties.
   b. A picture of a bunny made from a "fake fur" material and with a piece of cotton for a tail.
   c. A picture of your baby's favorite toy, made from a material similar to that which his toy is made of.
   d. A picture of some flowers like ones that grow near your home. You can make them from textured material such as crepe or velvet, and put some perfume on them to make them smell.
   e. A picture of your baby's favorite food, using some kind of flavoring rubbed in to give it an appropriate smell.
   f. Drawings or photographs of family members, each with some "prop" to help the baby recognize who it's supposed to be.
   g. A picture of a baby, with a small round mirror in place of the face, for your baby to look into and see herself.

3. Exactly what you put in your baby's book will depend on your baby and her particular experiences and interests. But, whatever you put in, make it more interesting by special feelings, smells, visual gimmicks, and even sounds if you can think of any sound-making objects that would fit in a book. Otherwise, you can provide the sounds with your

---

[8] Your baby won't be interested in the words for a while, but including them will get her used to seeing printed words in books and will enable you to use the book with her later to introduce her to the printed word.

voice. You might even have a page with "doors" (made from sewing on an extra flap of material to cover the pictures) for the baby to open and find a picture. Make it a book your baby can get involved with in as many ways as possible. You can make it longer, depending on your time, energy, and imagination.

4. Once the book has been made, then take the time to sit down with your baby and experience it together. Let her turn the pages. Stop when she chooses, to explore what's on each page. Don't try to make her read it like a regular book, going page by page. At this age, babies aren't interested in that kind of "reading." When she does show an interest in a particular page, show her how to feel the "picture," smell it if it has a special smell, play with any gadget you've included, and so on.

5. Talk to your baby about what she's experiencing in short, simple sentences: "Look, Margaret, that's Daddy. Feel his beard? Oh, he needs a shave." If the person or object in the picture is nearby, point to them to help your baby make the association between the picture and the object it represents.

6. By the way, you don't need to be a great artist to do such a book. Look at magazines for ideas, and trace your pictures onto the material you're

going to use. Then, cut out the material and sew it onto the page, using small stitches so it won't come off with a lot of use or trips through the washing machine. Something like the metal mirror would also be best sewn on instead of glued, so that your baby can't pull it off; use an awl or some similar tool to punch a few holes in the perimeter of the mirror, and then sew it onto the page.

**Purpose:**   To give the baby early experience with books, with two-dimensional representations of real objects; to give her practice connecting language with the experiences it represents; and to give her experience in using several senses to explore objects.

The most important impetus you can give your child to become interested and eventually competent in reading is to read yourself. Children model their behavior from that they see in those they care about (see "Behavior Speaks Louder than Words," pages 5–7, for further explanation), and if they see reading as an integral part of your life, it will become so with them also.

In addition, however, you can begin to give your baby positive early experiences with books so that when she's ready to really learn to read, she will be highly motivated to do so. Any experience shared in an enjoyable way with those she loves will continue to have positive associations connected to it for your child in later years.

**Variation:**   If you have neither the time, the skill, nor the motivation to make as complex a product as we've described here, you can still make books for your baby by cutting out pictures she likes from magazines and pasting them onto cardboard. Punch holes in the side of the cardboard, and join the pages with string, yarn, or a shoelace. If you have a limited amount of time to spend with your children because you work all day and have several children to care for, it's better for you to use what time you do have for interacting with them rather than for preparing materials.

## HIDE AND SEEK

**Participants:**   Eight- to twelve-month-old baby and adult. You can try this game with younger babies too by using the sound clue and only partially hiding the toy.

**Materials:**   Sound toy (e.g., bell, rubber toy that squeaks, toy that makes an animal noise), two plastic cups, cloth to cover toy.

**Explanation:** Learning that things which are out of sight still exist and can be found (object permanence) is an important thinking skill which babies develop in their first year through continued experience in "rediscovering" familiar objects and people. Developing an internalized memory of an object and its actions is one of their first steps toward the uniquely human skill of being able to think abstractly about things and ideas not directly accessible to concrete experience. The following is an example of a game that can be used to stimulate your baby's development of this important skill.

1. Make a noise with the toy while the baby is watching you. Move it above him, then to each side but not out of his line of vision, to get him to follow its movement.

2. Once you've got his attention, while he's watching you, move the toy to the side and then under a table or behind your back so the baby can't see it. Make the noise, and talk to him as you play the game: "Hear the bell? Can you find it? Where's the bell?" [9]

3. Continue the game as long as your child is enjoying it, hiding the toy in different spots out of his sight, but giving him a clue by making the noise. Whenever he gets tired of the game, leave it and come back to it or the following parts another day.

4. As you play the game, always hide the toy in the same place until your baby finds it every time with no effort. Then, hide it in a new place. Does he get confused at first and keep looking for it in the previous hiding place?

5. Play the game using the two cups. Make the sound with the toy, and while your child is watching, hide the toy under one of the cups. See if you can fool him into thinking it's under one of the cups when it's really under the other by putting the toy under one cup and then under the other.

6. Use the cloth to hide the toy. While your baby watches, put the toy under the cloth and make the sound. Leave just a little corner of the toy showing at first, then cover it up completely if your baby has no trouble finding it. See what happens if you pretend to hide the toy under the cloth and then you really move it from under the cloth to another hiding place. Can your baby follow your movements, or does he get confused and keep looking for the toy under the cloth?

7. Try the versions of the game that your baby can do easily when you use the toy's sound as a clue now without using its sound, or use another toy that doesn't make a sound. Does he have more trouble now?

---

[9] He'll probably be most successful and enjoy the game most if you use one of his own favorite toys if he has one that makes a sound.

**Purpose:**    To give the baby experience with hidden objects with and without an auditory clue to their location. The skill involved in playing this game requires the baby to (1) pay attention and (2) follow the path of an object, remember, and visualize its final location. When the sound is used, it helps the child both in attending and in locating the final position of the object. Without the sound, the child has to depend totally on his visual memory.

The game is also good in giving the child practice in developing flexibility in his approach to problem-solving. When you switch from one established hiding place to a new one, the child is required to change his mental "set" in order to find the toy in its new hiding place. Being able to play this game successfully, especially without the sound clue, though apparently simple to an adult, is quite an accomplishment for the baby, who in early infancy simply forgot about anything that wasn't in his direct sight.

## THE TOY BEHIND THE SCREEN

**Participants:**    Nine- to twelve-month-old baby and an adult. This activity will continue to interest many babies into their second year.

**Materials:**    A favorite toy of the baby and a clear acetate screen the thickness of heavy cardboard and large enough to cover the toy.

**Explanation:**    A baby's being able to perceive and find some means to get around a barrier between herself and a toy she wants is a complex task. It requires the baby first to understand what a barrier is and that one exists. Then she must apply problem-solving techniques to figure out how to overcome it. The following is an example of an activity which will challenge your baby's problem-solving abilities in this area:

1. With the baby sitting at her own table or on your lap at a big table, take her toy and dance it back and forth playfully to her and away from her until you have her attention.

2. While she watches, take the screen and place it between your baby and the toy.

3. Observe her reaction. Does she try to reach for the toy and bang her hand against the screen? Does she look perplexed and give up? Does she try to engage your help in getting the toy? Does she get frustrated and upset by the task?

4. There's no "correct" response; how your baby responds will tell you something about her developmental level as well as her problem-solving approach. You should use her response as a guide to (a) reduce the requirements of the task and (b) give her a little help so that she can be successful in solving the problem.

5. If your baby got very upset by the task, just reach around the screen to get the toy, give it to her, and put the screen away. You can try the game another time when she's more ready for it. Otherwise, show her how to reach around or over the screen in order to get the toy, and then see if she can copy you.

6. If it's still too hard, try putting the screen only partially in front of the toy so that she only has to pull the toy away from the screen. Then gradually, cover more of the toy with the screen as she is able to obtain the toy successfully until the toy is again totally blocked from her grasp by the screen.

7. If she runs into a problem again, try guiding her hand until she's able to grab the toy and pull it away from the screen to herself.

8. All of these steps may take a series of trials at different times. Continue the activity only as long as your baby is enjoying the challenge. If it becomes too frustrating, stop and try again another time.

**Purpose:** To give the baby practice in problem-solving, in figuring out why she can't reach something she can see in front of her and then coming up with a way to get at it. In addition, the task requires the ability to tolerate a certain amount of frustration and to delay gratification in order to find a solution to the problem; if the baby is overcome by frustration and anxiety over not being able to reach the toy, she'll be unable to use her energy to solve the problem.

On a concrete level, this task parallels the more complex and abstract kinds of problem-solving your baby will have to do all her life in order to successfully deal with "barriers" to things she wants. The most important requirement that characterizes both this concrete task and the more abstract problems she'll encounter as an adult is her ability to persevere calmly until the problem is solved.

This requires a belief in her capacity to be successful when she devotes time and energy to a problem. That belief-in-self is fostered in these early stages of her life by her meeting with success in her endeavors. You can help by by providing guidance, encouragement, and support; by not making unreasonable demands and restrictions on her; and by giving her opportunities to test out her developing competencies on tasks which are challenging, but still within her capacity to be successful.

**Variation:**　Try playing the game using as barriers things that your baby can't see through, e.g., a solid piece of cardboard, a small pillow, a cereal box. At first, when using solid barriers, leave a little bit of the toy sticking out so that she knows it's there. At an earlier stage, if you put a solid barrier in front of her toy, she'd just forget the toy was there since she couldn't see it. This kind of game helps her complete her understanding that things she can't see are still there and can be gotten.

## YOUR KITCHEN IS A LEARNING LABORATORY

**Participants:**　Babies nine to twelve months and older, and you as an observer.

**Materials:**　Pots and pans, especially double-boilers or other pans that nest; empty boxes with a few small things (e.g., pieces of macaroni, dried beans) to put in them, a metal spoon, measuring cups and spoons (plastic or metal), and so on.

**Explanation:**　If you can stand the noise and the mess, one of the best places you can allow your baby to play is in the kitchen. Set aside one low shelf or drawer with things in it you don't mind your baby taking out to play with, and let him sit on the floor and entertain himself. Your role in this activity generally is more just to keep an eye on him than to direct in any way. Following are a few of the kitchen games he might enjoy engaging in:

1. Putting pots inside one another, and putting things inside them.

2. Banging pots together or banging a spoon inside a pot to make noise.

3. Dumping a small amount of macaroni or dried beans[10] from the box into a pan or on the floor, and then picking them up and putting them back in the box; dumping them from one paper cup into another.

4. Waving the metal measuring spoons in the air like a rattle.

5. Trying to nest the plastic measuring cups.

6. You should take a couple of minutes occasionally to join your baby in play, following his lead, showing him a few new activities to try that he hasn't thought of on his own, and talking with him—giving words to his actions. Most of the time, he'll be content to play by himself while you work at something else.

7. One activity your baby will love doing, for which he'll need your supervision, is water play. Put some newspapers on the floor, and partially fill a shallow pan with soapy water. Give him a few things to play with—a sponge, measuring spoons and cups, paper cups, and the like. Then, just let him splash and dump and fill. You don't have to watch him like a hawk, but you should keep an eye on him, and he'll enjoy your playing with him some of the time.

**Purpose:** There are many things to be learned from this kind of activity. First, the baby gets an opportunity to play with "real" things, things that play an important part in the family's everyday life. It teaches him about the objects in his family-world and allows him to participate on his own level. (He'll also enjoy "helping" you around the house by this age, for example, bringing you things you ask for with words and gesture.)

In addition, the stacking and nesting and dumping and filling provide the beginnings of mathematical concepts—of quantity, of the size of one thing compared to another, of volume, and so on. And the handling of the small and large objects is good practice for the baby in developing his fine motor coordination with his fingers and hands.

---

[10] If your baby still puts everything in his mouth, it's better to give him larger items that he can't swallow or pieces of soft foods such as raisins that he won't choke on.

## THE TOY AT THE END OF THE STRING [11]

**Participants:** Nine- to twelve-month-old baby and adult. Some babies may enjoy playing a simplified version of this game as early as six months or whenever they're able to use their fingers to pick up a piece of string.

**Materials:** Three pieces of string, each a couple of feet long; a favorite toy of the baby's (something light-weight); a long table.

**Explanation:** In the second half of their first year, babies increase their skill using their fingers and thumb in a coordinated way to pick up very small objects. The following activity lets your baby practice this skill at the same time that it presents a challenge to her problem-solving skills.

1. Tie the end of one of the pieces of string to your baby's toy. Then line all three strings up on the table, parallel to each other. One end of each one should be close to the edge of the table so that the baby can pick up the strings without straining when she's seated in your lap at the end of the table. For the first parts of the game, your child should be able to see the far ends of the strings.

2. Show your baby how to pull a string toward her until she gets to its far end. Let her play with the strings in any way she chooses. If she pulls in

---

[11] After Ira J. Gordon, *Baby Learning Through Baby Play* (New York: St. Martin's Press, 1970), p. 32. This excellent "parent's guide for the first two years" is filled with activities for using your routine interactions with your baby as sources of special learning games to help her grow.

the one with the toy, exclaim "Oh, look! That one has a toy!" And, if she pulls one to its end, and there is no toy, say "No toy on this one."

3. Extend this game over as many sessions as your baby continues to enjoy playing it. Each time, you can add a little more. As always, play only as long in one session as your child is having a good time.

4. For the next step, line up the strings, and ask your baby to "Get the toy. Pull the string with the toy." Talk to her about what she's doing. If she pulls in the toy, make note of it. If she pulls in a string without a toy, note that there's no toy. Continue playing this way until your baby gets fairly accurate at pulling the right string.

5. Then, drape the far ends of the strings over the edge of the table out of your baby's view.[12] Ask her again to pull the string with the toy. Encourage her to practice for as long as she wants. Each time she's pulled in the toy, line the strings up again in the same positions as before. See if she can learn to find the string with the toy consistently without trial and error.

**Purpose:** To give the baby practice using her fingers and thumb in a pincer grasp to pick up and manipulate a small object (in this case, a piece of string). Having a toy at the end of one string serves both as a motivator in the task and, for babies who understand the task, as a problem to be solved: Which string has the toy? It requires the baby to remember the location of the toy, at first with the toy in view and then without being able to see the toy. In the first version, the baby has to *recognize* the toy's position. In the second, she has to *recall* it. (For further explanation of the memory process, see "More Memory Games," Two to Three Years, page 167.)

**Variation:** If your baby enjoys this activity very much and gets very accomplished at it, here are a couple of ways to make it more challenging.

1. Periodically change the position of the string with the toy. For example, you might put it in the middle every other time.

2. Color-code the strings. For example, make one red. Have it always attached to the toy, regardless of location.

These variations will give your baby practice solving problems on the basis of position, temporal, and color cues.

[12] For this part, you'll need to use a small, very light-weight toy, such as a little plastic animal, so it won't pull the string off the edge of the table.

## GIVE AND TAKE

**Participants:**   Nine- to twelve-month-old baby and another person. Some babies will continue to enjoy this or a variation of this game after their first year.

**Materials:**   A block, small ball, or some other object that can be held easily in the baby's hand.

**Explanation:**   Having developed the ability to grasp, most babies now are learning to let go. This is an example of a game that many babies initiate on their own. You can increase your baby's fun and learning if you join him enthusiastically when he starts the game and sometimes introduce the game yourself.

1. Give the object to your baby and say "Here's the ball (or whatever the object is)."
2. Then, put your hand out as if to receive it back, and when your baby places the object in your hand, take it and say "Thank you." If he imitates your "thank you," respond with "You're welcome."
3. Continue this give and take for as long as your baby enjoys it. If he wants to keep playing, he's still learning.
4. Give your baby the object and take it from him with enthusiasm and a spirit of fun to match his own.

**Purpose:**   To give the baby practice in letting go, using his hand muscles in a controlled way to let go of and release into another person's hand an object he's holding onto.

Also, it's a form of social interchange. It's the easiest and most pleasant way to teach appropriate language to accompany such an interchange (i.e., that when someone gives you something, you say "Thank you," and when someone says "Thank you," you reply "You're welcome").

At first, many babies get confused and say "Thank you" even when they are handing the object to another. After a while, they'll learn to discriminate which part of the interchange is correctly associated with which verbal expression.

*Don't correct your baby* if he uses the words incorrectly. Your model and the practice will be far better teachers than deliberate instruction and correction.

## YOU DO WHAT I DO

**Participants:** Nine- to twelve-month-old baby and adult.

**Explanation:** At different times when you're with your baby, take a few minutes to play copy-cat with any kind of movement you can think of that you know she can do too. Sometimes you can start the game by copying whatever she's doing at the time. Then see if she'll copy you.

1. Make a funny face at the baby and see if she'll make one too.
2. Stick out your tongue and make a funny noise. Will she copy you?
3. Wave bye-bye to her, say the words, and pretend to walk away. Does your baby wave back or try to say "bye-bye?"
4. Get on your hands and knees, and crawl or creep like her. Does she copy you in turn?
5. Open and close your eyes, then your mouth. Move your head from side to side and up and down. Will she do it too?
6. Play pat-a-cake with her. Will she join you or at least hold her hands up to play with you?
7. Pretend to drink from a cup, then hand it to her. Pretend to eat from a spoon, then give it to her to pretend.
8. Make some different kinds of sounds, and see if she'll try them. Make a coughing sound; whistle; make a kissing sound; make a noise like a howling wolf; sing a simple tune; say ba-ba-ba.
9. Babies this age generally like to play copy-cat. They will catch on to what you want them to do fairly easily, especially if you start the game by imitating them. If your baby doesn't try to copy you spontaneously, don't try to "teach" her. When she's seen you do the action enough times, and she's ready to do it herself, she'll copy you. And the more times you repeat any action and give your baby a chance to practice it herself, the better she'll get at it.

**Purpose:** To give your baby practice imitating someone else's behavior. This is a complex skill. The baby has to pay attention to the movements she sees, form a visual image of them in her mind that corresponds to the movement, and then perform that movement. Thus, copying gives the baby practice visualizing and matching her own movements to those she sees. In the case of sound-making, she also has to form an internal "image" of the sound which she then tries to match. Imitation is an important form of social interaction. It is a variant of modeling, one of the principal means through which children learn those behaviors which human society in general, and their own culture in particular, requires of its members.

## A CUP IS TO DRINK AND A BELL IS TO RING

**Participants:**   Nine- to twelve-month-old baby and adult.

**Materials:**   A plastic cup, a bell, a rubber squeeze toy, a spoon, a big crayon and a piece of paper, and other simple objects from the baby's environment that have a specific function.

**Explanation:**   Most babies before this age and some of this age respond to all objects they encounter in the same way: They bang them, wave them, mouth them, and so on. This activity is one you can do as a special game or just any time as part of your daily routine to give your baby practice learning to use different kinds of objects appropriately, according to their particular function.

1. Present the objects to your baby, one at a time, and see what he does with each one.
2. Does he pretend to drink with the cup or to give you a drink?
3. Does he ring the bell and squeeze the toy?
4. Does he pretend to feed himself or you with the spoon?
5. Does he know the crayon is for scribbling on the paper?
6. After seeing what your baby does on his own, show him what to do, one at a time, with the objects he didn't use appropriately. You do it, then hand the object to him.
7. Talk to your baby as you play the game, e.g., "Look, I'm going to draw a picture." "Now you do it. You draw a picture." "Oh, look at the picture Michael drew! What a nice picture." (It won't be much more than a couple of scribbles, but it's the first step in his artistic development.)
8. Don't correct your baby's way of performing a particular task; the point is to give him a model and then to allow him to practice using different tools. He will learn to use them more skillfully as he gains practice.

**Purpose:** To help the baby learn to use objects appropriately, i.e., according to the use specified for them in his culture. To give him practice in fine motor coordination, using his hands to accomplish such tasks as picking up a cup and bringing it to his lips as if to drink, holding onto a crayon and bringing it to a piece of paper to make a mark, and so on. It requires sophisticated thinking skills and well-developed fine motor coordination with their hands for babies to use each object differently according to its particular function in their culture.

# 3

# One to Two Years: Shifting Gears

From one to two years, children refine previously acquired skills and develop new ones. They learn to walk, improve their balance and coordination in an upright posture, and learn more difficult walking-related motor acts such as trotting, running, climbing, and going up and down stairs. They gain voluntary control of their hands for controlled letting go now, in addition to their previously acquired skill of grasping and holding. So dropping and throwing become favorite pastimes (they usually begin toward the end of the first year). Children learn about gravity, also, from these "experiments." In addition, they learn better control of tools such as a cup, a spoon, and a crayon. By the end of the year, most children will have gained enough control of their sphincter muscles, both for holding in and for letting go, that they can be toilet trained.

Children's ability to discriminate the sounds and the meaning of the language spoken around them improves as does their ability to imitate and produce speech sounds themselves. Because of their preoccupation with motor learning, children may make very slow progress in language development in the first part of the year. Toward the latter half of the year, however, they will make fast gains in vocabulary (from an average of ten or twenty words at eighteen months to over two hundred at two years) and will begin speaking in short phrases. Most children, in this period, go from a few words mixed in

91

with a lot of jargon to mostly all real words. In the second year of their lives, children's memories increase—for things, people, places, and ideas. They not only recognize the familiar now. They begin to show the ability to recall and reproduce recent memories of words, actions, behaviors, and experiences. In solving new problems, children now bring to bear old experience. They try out different known procedures of action in the new situation and begin, toward the end of the year, to develop new procedures through combining and changing old ones. Children are beginning to have representations of real things in their heads (memories of pictures, sounds, feelings, etc.) that help them to think about something without its being physically present.

Between one and two years, also, children begin to develop a sense of themselves as persons. They begin to respond to and call themselves by their names; to claim possessions as "mine," and to recognize their mirror images. By two, they may even begin to want to hear stories about themselves. In this period, children are still very attached to and realistically dependent on their caregivers. But the skills they are learning enable them to become increasingly self-reliant in contrast to the helplessness of much of their first year. They are learning to feed themselves; help undress and dress themselves; control their bowels and bladder; eat solid, nonsimplified foods; and of course, get around well on two feet. In addition they are learning the power of words, on their own and others' behavior.

All the new skills children gain in this stage make them increasingly more independent. As a result, their relationship with those caring for them undergoes significant changes from what it was when they were more dependent. In particular, it has been suggested that the time period between ten and eighteen months constitutes a turning point in children's development and in their relationship with those adults closest to them that will have a profound impact on whether they grow to be healthy competent individuals or whether they have problems coping socially and intellectually.[1]

The combination of factors occurring in this period—the growth in children's ability to understand language, not yet matched with any significant competency in its use; the development of the ability to get about on their own and get into things; an intense curiosity about things, not matched by an understanding of danger (e.g., of playing with razor blades) or by an appreciation of other people's property rights; and an emerging sense of themselves as persons having separate identities and who can have an effect on their world—makes this a period that can challenge caregivers to the limits of their skills and patience.

[1] See Burton White and Jean Carew Watts, *Experience and Environment*, Vol. 1 (Englewood Cliffs, N.J.: Prentice-Hall, Inc., 1973). See also the chapter on this subject in J. and L. Braga, *Growing with Children*.

## DUMP AND FILL

**Participants:**   Twelve- to eighteen-month-old baby by himself.

**Materials:**   A small wastebasket and some "junk mail"; a basket or bowl and some blocks; a paper bag and some wood or plastic clothespins; or any other container and objects to put in it.

**Explanation:**   For times when you're busy doing other things, your baby can entertain himself for long periods of time "dumping and filling."
1. Give your baby a container and some objects to put in it. Then, keeping him within hearing distance and checking on him regularly without making him feel "watchdogged," let him be.
2. He'll have great fun dumping out the contents of the container and then putting it all back again, piece by piece by piece. You'll be surprised how long your baby can keep himself busy with this activity.
3. You might want to take a couple of minutes off from your work to join him in his game or to start him off, but as a rule, this is one he'll enjoy on his own.

**Purpose:**   To give your baby practice using his hands to let go of objects with control. As you remember, your baby learned to grasp fairly early in his first year, and throughout the year he improved and refined his grasping ability. Letting go—releasing objects by opening up his fingers slowly and not expulsively—takes longer to learn. "Give and Take," Birth to One Year, page 87, is an example of one of the first games many babies play to practice letting go. Dumping and filling is another way that many babies practice this skill. In addition, this activity has value because it enables your baby to have some time alone, to play without direction or instruction—without anyone to tell him what to do, how to do it, or how well he has done.

## I'LL FEED YOU AND YOU FEED ME

**Participants:**   Twelve- to eighteen-month-old baby and adult.[2]

2 See "Variation" for some notes about feeding at eighteen to twenty-four months.

**Materials:** Regular mealtime utensils plus an extra spoon for the baby.

**Explanation:** Feeding should be a special time for interaction between you and your baby now as it was in the first year (See "Eating Is More Than Filling Your Belly," page 64). Toward the end of her first year, your baby probably began trying to feed herself. This year, she will be increasingly more deliberate and effective in these efforts. Gradually she'll take over more and more of the feeding process herself. Therefore, part of your feeding responsibilities include helping your baby learn to feed herself.

1. You can "teach" this skill best by giving your baby encouragement, opportunity for practice, and patience. Let your baby have her own spoon while you feed her with another. Thus, you can make sure she gets some food in her mouth while she practices her skill. As long as you're not overly concerned with cleanliness, efficiency, and speed, the two of you should be able to work out a relaxed, comfortable system of "taking turns."

2. Sometimes you can help out by pouring food from your spoon into your baby's. And sometimes, if she doesn't mind, you can hold her spoon with her, helping her guide it to her mouth. But, ultimately, your baby will learn to feed herself only through practicing on her own.

3. While she is learning, your baby will turn the spoon over often before it gets to her mouth. She may feed as much food to the floor or table as she does to herself. With your patient understanding and tolerance, by the end of the year your baby will learn to feed herself fairly neatly and efficiently.

4. Sometimes feeding you will help your baby practice. Since she can see your mouth, she can be more successful at aiming and reaching it with the food. So, stop your feeding once in a while to let your baby try her skill at using the spoon to put some food into *your* mouth.

**Purpose:** To give your baby opportunity to practice feeding herself with a spoon. This skill requires the development of fine motor coordination in using her hands for manipulating tools. Also, it gives the baby feelings of competence and self-worth to learn the skills she needs in order take responsibility for her own feeding. This is especially true because it increases her control of her own behavior in a situation in which she previously was entirely dependent on her caregiver.

**Variation:** If you've been patient with your baby's efforts to feed herself in the first half of the year, your patience is soon to be rewarded. Between eighteen and twenty-four months, she will become increasingly able to care for herself at meals and should be allowed to do so. Your cleanup afterwards will be progressively easier, and your baby probably will enjoy helping.

In this age period, your baby may become interested in learning to use a child-sized fork to spear small chunks of food. Show her how, and let her practice. To avoid spilling, fill your child's glass only half-way with liquid. Then let her drink from it by herself. Be sure not to give your baby any breakable dishes or glasses. If you're not around to take her plates when she's done eating, she's likely to drop them on the floor, as if announcing the completion of her meal.

## BABY'S FIRST PUZZLE

**Participants:**   Twelve- to eighteen-month-old baby and an adult.

**Materials:**   Heavy cardboard or posterboard, clear contact paper, paste or glue, a felt-tip marker, scissors or X-acto blade for cutting the cardboard.

**Explanation:**   Your baby learns to use his hands skillfully through practice in manipulating many different kinds of materials. Puzzles are one of the materials that can help a baby develop control and coordination of his hands. The first puzzles your baby will be able to handle are simple one piece "formboards." Following are instructions for making such a puzzle.

1. Cut several circles out of square pieces of heavy cardboard. The circles should be all the same size, bigger than your baby's hand. When you cut out the shapes, be careful to leave the square forms you cut them from as whole pieces; they will be put together to make the outline for the puzzle. Paste all the circles together and all the circle forms together.

2. Paste together several square pieces of cardboard the same size as the forms from which you cut the circles. Paste the outline form to the solid sheet of cardboard, and cover the whole thing with clear contact paper. Cut away the part of the contact paper which is covering the circular indentation.

3. Using crayon or magic marker, draw a happy face on the circle. Cover the circle with clear contact paper. You now have a simple, sturdy "formboard" for your baby.

4. Your baby probably will begin to enjoy this formboard at about twelve to fourteen months. The first time you give it to him, sit down with him and show him how to take the circle out and put it back in. Then let him practice.

5. It will take your baby a little while to get the knack of (1) grasping the edge of the circle to get it out and (2) getting it in just the right position so that it'll go back in. But unless he gets really frustrated and upset with the task, let him work at it himself. This is another good toy for your baby to play with on his own.

**Purpose:**  To develop your baby's fine motor coordination of his hands, through practice using his fingers and thumb to pry out the circular puzzle piece. In addition, this task requires the baby to make a spatial judgment, matching up the circular form with its space and getting the form placed just right in order to get it into the formboard.

## Variation:

1. When your baby is able to accomplish this formboard with so much ease that it no longer interests him, make him a new one, this time a square one. When he can do that one well, make him one in the shape of a triangle. And when he can handle that with ease, make him (or buy) a formboard with places for all three shapes on the same board.

2. Toward the second half of the year, as your baby becomes more skilled, he'll probably enjoy slightly more complex two- and three-piece jigsaw puzzles. The best ones for him at first are those in which each piece is a

whole picture. There are some good wooden ones commercially produced, or you can make your own. Mount magazine pictures or photographs of things familiar to your baby on cardboard, and cut them out. Cut a puzzle form out of several thicknesses of cardboard pasted together, and cover the whole thing with clear contact paper.

## WAIT IS A BETTER WORD THAN NO

**Participants:**   Babies, one to two years and older, and adults.

**Explanation:**   When babies are able to get about on their own, they generally are more adventurous than cautious at first. This poses a behavior management challenge to their caregivers. At this age the function of "discipline" or controls should be to monitor children's behavior so that they don't hurt themselves or others, not to "punish" them. You shouldn't draw any more attention than is necessary to problem behaviors. Children go through a couple of negativistic phases between one and three years in which they're likely to do the opposite of what you say, especially when you use an emotionally-charged word like "NO!" The word "Wait!" can be a useful tool in your behavior management tool kit during this time.

1. When you notice your baby approaching a situation that you wish her to avoid (e.g., if she's about to stick her fingers in the electric outlet), or when you see her engaged in an activity you want her to stop (e.g., playing with matches, scissors, razor blades, or something equally dangerous), call out to her in a strong, loud, but calm voice, "Wait!"

2. This usually is much more effective at preventing a crisis than is "No!" since for many children this age, *no* has very negative connotations. It is just as likely either to frighten the child or make her deliberately continue her action in defiance of the order as it is to make her stop. "Wait!" is a much more neutral word emotionally, both in the way it is delivered by adults and in the way it is received by children.

3. In addition, using "Wait" gives you a few seconds to gather your resources and decide what action to take next. It will work especially well as your baby begins to understand that "Wait" means to stop temporarily what you're doing.

**Purpose:** To develop a consistent method that works to inhibit your baby's behavior. This is particularly useful in times of near crisis when you're too far away to intervene physically by removing the child bodily from the danger situation. In addition, "Wait!" can be used in place of "No!" in less drastic and more routine situations when you need to get your baby to stop what she's doing long enough for you to distract her from the activity in question.

## HOW DO YOU SAY NO TO A BABY?

**Participants:** Babies from the time they can get about on their own until they understand spoken language well enough to be reasoned with, and adults.

**Explanation:** You can't curb the active, exploratory nature of babies this age through reasoning. You can't explain to them *why* they shouldn't play with matches or dump all the contents of your drawers on the floor. And you shouldn't use methods of control that will frighten your baby or interfere unnecessarily with his initiative in learning. Fortunately, there are several techniques you can use to prevent some problems and deal with others when they occur.

1. *Prevention.* When your baby can get around well on his own, he no longer needs to devote all his attention to self-propulsion. Now, he can move

about and destroy property at the same time. As he grows older, he'll learn respect for other people's property. Until then, you'll save him and yourself a great deal of pain by "baby-proofing" your living environment. Clear it temporarily of objects within his reach that he could damage or hurt himself with.

This doesn't mean that you have to put away everything you own. Simply remove from temptation those items that are sure to attract your baby's attention and your anger if he harms them. Also, cover electrical outlets and put matches, knives, razor blades, pills, cleaning solutions, and other potentially dangerous things in a locked cabinet where your baby can't get at them

2. *Modify your expectations:* both of your baby's behavior and of the condition of your living environment during this period. It's unrealistic to expect to keep your home perfectly neat, orderly, and spotless with a child this age. Trying to do so can cause only frustration and anxiety for you and your child. Most mothers realize this fairly quickly even if they formerly were very concerned about the condition of their home. But fathers who work away from the home all day and don't contribute to the housekeeping responsibilities sometimes may be unreasonable in their expectations of a neat and clean home.

We ask you fathers who are fortunate enough to have only one job to do each day to understand that taking good care of children and keeping a house clean and neat are both very demanding jobs. Sometimes they are mutually exclusive. Babies this age are very active, and it takes time to supervise or keep an eye on them. Learning to tolerate a bit of mess is an investment in your child's growth. It will enable you to spend your time together productively rather than watchdogging your baby's every move or barricading him or most of your home from him.

3. *Distraction.* Babies this age have short attention spans. They forget quickly about something that is removed from their attention. If your baby is doing something you want him to stop, remove him from the situation or take away the item you don't want him to play with. Distract him with an activity he enjoys, a toy, a funny face, a silly noise, or something you know will attract his attention. This is not the time to teach your baby lessons. He'll only be frightened by your yelling or hitting him, and he won't understand why you did it. Instead, just remove him calmly from the problem situation.

4. *Remember this rule:* If you want to see a behavior again, pay attention to it. If you don't want to see a behavior again, ignore it and pay attention to a competing or incompatible behavior. For example, ignore your child when he plays with his food. Give him lots of positive attention when he eats neatly with a spoon or fork. He'll soon stop

playing with his food. Pay more attention to your child's "good" behaviors than to his "bad" ones, and you'll see more good than bad behavior.

5. *Eye control.* If your child's within your eye's view when he starts to do something harmful or dangerous, give him a look that says in no uncertain terms, "Don't do it." You don't have to look threatening or mean. Just let him know through your look that you will not be pleased if he continues. If he does continue, go over and remove him from the situation. He'll get the message without your having to get angry.

6. "No!": Use with discretion and conviction. Sometimes the best way to stop your baby from doing something is to say "No!" in a strong, definite—but not mean or frightening—voice. In some cases, "Wait!" may be better; see the preceding activity. If your baby is beginning to feel that "No!" is the only word you know, you're overusing it. Examine your behavior management techniques and see where you could substitute some of the ones we've suggested.

7. Never hit babies this age. It serves no useful purpose. It only frightens them and shows them that aggressive behavior is acceptable. Aggression breeds aggression. When you hit or yell, you teach your children to do the same. And you create feelings of anger and resentment. If you can use other methods that work as well or better without such unfortunate consequences, it makes sense to do so.

8. Don't set up win-lose situations with your baby. For example, if you say "Come here," and your baby walks the other way, be careful not to turn it into a showdown. If it doesn't matter, just ignore him and go do something else. If it is important, calmly go to him.

9. Humor can be a useful tool to relieve the tension in this kind of situation. When your baby does just the opposite of what you ask, then ask him to do the thing he just did. Use a tone of voice that turns it into a game. For example, tell him playfully to "Go away." You may finally get him to come to you as you originally requested.

10. The important thing to understand is that your baby is beginning to develop his identity as a separate person, all his own. He needs guidance and firm limits to keep him from hurting himself or others. But don't take his testing of his limits so seriously that you allow yourself to get into games of tug-of-war with him.

11. Provide a steady and dependable source of strength and loving support for your child. Keep your expectations and demands reasonable, consistent, and predictable. Help your child grow through this and later stages of negativism rather than get stuck on some unending merry-go-round of unproductive behavior patterns in which no one really can win.

**Purpose:** To help you develop some workable, nondamaging, and growth-enabling behavior management techniques to use with your baby in a stage in his growth that can challenge and frustrate even the most patient caregiver.

## PLAY BALL³

**Participants:** One- to two-year-old baby and adult.

**Materials:** Large rubber ball or beach ball.

**Explanation:** Many babies this age enjoy simple games with balls. Ball play develops both fine and gross motor control and coordination. It also is an enjoyable form of social interaction. Following are guidelines for playing ball with your baby.

1. Sit on the floor facing your baby with your legs spread, your feet touching hers. Gently roll the ball to her. Urge her to grab hold of it with her arms and hands. Talk to her as you play, "Here comes the ball," "Catch the ball," and the like.

2. Show your baby how to push the ball back to you. At first, her aim won't be too good. If you sit close, with your feet touching to make an enclosed space, you should be able to catch her "throws." If the ball does go outside your "circle," it's good exercise for her to go after it and bring it back. As your baby gets better at the game, you can move farther apart, making a space between you. Continue talking with her, giving words to her actions and your own.

3. Toward the latter part of this time period, many babies can begin playing ball standing up too. Again, start close, and almost place the ball in your baby's arms when you "throw." Throwing will be hard for her at first. It takes a lot of skill to coordinate the throwing, letting go, and aiming parts of the action. With practice, she'll learn how to do it.

**Purpose:** To give your baby practice in the following fine motor, gross motor, and thinking skills required to throw and catch a ball: aiming the ball in the right direction; letting go of the ball with control; using just the right

³ See "Feed the Bear" (page 140) and "Kickball" (page 156) Two to Three Years, for more ball-playing activities for older and more skilled children.

amount of effort to push or throw the ball where she wants it to go; keeping her balance while she stands and throws or catches; positioning herself so she can catch the ball; extending her arms to catch the ball and pulling them in just the right amount to capture it in her arms; and closing her fingers around the ball to catch it in her hands and arms.

**Variation:**   By the second half of this year, your child can learn to kick a large, lightweight rubber ball. Show her how, and let her try while you hold her hand. Guide her foot if necessary. Kicking is hard because the child has to balance on one foot while she kicks with the other. With practice, your child will learn to walk up to the ball and kick it herself.

## TALKING AS YOU GO

**Participants:**   One- to two-year-old baby and adult. The same principles apply to younger babies and older children too.

**Explanation:**   Whenever, you're with your baby, talk to him about what you're doing. Accompany your activities with words to match your own and his actions.

1. For example, when you're giving your baby a bath, talk to him about the temperature of the water, the procedures and objects you're using to wash him with, and so on: "Let's feel the water. Ummm. It's warm. Not too hot and not too cold. Just right." "Now let's soap you up. Look at the bubbles." "Hand me your washcloth. There it is." and so on. (See "Fun in the Bathtub," Birth to One Year, page 72, for ideas to make bathtime experiences enjoyable and entertaining.)

2. Use your own words to describe what's going on at the time. Your baby's vocabulary will expand by hearing the same words used over and over to accompany routine activities such as bathing, eating, getting dressed and undressed, going to sleep, and so on. Remember that your baby understands words before he uses them himself. Thus, you should judge his vocabulary by how much he understands rather than by how many words he can say.

**Purpose:**   To help expand your baby's receptive vocabulary, i.e., the number of words he can understand. To give him practice hearing the names of common, everyday activities and objects in his life used along with these activities. Sharing a common language with those around him gives greater consistency and predictability to your baby's life. It adds to the stability of the routines in his life and thus provides an important structure to his existence.

Life for your baby could be compared to your moving to a foreign country where at first you knew no one, didn't speak the language, and didn't understand the customs. As you got to know some people, established some routines in your life, and heard the language spoken repeatedly in the context of those routines, you'd gradually be able to connect some words to the actions and objects you observed. And the more you came to understand, the more comfortable you would become. For your baby, it's very much like that. You can help him become a "native resident" and member of the community rather than a foreign visitor by providing consistency in all areas, including language.

## Variations:

1. Ask your baby to give you things when you're doing things together. For example, when you're dressing him, ask him to hand you each item as you're ready to put it on him: "Hand me your pants," "Now give me your shirt," "Get me some socks from the drawer," and so on. This will give you an idea of how much your baby understands. And it will give him practice connecting his actions to words and words to his actions.

2. Children this age generally enjoy helping around the house. Have your baby go get things and bring them to you. Though it may slow you down, it's an invaluable learning experience for him. It contributes to his understanding of language as communication. And it makes him feel that he's a contributing member of the family rather than a boarder.

## WHERE IS IT?

**Participants:**    Twelve- to eighteen-month-old baby and adult.

**Materials:**    Objects around the baby's environment.

**Explanation:**    Babies get better at communicating their needs so adults can understand them as they learn labels for the things around them. You can help by playing games such as this and the preceding activity which give your baby practice connecting objects with their names.

1. Look around the room you're in and ask your baby, "Where's the ball?" After searching, "find" the thing you're "looking for" and say, "Here it is. Here's the ball." Keep playing until your baby tires of the game: "Where's the window?" "There it is. There's the window." "Where's the spoon?" "Here it is. Here's the spoon," and so on. Try to be very enthusiastic as you ask and answer the questions.

2. Encourage your baby to point to the objects you ask about. When she points correctly, get very excited, praise her, and say, "That's right. There's your bear," and so on. Play the same game with your own and her body parts, her clothes, kitchen utensils, foods she eats often, people who are around, and so on. Do it as a special game and just as a routine part of your time together.

3. Most babies this age will especially love playing the game with the baby as the lost object: "Where's Kathie? Has anybody seen Kathie? I can't find Kathie. Where is she?" Carry this one on for a while to increase your baby's delight before you say, "There she is! There's Kathie." Occasionally, a baby will become upset if you do it too long, because she'll be afraid you don't see her or upset at your failure to acknowledge her presence. If your baby appears to be getting upset, "find" her right away.

**Purpose:** To increase the baby's receptive vocabulary, that is, the number of words she can understand and connect with the objects they represent. Understanding language precedes expression, and the baby needs to learn to associate words with objects and actions before she'll be able to use those words herself. Babies' first words refer, to a great extent, to tangible, visible, concrete objects—things they can touch and feel. Continuous experience hearing language used to accompany their activities plus some special learning games such as these will help your baby learn to use these words herself.

## WHICH ONES ARE THE SAME?

**Participants:** Babies fifteen to eighteen months and older, and an adult.

**Materials:** Magazine pictures or realistic drawings to match common, familiar objects, e.g., pieces of fruit, a ball, articles of clothing (shoe, sock, hat), kitchen utensils (pot, spoon, measuring cup), hairbrush, toothbrush, doll, stuffed animals, blocks; clear plastic bags or refrigerator containers to put the objects in and to which to tape the pictures; scotch tape.

**Explanation:**   Learning to associate pictures with the objects they represent is another example of human beings' capacity to represent experience in different ways. When your baby first experiences pictures, he responds to them as if they were three-dimensional. He may try, for example, to pick up an "object" in a magazine picture. This activity can help your baby learn about pictures and connect them with the objects they represent.

1. Draw, or cut from a magazine, pictures to match two objects with which your baby is familiar. Tape each picture to the top of a clear plastic container or to a clear plastic bag.

2. Hand your baby one of the objects. Ask him to "Put the orange (or whatever the object is) with its picture." If he doesn't understand the task, see if he can identify the pictured object: "Where's the orange?" "Is this an orange?" Hold the object next to its picture and ask, "Are these the same?" If necessary, show your baby that the picture and the object are the same, and put the object in the container with its picture on it. Repeat the process with the other object.

3. As your baby gets better at the game, increase the number of object-picture pairs. To make it even harder, put out all the objects and pictures at once (rather than presenting one object at a time), and ask the baby, "Which ones are the same? Put the things with their pictures. Put the same ones together."

4. When you first begin the game, be sure to select objects that are very

different from each other (e.g., an orange and a spoon). As the baby gets better at the game, you can use objects that are more similar to each other (e.g., an apple and an orange). One further way to make the game harder, in order to continue to challenge your baby's skill, is to present one more object than the number of pictures or vice versa.

**Purpose:**   To help your baby learn to associate different ways of representing objects with the objects they represent—to give the baby practice associating two-dimensional pictures of objects with three-dimensional objects and with the verbal label that is used for both. As adults, we take this skill for granted. But research with other cultures tells us that deriving meaning from pictures is a learned skill requiring experience. Games such as this as well as reading books with pictures and looking at television contribute to the child's learning about these different ways of representing objects.

## SCRIBBLING IS ART TO A BABY

**Participants:**   One- to two-year-old baby and an adult to start.

**Materials:**   A big, fat crayon and paper.

**Explanation:**   Drawing is a human capacity which many adults have not developed. They may not have had the opportunity to draw when they were children. Or, they may have been "taught" how rather than being allowed to develop their skill at their own pace, according to their own inner developmental guide. This activity gives you some guidelines to help your baby begin the developmental process of learning to draw.

1. Put a piece of paper on a table in front of your baby or on the floor. Make a mark on the paper with the crayon. Then hand the crayon to the baby, and tell her "Now you do it," making a gesture that indicates you want her to mark the paper with the crayon.

2. Once she understands that the crayon is to be used to draw on the paper, and she gets the knack of doing it, then just provide her with paper and let her go. It's a good idea to put newspaper under her paper so you don't have to worry about her keeping her drawing on the paper.[4]

[4] If at first your baby has trouble coordinating both hands to hold down the paper with one while she draws with the other, tape her paper down on the table or floor with masking tape.

3. If you're running low on drawing paper, you can just let her use old newspapers to draw on. Also you can save junk mail for her to use, cardboard from laundered shirts, or bags in which you've gotten purchases. In addition, ask friends and neighbors without children or places where you do business to save you scraps of paper for your baby's drawing.

4. By about eighteen months, most babies enjoy scribbling on paper on their own and can be given crayon and paper to amuse themselves while you're busy working. Keep an eye out to make sure your baby doesn't get carried away and decorate your walls,[5] but otherwise leave her be to practice drawing on her own.

**Purpose:** To give the baby the opportunity to practice using crayon to draw. This serves several functions:

1. It gives the baby practice using her hands in the fine motor coordination necessary for using tools. She has to learn to use one hand to hold the paper down while she uses the other to grasp and use the crayon. This technique of holding with one hand and manipulating with the other is an important human skill related to tool use.

2. It provides the baby with experience in the first stage of graphic art. Children do not learn to draw by being taught. They learn through their own experience—through having the opportunity to use the tools and to take themselves through the developmental stages of drawing.

3. This is another area in which the baby can be self-directive, working and playing according to her own timetable, choice, and judgment.

Be sure, now and in the future, that you do not criticize your child's "products" or try to correct her way of doing it. For example, you can expect her to hold the crayon tightly in her fist at first, because she's learning a motor skill as well as beginning artistic expression. Also, it will be a couple of years before she'll be interested in the products of her work. For now, she's concerned with the process of doing, not with what she's done.

**Variation:**

1. Occasionally, your baby may enjoy playing a game in which you make a mark on the paper with a crayon, then she does; then you make another mark, then she does. Or, turn it around the other way, and you copy her. Keep it simple, since at this age her skills are only up to making vertical and circular scribbles.

2. From eighteen to twenty-four months, many babies will enjoy trying

[5] You might also designate one wall in her room as a drawing wall and keep it covered with paper which can be taken down and replaced when all the space is used up.

other media such as clay or "painting" with water. Again, remember it's the process of learning how to use the materials and tools that's important now, not a particular way of doing it or what the product is.

3. If you give your child a chance to practice, as she grows older she will experiment with different kinds and combinations of artistic symbols. By the time she's five or six, she'll begin to create designs that resemble "real" things, though her purpose at this stage probably is to create something aesthetically pleasing rather than to represent the real world.

4. There is a predictable sequence of artistic development that all children throughout the world go through. They do not require teaching. But they do need the opportunity to experiment with different kinds of materials. And they need a chance to practice, at their own pace, in an atmosphere that is encouraging, accepting, and not overly directive. Following are some of the kinds of materials which should be made available[6] to children two years and older.

   a. different-colored poster paint, different-sized brushes, sponges, and an easel.
   b. finger paints
   c. different-colored soft chalk
   d. crayons
   e. paper
   f. clay
   g. scissors
   h. materials for *collages* (pictures made from combining various materials on paper). Common household materials such as pieces of fabric, foil, plastic wrap, wrapping paper, small boxes, magazine pictures, popsicle sticks, scotch tape, paper bags, and so on can be used for collages.
   j. materials to combine with clay or with each other to create *constructions*. Again, there are unlimited numbers of common household and classroom items that can be used, e.g., empty food containers, empty spools of thread, pipe cleaners, popsicle sticks, toilet paper and paper towel rolls, pieces of broken toys. The list is only as limited as your imagination.

[6] There are a number of excellent resources which give detailed information about materials to use in arts and crafts activities with young children. Two that you may find very useful as (1) guides to buying and making materials and equipment, and (2) sources of interesting activity ideas and general suggestions of how best to facilitate children's spontaneous artistic expression are Jane Cooper Bland, *Art of the Young Child* (New York: The Museum of Modern Art, 1968), and Doreen Croft and Robert Hess, *An Activities Handbook for Teachers of Young Children* (Boston: Houghton Mifflin Co., 1972), Part three, pp. 83–100.

You make it possible for your child to develop her artistic skills by providing materials, time and space in which to use them, and encouragement. An occasional open-ended suggestion also can be helpful, e.g., "I'm going to put on some music. Why don't you try painting the way the music makes you feel?"

Resist the impulse to show your child how to do something (unless she asks. Even then, encourage her to do it *her own way*.) Also, be careful not to make comments about what she's doing that "tell" her what you expect her to do. For example, don't respond positively only to realistic-looking drawings.

When your child asks for your feedback, compliment her use of space and color, the way she combined materials, the feelings her work conveys to you, and so on. Also, turn her questions back to her, e.g., "How do *you* like it?" This will help her get used to evaluating her own work rather than looking to others for approval.

Don't forget to participate yourself. Try out the various activities you provide for your child. It's not too late for you to develop your own capacity for creative self-expression.

### THIS IS ME

**Participants:** One- to two-year-old baby and adult. The idea can be adapted for any age child.

**Materials:** Sturdy paper, cardboard, oaktag, or cloth to make into a book; heavy string or yarn to bind it; magazine pictures, photographs, and drawings of things related to the baby.

**Explanation:** Your baby is becoming increasingly more aware of himself as a person in relation to other persons and things in his life. He is becoming more conscious of who *he* is, what he likes and dislikes, what he looks like, what things belong to him, which people are important in his life, and so on. You can help make these ideas more concrete by making a book for your baby all about him.[7]

1. On each page of your child's book, put a picture. Following are things you might include:
   a. a drawing of his favorite toy
   b. pictures of his favorite foods

---

[7] See "Baby's First Book," Birth to One Year, page 76, and "Read Me a Picture," Two to Three Years, page 142, for some instructions on making your own books. It's common for babies this age to tear the pages of books, so be sure to make the book out of something sturdy.

    c. photographs of each of the members of his family

    d. photographs of him, shot from different angles (full face, profile, full length from the front, sides, and back, even individual body parts).

    e. tracings of his hands and feet

    f. a small metal mirror attached to the page for him to see himself

    g. a picture of where he lives, and one of the room he sleeps in

2. Label each picture with a simple caption, e.g., "This is my Mommy." "Here's what I like to eat." Print the captions in large, neat capital letters at the bottom of the page.

3. You might want to divide the book into two sections. In the first part, have pictures of the baby, the tracings of his hands and feet, and the mirror. In the second part, include pictures of where he lives, what he likes to do, what he likes to eat, and the important people in his life.

4. When the book is done, read it with your baby. Let him turn the pages and take the lead, deciding which pages he wants to look at. Talk with him about who and what's in each picture he turns to. Ask him questions, e.g., "Who's that?" "Is that Ari?" "That's right. That's you. That's Ari's back." "Is that your foot or your hand?" In general, give him two names to choose between on pictures for which he doesn't spontaneously give a name. If he still can't answer from a choice of two, ask him yes/no questions, e.g., "Is that your bear?"

**Purpose:** To contribute to the development of the baby's self-concept—to help him recognize what he looks like from many viewpoints (thus increasing his body awareness) and to make a record for him to see of important people, things, and activities in his life; to give him further experience "reading" something of personal interest to him as a prelude to reading about other things.

**Variation:** Make a couple of pages with "pockets" to keep other items relating to your baby.

1. If you have a tape recorder, make a tape of your baby's voice at periodic intervals—talking, singing a song, laughing—and play them back to him.

2. Make a one- or two-piece puzzle of your baby's face by mounting a photograph on heavy cardboard, covering it with clear contact paper, and either cutting it in two pieces or making a form into which to fit the one-piece "puzzle" (see "Baby's First Puzzle" page 95 for instructions).

3. Get a long piece of newsprint, and trace your baby's entire body onto it. Fill in the clothes and body details with crayon and props. This life-size paper doll can be taped to the wall. When he grows older, your child will enjoy cutting out his form and filling it in himself.

4. On another piece of newsprint, or on several strips of cardboard taped together, make a growth chart, marking at periodic intervals how tall your baby is, and noting his age and the date.

5. On another piece of newsprint, let your baby step in washable paint and then along the newsprint to make a footprint path.

## THE LITTLE ONE GOES INSIDE THE BIG ONE

**Participants:** Fifteen- to twenty-four-month-old baby alone or with an adult. The materials you make or buy for this activity will continue to be enjoyed by most two- to three-year-olds and some older children.

**Materials:** Empty cans of graduated sizes; contact paper to cover them.

**Explanation:** Learning about the relationships of different sized things to each other is a concrete skill that underlies more advanced, abstract mathematical concepts children will confront later in school. Even more important, however, is that it is the basis of skills we use all the time in our daily lives without even thinking about it (e.g., estimating whether a shoe will fit our foot before we bother to try it on; deciding on which shelf in the refrigerator to put a bottle). This apparently simple skill which we all take for granted must be learned by children through experiences with their own bodies in relation to different-sized spaces and with different objects in relation to each other. The following activity can help your child develop this basic mathematical skill.

1. Save three food cans of different sizes, remove their labels, and hammer down any sharp edges on the open end. Cover each can with contact paper of a different color (e.g., red, orange, and yellow). Give them to your baby to play with.

2. At first, your baby may try to put the big one into the little one, or she may be able only to put the smallest can inside the biggest one. With time and practice, she'll learn to stack them all inside each other correctly.

3. You can play with your baby and demonstrate how to nest the cans correctly. But she will learn most through trial and error and practicing on her own.

4. When your baby has learned to nest all three cans easily (which may

not occur within this age period), add a few more cans of different sizes.[8] The closer to one another the sizes of the cans are, the more difficult your baby will find the task.

**Purpose:** To give your baby experience in beginning mathematical concepts—of size and quantity—more and less, bigger and smaller. These conceptual understandings first must be learned by the baby at this age through active manipulation of objects. Having had such motor-based experiences, when she is older your child will be able to learn the generalized principles in the abstract. This activity also gives the baby practice using her hands for grasping and manipulating objects.

**Variations:**

1. Collect a set of different-sized boxes for your baby, e.g., an empty match box, a small gift box, a larger gift box, and a shoe box. Removing and replacing their lids, putting them inside each other, stacking them on top of each other, and so on provide good practice for fine motor and thinking skills.

2. Make a cone from a piece of shirt cardboard. Starting at one corner, roll the cardboard into a cone shape, and tape it; cut the wide bottom part so that it's flat. For a base, cut out a square piece of cardboard bigger than the largest doughnut, and cut a circular line into it so that you can fit about a quarter-inch of the base of the cone through it. Make cuts along the quarter-inch of the cardboard of the bottom of the cone; fold the flaps of cardboard down, and tape or glue them to the underside of the cardboard square. Cut cardboard doughnuts in graduated sizes and with holes of different sizes such that they fit over the cone from bottom to top. Cover all the parts of the toy with different-colored contact

[8] Cover them in other solid colors—green, blue, and purple. This will give your baby a set of colored cans which includes the entire spectrum of the rainbow. (Look at the book's cover for the order.) Children are very attracted to the rainbow spectrum, and they will learn about the color spectrum through their play.

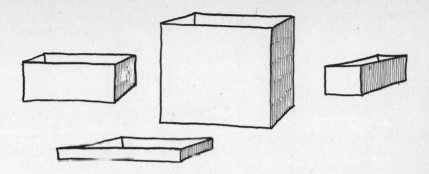

paper, making the doughnuts correspond to the rainbow spectrum. You can buy such a toy made of plastic or wood if you don't have the time or motivation to make one.

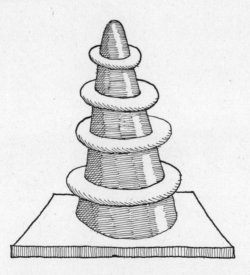

3. Give your baby a bunch of blocks, stones, dried beans, acorns, or some other collection of objects that are all about the same size for her to use with the nesting cans and boxes. Play along with her. Guide her to discover what happens when she fills a big container with objects and then dumps its contents into a smaller box or if she fills a little can and dumps its contents into a bigger can—these are further lessons in quantity. Leave her to entertain herself with these materials too.

## ALL GONE, YOU AND ME, FULL AND EMPTY . . .

**Participants:** Eighteen- to twenty-four-month-old baby and adult.

**Materials:** An empty coffee can and some blocks, wooden beads, or other group of objects, enough to fill the can.

**Explanation:** Babies in this age range often are ready to learn vocabulary such as *you* and *me*, *full* and *empty*, *all gone*, *more*, *no more*, *another*, and *one*. Such words are learned through repeated experiences involving the expressions. Usually, babies pick up the expressions in time through hearing them used and trying them out. Games such as this are fun and can help reinforce your child's learning these words.

1. Play with your baby, handing him the objects one by one until he has put them all in the can. As you hand him each one, say: "Here's one for you." "Here's another one for you." "One more for you," and so on.

2. When you've given him the last object, look around for others and when you don't find them, say "That's all." "No more." "All gone." As you say the words, make a gesture to show that there are no more.

3. Then, motion and tell your baby to dump out the contents of the can and give the can to you, saying "*You* take the blocks. Give *me* the can."

4. Then hold out your hand for a block, and say "Give me one block." Take it and put it in the can. Hold out your hand again, and say "Give me *another* block," or sometimes, "Give me *one more* block," until you've put all the blocks in the can.

5. When your baby has no more blocks to give you, ask him for another. When he communicates to you in word or gesture that there are no more, ask "No more? All gone?" Then the two of you together can say: "That's all." "No more." "All gone," as you make a gesture to show that there are no more.

6. Play the game for as long as your baby wants. Many babies this age delight in this kind of repetitive game. So be prepared to be involved for a little while. It should be quite animated and enthusiastically played as the baby learns to join you in proclaiming "All gone!" and so on.

7. You also can introduce the words *full* and *empty* as you fill up the can with blocks and as you empty it again. When the can has been filled and you've gone through your "All gone . . ." routine, point to the can and say: "Look, Jimmy, the can is full." When he has dumped the contents out, point to the can and say "Now the can is empty." Pick it

up, look inside it, and give it to your baby to investigate. Put your hand in, and feel around as if to find something, and say "There's nothing here. It's empty." "Let's fill it up again." Then start your game again of putting the blocks in the can.

**Purpose:**   To increase the baby's functional vocabulary, the expressions he can understand and use. Through the continuous repetition of the actions and accompanying words of this game, the baby can learn to understand what these words mean and learn to use them himself. In addition to teaching vocabulary, this game provides the baby with further experience with beginning mathematical concepts. One, one more, many, full, empty, all gone, and so on all relate to quantity and volume; they too must first be learned through concrete experiences such as this game provides.

**Variation:**   Make up similar games to give your baby practice in understanding and using pairs of opposites such as *hot* and *cold* (e.g., with different temperatures of water); *hard* and *soft* (e.g., with a collection of hard and soft materials); *happy* and *sad* (e.g., "Happy Face, Sad Face," page 121); *big* and *little* (e.g., with a collection of objects, each in two sizes) *open* and *shut* (e.g., play an open-shut game with a box, a jar, or a door); *quiet* and *noisy* (e.g., use a radio or record player or voice, on and off); *slow* and *fast* (e.g., make toy cars move at different speeds); and so on. These games will continue to be useful into the third year, until the children can understand and use these word opposites correctly.

## DO AS I DO, DO AS I SAY

**Participants:**   Eighteen- to twenty-four-month-old baby and adult.

**Materials:**   Two chairs, at least one small, child-sized one.

**Explanation:**   In their first two years, babies are primarily action-oriented. They learn everything by doing. With time and practice, they learn to connect those actions with words. After the first two years, children gradually learn to internalize language. They learn to use words by themselves in the absence of the objects and actions they represent. Eventually they will be able to think about and formulate ideas that have no specific, concrete, physical referent. The following activity can help your baby in the beginning stages of this process.

1. Sit facing your baby. Stand up, and as you do, say to your baby, "Stand up." Then, say "Sit down," and both of you sit down. Repeat this for as long as your baby wants, until you sense she's ready to move on to a new action.

2. Then, while standing up, say to her "Turn around," and do so yourself. If she doesn't follow you on this or any other action, guide her until she gets the idea. For example, for "Turn around," put your hands on her upper arms and gently turn her as you say the words. Then demonstrate again while you say it.

3. Alternate "Turn around" with "Jump up and down." Do it with her as you give the command, and if necessary, take her hands and help her.

4. When your baby tires of "Turn around" and "Jump up and down," tell her to "Sit down," and try some seated activities:[9] e.g., "Open your mouth." "Close your mouth." "Open your eyes." "Close your eyes." "Stick out your tongue." "Clap your hands." "Touch your ear." "Touch your hair." "Touch my ear." "Touch my hair," and so on.

5. Always start off with one command, and when you know your child can do it, introduce another one; then alternate between those two until your child tires of that pair. Don't overload her with too many different commands in one session. You can add one or two new actions and instructions each time you play the game.

6. When your baby can do a number of actions with you, try giving her just the verbal command without a demonstration by you or any kind of nonverbal gesture. Are there some she can't do if you don't demonstrate? Give her a number of different action-instructions, one after another, rather than alternating between just two. Is this confusing to her?

7. Try giving your baby two action-instructions together, e.g., "Stand up and turn around," or "Clap your hands, then stick out your tongue."

8. When she gets really good at a particular action series, see if you can fool her, for example, by saying "Open your mouth," then "Close your eyes." instead of your usual "Open your mouth," then "Close your mouth."

9. Think of more of your own action-instructions to do with your baby when the ones you've done become old hat. See how many instructions in a row your baby can follow as she gains experience.

**Purpose:** To give your baby practice matching her actions to words, first by accompanying the words with a demonstration of the actions, and later by

---

[9] This, like all the activities, is intended to be played many times. As always, how much of the activity and which parts of it you play at any one time will depend on your child's interest. Continue it as long as she enjoys it, and stop when she gets tired and distracted.

using the words only to direct her actions. As we've said, babies learn language first in relation to their own activity. Only later will they learn to be able to use words alone to think about things apart from their actions.

This kind of activity is good because it takes the baby through two steps toward that process: First, by actually doing the activity at the same time as the words are spoken, the baby learns the connection between the words and the action they represent. When you use just the words alone to prompt the action, those words take on the meaning of the action. After she's learned the connection between the words and the action they represent, then in the future when she hears those words, the child will be able to picture the action in her mind without having to perform it. This is an important part of the process of learning to use language to think.

## SING ME A SONG[10]

**Participants:**   Eighteen- to twenty-four-month-old baby and adult. The same basic approach can be adapted for use with older children.

**Materials:**   Record player and records; records should be of simple, rhythmic, melodic tunes with repetitive, easy to say words, e.g., "Me and My Teddy Bear," "Old MacDonald," simple folksongs.

**Explanation:**   Singing is another potential human capacity which remains relatively undeveloped in many people. Children generally are not encouraged to practice singing enough to develop their skill. Or they are "taught" in ways that inhibit rather than enhance their capacity to sing. As in any other area, you teach children to sing most effectively through your model. The following activity offers some suggestions of how to do this.

1. Play some different selections of music for your baby while he's playing. Watch to see if he especially likes a particular song. Some cues to look for include: if his face brightens, his eyes widen, he stops what he's doing momentarily to attend to the music, or he tries to sing or dance to the music.

2. Put on a song your baby seemed to like later. Hold your baby on your lap facing you. Sing to him along with the song while he watches your face. Your facial expression should be animated and your singing

---

[10] See "Singing and Dancing," Three to Four Years, page 176, for more ideas on singing with older children.

enthusiastic. When your baby begins trying to sing along, choose one simple refrain of the song to "teach" him.

3. Emphasize that part as you sing the song to the baby, and encourage him to sing it along with you (e.g., "Ee Eye Oh" from "Old MacDonald"). When he's learned that part well, you can introduce another part of the song in the same way. Your general approach should be low-key, getting your baby to join you because you're having fun rather than because of pressure for him to do it in a particular way.

4. Babies with good language skills may be able to learn a whole song within a few months. Others may be unable to learn a whole song until they're older and more skilled. But they'll enjoy singing along with parts of a few favorite songs.

5. Once your baby has the knack, learning more songs will be easier. You can expect to extend this activity over many sessions, because babies this age have short attention spans for adult-directed activities. The more genuinely joyful, uninhibited, and childlike you are in singing with your baby, the longer you'll sustain his attention. You should spend only as much time at one sitting as your baby enjoys; then quit and take it up another day.

6. The model you present your baby as part of your daily routine is even more important than a special activity for learning to sing. If singing is an integral part of your life, then your baby will sing too. Sing to him, sing along with the radio and records, and sing while you work and play with him. If you're not used to singing, try it. Not only will it provide your baby with a good model, but it might brighten your day too.

**Purpose:** To give the baby practice early in using his voice for singing; to expand his vocabulary through learning words to songs; to provide him with experience in rhythm-related activities. Although many of us (perhaps the majority) feel we can't sing, most of us could learn to sing quite well with practice.[11] But we learned early that singing was not for us, and so we failed to develop one of our natural human capacities.

By giving babies the opportunity to listen to music and learn to use their voices to accompany it, we stimulate that capacity. Thus, we enable them to develop a very important means of human expression and communication. Singing is a potential source of joy both to the singer and to the listener and should be encouraged from an early age. It shouldn't be pushed, but just allowed to develop at the baby's own pace.

[11] It's the combination of lack of sufficient practice and self-consciousness that inhibits most adults' ability to sing.

Further, singing with your baby will help you grow too, through enabling you to develop further your own human capacity for song.

## Variations:

1. Teach the baby simple gestures to go with the songs he's learning.
2. Make up picture books for the baby to accompany his songs.
3. Make up and sing songs about your baby or using his name. If you don't feel competent at composing your own tunes, borrow them. For example, you can sing "Happy Birthday" as "Good morning to you. Good morning to you. Good morning, dear Kenneth. Good morning to you." Or you could make up words to the tune of "Old MacDonald" much as "Kenneth has a blue shirt on. Eee Eye Eee Eye Oh. And, on his shirt, he has some buttons. Eee Eye Eee Eye Oh."

## LET'S TAKE A WALK

**Participants:**    Eighteen- to twenty-four-month-old baby and an adult.

**Explanation:**    Having spent the first half of the year becoming adept at getting about on two feet, babies this age really like to push their new skill to maximum effort. They enjoy going on long walks, as much as a mile or two, stopping to explore, walking slowly, and observing everything on their way. Take a walk with your baby. Leave yourself an hour or more, and let your baby set the pace.

1. Let your baby be your guide in noticing sights and sounds and things of interest in your neighborhood and elsewhere. As adults, we're often too busy to take the time to notice what's around us. We're always rushing through our lives to get things done. Children live today. They notice all the details of events and things around them. Take the time to go on a long, leisurely walk with your baby and to see the world through her eyes.
2. Go on a city walk. Walk in places where there are shops, and stop to look in interesting windows as your baby chooses. Go slowly enough that you can notice trees and bushes, leaves on the ground, flowers in the spring, snowflakes in the northern winter, and so on. Stop to talk with friendly people, pet a dog, watch a squirrel, listen to a bird. Listen for the traffic noises and airplanes overhead. Do they make it hard to

hear yourself talking or to hear the song of a bird? Stop and watch the goings-on at a construction site. Lift your baby up so she can see the machines, the holes in the ground, the foundations going up. Take a detour to a playground, and spend a few minutes on a swing, a slide, in the sandbox, or just running up a mound of dirt (Don't just watch; get involved.). Talk with your baby about all the things you see and do.

3. If you're fortunate enough to live in the country or to have transportation far enough out of town, take your baby on a country walk. Here your main events are found in nature—a caterpillar on a leaf, the city of insects under a rock or log, the variety of trees and plants and flowers and small creatures, the different kinds of places to walk and run and climb, the wonder of an unobstructed skyline.

4. Take along a bag for collections—gather some leaves, some rocks, and other things of interest. The rocks can be used in games like "Dump and Fill," or you can paint faces on them or separate them into piles of big ones and little ones. You can make a pretty picture with the leaves or see if you can tell which ones come from the same tree. Or, your baby may just like to have a few special things of her own that she collected.

5. A walk in the suburbs can provide your baby with city and country sights. In addition, walk along a house-lined street and look at all the different houses; notice and talk with your child about the ways in which they're all alike and the ways in which they differ. Stop to look at the different foliage. If it's warm, take off your shoes and walk barefoot on the grass.

6. Wherever you take your walk, see what interesting things you notice that you'd never seen before. Let it be a time of slowing down, of "being" now instead of going somewhere, and of enjoying time shared with your baby, living life for just a little while at her pace.

**Purpose:** To give your baby the opportunity to get out and investigate the world around her—to take the time to explore the sights and sounds and smells of her environment. In addition, long walks are good exercise for her developing muscles. Babies this age enjoy long walks. Whenever you can take the time, it's an excellent investment in your own as well as your baby's healthy development.

## HAPPY FACE, SAD FACE

**Participants:**  Eighteen- to twenty-four-month-old baby and an adult. This activity will continue to appeal to many children older than this also. See "Mirror Games," Birth to One Year (page 74) and "More Mirror Games," Three to Four Years (page 184) for other activities using mirrors.

**Materials:**  Large mirror that can be stood up on a table or one that's attached to a door or wall which you can sit in front of.

**Explanation:**  Babies recognize positive and negative emotional states early in infancy, but it is on a nonverbal, gut level, not on a conceptual level. Learning to become consciously aware of nonverbal behavioral signs of how people are feeling is a skill that can be very helpful in interactions with others. The following activity can begin to help you and your baby become more alert to your own and others' facial expressions, one important nonverbal signal.[12]

1. Sit with your baby in front of a mirror. Make a happy face, and say "Look at me. Daddy's face is happy," as you point to your face in the mirror. Then say to the baby, "You make a happy face." "Make a face like mine." When he does, say "Oh, look at you. Your face is happy too." "Trenton has a happy face."

2. Then, make a sad face, and point it out to your baby. "Look at my face. My face is sad." "Can you make a sad face?" When he does so, point to his mirror image and say, "Now your face is sad. You have a sad face."

3. Keep playing for as long as your baby is interested in the game, alternating between happy and sad. Make a face, and ask him to tell you what kind of face you're making, and do the same for him.

4. Most adults have had very little practice observing their own facial expressions, and you may become self-conscious when you're trying to make your face look a certain way while watching yourself. It may help if you imagine a happy or a sad experience while you're trying to produce each kind of expression.

5. Mirror play is an artificial way of teaching your baby to make the connection between his gut reactions to positive and negative emotional states in himself and others and the facial expressions associated with those emotions. But, the game can help to make it concrete, especially by enabling your child to see his own facial expressions.

[12] See "How Do You Feel?" Three to Four Years, page 181, for further illustration of ways to get more in touch with your own and others' nonverbal expression of feelings.

6. To be really effective, however, you should follow up this type of activity: Use the words in your day-to-day life to help your baby recognize and give labels to the ways you, he, and others feel at different times and the ways your facial expression reflects those feelings.

**Purpose:** To help your baby learn to connect the words to describe the emotional states, happy and sad, with the facial expressions exhibited by people feeling those emotions; to give the baby practice associating his own and others' facial expressions with the emotional states to which they correspond.

**Variation:** If your baby has trouble making his facial expression fit the words, just have fun making any kinds of faces (e.g., silly faces, sticking out your tongue, puffing out your cheeks, widening your eyes), and try again another time. Meanwhile, next time he has a particularly animated expression on his face, take your baby to a mirror (or a hand mirror to him) and show him how he looks, saying, "Look, Trenton, your face is sad," or "Look at your face. You look angry," or "Look at your happy face."

## WHAT'S THAT?

**Participants:** Eighteen- to twenty-four-month-old baby and an adult.

**Explanation:** The period beginning about this time for most babies is characterized by an explosion in language development. Gross and fine motor skills (especially, learning to walk and feed themselves) preoccupied much of their energies in the first half of the year. Now babies' energies are freed to concentrate on learning to give words to their actions and to the things around them. The game that follows is borrowed from a favorite activity that babies this age engage in with adults to find out the names of things; here, we just turn it around.

1. Go around your home with your baby and point to objects that are familiar to her—those whose names she is certain to have heard many times, even though she may never have said them. Do include some things you know she can name to give her a feeling of success.

2. As you point to an object, ask your baby, "What's that?" If she answers correctly, respond with great enthusiasm and praise, and reinforce her

answer, saying, for example, "Right! That's a window," or "Yes! That's soap."

3. If your child says nothing, ask her (giving an incorrect name the first time, something silly you know that she'll know is wrong), for example, "Is it a nose?" Then, the correct answer: "Is it a table?" If she nods yes, say "Yes. It's a table. Can you say its name—table?" If she doesn't respond, drop it for the time being.

4. Another way of phrasing the question to your baby if she doesn't name an object on her own, or if she gives it the wrong name, is to ask "Is it a table or a chair?" giving her a choice of two, one of which is the correct answer.

5. If your child then says the name, applaud her answer, and say "Good! That's right. It's a table." Don't try to correct her way of saying the words. It takes time and practice for children to develop the movements needed to say all the sounds of their language correctly. Your corrections won't speed that process; it will only make your child feel bad and less willing to try in the future.

6. As long as the name the baby gives something is near enough to its name that you and others know what she's referring to, that's all that's important. Your model and her opportunity to practice without the fear of failure are your child's best "teachers."

**Purpose:**  To give your baby an opportunity to practice naming the things around her and to receive some positive reinforcement for doing so; to increase her vocabulary, attempting to add to it a new name or two each time the game is played; and, even when no new names are added to her expressive vocabulary, to reinforce her understanding of the connections between objects and the words used to represent them. In sum, to give your baby a chance to show off what she knows already at the same time that she learns some new words.

**Variations:**
1. Play "Where Is It?" (see page 103) with those objects your baby couldn't name to see if she understands the words even though she can't yet say them.

2. Play "What's That?" with the baby's books.
   a. Make a book together, filled with pictures she selects from magazines, and play the game with that book.
   b. Make up a book filled with drawings and/or magazine pictures of the objects around the house that she can name. Then let her take you around and point out and name the objects that are the same as the pictures in the book you make together.

## DANCE WITH ME

**Participants:** Eighteen- to twenty-four-month-old baby and an adult.

**Materials:** Record player and records; the selection of music should range from rock to marches to gentle waltzes.

**Explanation:** Moving to the rhythm of music is both therapeutic and beneficial to your baby's development and to your own. Coordination is gained from learning to match your movements to the music. Relaxation is achieved by letting your body respond to the rhythm. These benefits can help you learn to become more in tune with your own inner body rhythm and to carry yourself and move with greater comfort, grace, and personal expressiveness. Take the opportunity to really get involved in dancing with your baby, on his level, unself-consciously. Both of you will have a good time, and you will grow.

1. Put on some music, take your baby by the hands, and "dance" together. Move as the music makes you feel, from the inside out, and follow your baby's lead in any movements he makes.

2. "Waltz" around, taking big, sliding steps to circle 'round the floor. "Bounce" to the beat of some rock music. March along behind your baby in bunny-hop style, or with him behind you. And so on.

3. Occasionally, your baby might enjoy being picked up and held in your arms while you dance.

4. Sometimes the two of you may have fun dancing in front of a mirror, to see how you look or to take turns copying each other's movements in time to the music.

5. If your baby prefers to dance by himself, that's okay too. Just put on some music and let him enjoy himself. You can dance by yourself too, or leave him be while you do something else.

**Purpose:** To give the baby practice in a rhythm-related activity—listening to music and moving in response to its rhythm and mood. It will be a while before your baby will learn really to match his movements to the beat and tempo of a particular piece of music, but for now, he can begin to get the feel of different kinds of music. At the same time, you can use his model of spontaneity, lack of self-consciousness, and gaiety as a stimulus to loosen yourself up.

## SAY WHAT I SAY

**Participants:**   Eighteen- to twenty-four-month-old baby and an adult or older sibling.

**Explanation:**   This activity is an expansion of one many families spontaneously do with their babies this age: They chance upon a few expressions that perhaps the baby said herself the first time, and they ask the baby to repeat this "saying" all the time for other people.

1. Choose an expression you know your baby can say already, a two- or three-word "sentence" such as "Mommy talk" or "Baby eat." Say to the baby, "Say: 'Baby eats.' " If she cooperates (as babies this age are notorious for becoming suddenly silent when you want them to talk), change the expression by using a different subject, and ask the baby to "Say 'Daddy eats.' "

2. Continue as long as the baby is interested, changing the subject at first and then the verb. Then try a new expression once you're sure she's got the point of repeating what you say. Make the new expression one word longer than you've been using, e.g., "Say: 'Tommy loves Michelle.' "

3. When your baby tires of this game, try changing the content to sounds instead of words: See if you can get her to copy you barking like a dog, meowing like a cat, quacking like a duck, honking your horn like a car, squeaking like a squeaky door, and so on. Silly, made-up, "nonsense words," made from combining syllables your baby can say, may also be enjoyed.

4. Babies this age usually really love pretending to talk with someone on a toy telephone. You can vary the game and make it more interesting, sometimes, by turning it into a telephone conversation with your baby. You say something into the phone, then hand it to her to talk; she'll probably copy you.

**Purpose:**   To exercise the baby's attention span and memory for words and sounds; to give her practice in listening and reproducing what she has heard. Babies do not learn to speak through direct imitation of what others say. If they were dependent on adults to teach them to talk, they'd never learn. This activity will not expand your baby's level of language usage. For example, if your baby is talking in two-word sentences, you won't teach her to use three- or four-word sentences through this activity. As a matter of fact, try getting your baby to repeat a sentence such as "My baby wears pretty blue socks." You'll get a response on the level of her spontaneous sentence production such as "Baby wear socks."

What an activity of this sort can accomplish, however, is to help your baby learn to increase the amount of time she can pay attention. Babies this age typically don't have long attention spans, and their attention span for this kind of activity is generally shorter than for a self-chosen activity. But if you make the activity fun and don't carry it out longer than the baby's interest holds out, you'll gradually, over time, help her learn to pay attention and listen, an important skill she'll need later in school.

# 4

# Two to Three Years: From Babyhood to Childhood

The two- to three-year-old is undergoing some important changes. In a sense, this is a period of transition—from the babyhood of the first two years to the early childhood or preschool period of the next few years. Before two, children are very motor-minded; they not only expend a great deal of energy learning control and coordination of their bodies' movement, but they "think" primarily with their bodies. Gradually in those infant years, children began to develop internal memory images of some of the things and people around them as well as of their own behaviors. By two, most children not only have internalized images of their world, but they can begin to act on the world through the manipulation of those images in their heads. They are no longer bound to their immediate experience; they can think about things that aren't right there in front of them.

From two to three, children develop more efficient ways of representing their experience. They translate what they have learned before through direct sensory-motor experience into different shortcut codes. For example, most children expand their understanding and use of language in this period.

Many two-year-olds accompany their activities with talking. But the talking doesn't direct the actions. The actions lead, and the words seem to arise from the experience as if the children were trying to give their actions a name, to translate them into an efficient, mentally manipulable form. By three, most children's behavior is more under the control of language. They are able, for example, to begin or end an activity according to verbal directions. Between two and three years, children are learning their language; so that by three they will be able to use it to learn other things. But for the two- to three-year-old, actions are still more a reality than are words.

The average number of words in the vocabularies of two-year-olds is two hundred fifty and of three-year-olds, nine hundred. This increase in number is indicative of the growth in language skills at this age; but more important are the changes in the kinds of words used, the kinds of sentence structures used, and the purpose and function of language in this period. Most two-year-olds speak, to a great extent, in telegraphic sentences, leaving out all but the essential words. Also, their repertoire of language probably includes several stereotyped one-word "phrases" to which they attach a whole variety of subjects, e.g., "*See* cookie, boy, dog, man. . . ." By three, most children's language includes a greater range of types of words and sentences, their sentences are more complete, and the structure of their sentences is becoming more like those of adult speakers.

The further refinement of motor skills does not, of course, stop with infancy. Most children from two to three are gaining total mastery of the upright posture. At two they can run, but not well; by three they are beginning to learn running maneuvers such as stops and starts, turning corners, and avoiding obstacles. At two most children can climb stairs, but they take it one tread at a time, bringing both feet together at each tread. By three, most children alternate feet going up stairs, and also in riding a tricycle. Between two and three most children also learn to jump with both feet, walk on tiptoe, balance briefly on one foot, kick a ball, and throw a ball into a basket.

All of these larger motor skills require, also, more complex thinking about spatial relationships than most children show before this time. In order to accomplish many of these acts, children must be aware of their position in space in relation to other things as well as the position in space of things in relation to each other. And, to make it even harder, the children must understand these relationships when either they or the things are in motion.

The development of more refined fine motor skills contributes to children's growing independence. They are learning increasing numbers of self-help skills such as undressing themselves (and helping with the dressing), going to the toilet on their own and washing themselves (though still not very well), feeding themselves very adequately, using a spoon and cup well without spilling and a fork to spear chunks of food.

Fine motor skills improve also, with practice, for such tasks as cutting with scissors, drawing, and manipulating puzzles. From two to three children really enjoy art activities such as drawing, painting, modeling with clay, snipping paper and pasting, and so on. They enjoy the process of using their hands and a few simple tools more than they care about producing anything. They're not very interested in the things they make; they're more interested in the making.

From two to three, children also are changing their relationships with other people. Whereas through age two, most children are more responsive to adults than to other children, by three they are beginning to play together. The two-year-old might play side by side with another child, but even though they might be playing at the same activity, they will not do it together. So the two-year-old engages in role-playing and make-believe behavior, but she plays all the parts herself. By three, if she has had some experience with other children, a child will join forces with one or two others to play together at the same activity.

The period between two and three years is perhaps best known as "the terrible twos." Some people who study children have suggested that in this period, children's behavior is characterized by rigidity and inflexibility. They want things just so and no other way; they don't like change, can't wait, won't give in; they often do just the opposite of what they're told. Although this kind of behavior can occur, and when it does occur, it can be annoying, it should not be thought of as *bad* behavior. There's a very good reason for it.

Children at this age have just begun to figure out things about the world they live in. They're beginning to have "ideas" about the way things are. But their ideas aren't yet secure. Therefore, they don't feel comfortable with a lot of change; that makes it harder to be sure about things. Also, children are beginning to gain command over many new skills, most notably understanding and using speech. Much of their behavior is the result of their checking out the power of their new skills. For example, if you say "come here" and your child walks in the other direction, he's showing that he understood you well enough to do just the opposite—quite an accomplishment.

Finally, this is an age when children's "eyes are bigger than their stomachs," in terms of trying to do things. They can't do everything they try to do, and that's frustrating. They have not yet learned to find reasonable solutions to feelings of frustration. At this age, they still just become enraged. Patience and sympathy will see them through this period until they become more secure and more in command of their own emotions.

## HOW DO YOU FEEL ABOUT ME?

**Participants:**    Two- to three-year-old child and the important adults in her life. Since the nurturant and caring role so important to "mothering" [1] also is

---

[1] "Mothering" can be engaged in by women or men. The choice of this word rather than parenting or fathering is related to the connotations each term has, not to the sex of the person.

a model for all human relationships, the principles explained in this activity are applicable at any age level, to children and adults.

**Explanation:** The way you treat your child in this period of growing self-awareness in relation to others is very important to her development of a positive self-concept that will enable her to be effective in whatever area she puts her energies and not be burdened by crippling fears and self-doubt about her worth and ability to be successful.

1. Treat your child in a manner that demonstrates concern and respect for her thoughts and feelings as a human being. She needs from you gentle guidance and understanding of her moods, her ups and downs, her stops and starts, her bouts of self-assertion, and her retreats to "lick her wounds," regroup, and try again.

2. Children this age frequently seem to get upset suddenly, apparently over nothing, for no reason at all. What's often occurred is that the child has formed an idea inside her head of something that's going to happen a certain way, and then it doesn't happen as she planned. If you understand this, you can deal calmly with her temper and help her learn to communicate her thoughts and feelings better to you in the future. Think of how you feel when you're upset and there's no one you can turn to who'll be calm and understanding. Probably you feel lonely and frightened. Help your child avoid these feelings; be to her the kind and gentle guardian we all long for, even as adults.

3. In all things, allow your child to practice as much responsibility as is consistent with her developmental needs and capabilities. Give her a chance to test her limits, to try her hand at doing for herself. At the same time, be understanding of the times when she would rather revert to being cared for, with no demands or expectations. We all have times when we feel capable of doing anything we try and others when just getting out of bed seems like a supreme effort.

4. Show your child by the way you treat her (and yourself) an understanding and supportive model. Try to respect her different moods: Let go and urge her onward when she's up. Lessen demands and deal gently with her failures to accomplish even easy tasks when she's down. And help her all the while to learn to seek more of a balance. If you do these things, then when she's an adult and has internalized and made part of herself the ways you treat her now, perhaps she will treat herself with similar kindness and understanding. And what a welcome change that would be from the harsh, critical, and demeaning "monitor" too many adults carry around inside their heads today.

5. Encourage your child and give her opportunities to gain skill and be successful with people and things in the world around her, so that she can feel that she's a good, capable, and worthy person. The development of self-esteem in a child (essential to continued growth) requires that she receive and come to expect esteem from others as a matter of course and not worry about it. When this is true, then she doesn't have to direct her energies continually to seeking others' respect and esteem, and her energies are released for more productive enterprises. In addition, she becomes capable of showing concern for others' needs when she is released from always having to worry about their meeting hers.

6. Throughout life, esteem from others is increased by displays of competence. Competence, in turn, is the product of having opportunity for practice in a skill combined with a sense of confidence that you can be effective at it. Thus your child needs from you—now and in the future—the chance to develop, test, and use her skills within a context of support, respect, and trust from you in her capacity for growth toward competence with people and with things.

7. This means, particularly, that you never demean her actions and that instead, you act as a guide and a facilitator to her learning, not as a trainer without whom she'd never learn. Children learn better through being given opportunity, trust, and the chance to make their own mistakes without the fear of ridicule or accusation than they ever do through deliberate training.

8. Talk to your child with respect. Do you remember how it felt when you were a child (and how it still does now) to have someone yell at you or belittle you? If you have ever been hurt that way, don't do it to your child. Stop and ask yourself next time you start to tell your child that she or her actions are stupid, bad, ugly, and so forth, or that she should be ashamed of herself: "How would I feel if our places were exchanged?"

9. Try not to talk to your child impatiently, thus communicating through your tone of voice that she is bothering you or that she's too much trouble or that she's not smart enough to understand you. Remember how it makes you feel when people let you know, through their words or their behavior, that they don't value you and are not concerned about your feelings.

10. If you're in a bad mood, or if your child does something to annoy you, let her know exactly what the problem is in clear and honest terms. Don't send disguised and confusing messages. She can only interpret them as something wrong with her to make you act this way toward her. And, don't take every opportunity your child does anything

wrong to bring up every single thing she's ever done wrong in the past, thus making her feel she's a terrible person who's always making mistakes. Be as kind to your child as you'd like others to be toward you.

11. Pay attention to your child when she talks to you, especially when she calls your name. You'll save yourself many "discipline problems" if you don't wait to respond to her until she has to resort to whining or a tantrum. In general, talk with your child as you would wish her to talk with you if your positions were reversed.

12. Let your child know, in words, but most of all through your behavior toward her, how much you love her and how special she is to you. Don't assume she knows. Make sure she understand you love *her*, not the way she acts or what she does or doesn't do. Let her know by your behavior that nothing she does can change or threaten the love you have for her, that your love is absolute, not relative to her behaving in a certain way. Make sure she understands that although you may get angry at something *she does*, you *never* stop loving her, no matter what.

**Purpose:**   To communicate to your child feelings of love, supportiveness, and respect that will help her develop feelings about herself of competence and self-worth and feelings about the world of trust, security, and confidence. If you do this for your child, not only will you enable her to grow to be all that she can be, but you also will grow yourself.

## REMEMBER AND DO

**Participants:**   Two- to three-year-old child and an adult. This activity could be played with a group of children, this age or older. The older children should be able to remember and carry out a longer series of instructions.

**Materials:**   Several objects that are familiar to the child, table and chairs, a room with a door.

**Explanation:**   Being able to follow a series of instructions correctly is a skill that is necessary both in children's routine daily activities and in school learning. All day long, children are being asked to do things. Usually they are given a series of requests rather than a single one, e.g., "Come into the house, take off your coat, hang it up, and then come in the kitchen for lunch." The activity which follows can help you (1) find out just how many things in a row you can reasonably expect your child to remember and do and (2) make it possible for him to increase his skill at following verbal instructions, to the limits of his developmental capacity to process them.

1. Prepare the room for the activity: Close the door, put a few objects on the table (e.g., a ball, paper, and a pencil), and sit down with your child at the table. Tell him you want to see if he can do what you say. Then, say to him, "Stand up." When he does so, tell him to "Open the door," then "Close the door." Then ask him to "Come here," then "Bounce the ball," then "Put the ball on the chair," then "Make a mark on the paper," and "Sit down."

2. In each case, wait until he's carried out the former instruction before you give another. If he doesn't understand what to do in any instance, show him as you give the instruction. Then give the instruction again without a demonstration. Drop from the activity any instruction that he still doesn't follow correctly.

3. When you have established that your child understands and can carry out each of the instructions when given individually, try combining them in twos, e.g., "Stand up and bounce the ball." "Open the door and then close it again." "Make a mark on the paper and then sit down." Don't gesture or give away in some other nonverbal way what you want the child to do; just say the words.

4. If your child can do all these easily, think up some different instructions (e.g., "Turn around." "Stand on one foot." "Put the pencil on the floor." "Jump over the pencil." "Roll the ball." "Throw the ball to me." "Put the ball on the paper."), and make sure he can carry out each one. Then use them in combinations with each other and the previous instructions.

5. This activity should be fun for both you and your child, not a boring procedure of you telling your child to do something and his doing it. Once he understands the game, try getting more into the spirit of it by letting him give you instructions to follow. How long you spend on the activity at any one sitting, and how many instructions your child follows, will depend on his level of skills and his interest. The more you really get into the spirit of the activity as a fun, shared, sometimes silly game, the more your child will want to do it again.

6. Toward the end of the year, with repeated experience playing this game, your child may be ready to carry out more than two instructions in a row. Try three, using combinations of ones he's used to doing in combinations of two, e.g., "Stand up, bounce the ball, and open the

door." "Close the door, jump up and down, then sit down." The most difficult part of the activity at this stage is for your child not only to remember all three instructions long enough to carry them out, but to remember them and do the actions in the right order.

7. Keep a note in your child's book (see "The Baby Book," Birth to One Year, page 62) of how many and what kinds of instructions he's able to follow at different stages. The next time you play the game it will be useful to you to know where to begin. Even more important, however, the record of the length and complexity of sentences he's able to understand will make you more informed in your general "language feeding," using the kinds of sentences that are close to, but just a bit beyond, his present level.

Furthermore, it will remind you how much you can reasonably expect your child to remember. This will help you gear your routine instructions to him accordingly and not get upset when he sometimes forgets something you told him or doesn't carry out instructions you give him in the context of daily activities.

**Purpose:**   To give your child practice in paying attention, listening, remembering, and acting on verbal instructions. As we noted, this is an important skill in day-to-day life, necessary in learning to respond to other people's verbal communications. In a general sense, also, it is a prerequisite for learning any kind of verbal material. Therefore, it is involved in much of children's school experience. Your giving your child practice in following a series of verbal instructions will help him become used to and successful at this mode of learning.

**Variation:**   This activity doesn't have to be a formal game. Play it any time you and your child are together, giving him an increasingly larger number of instructions to carry out for you in the context of routine activities. For example, at the grocery store, you can start out by asking him to get you one item. Then see if he can remember two items long enough to find them and bring them back to you, and so on.[2] Don't expect him to do much better than carry out correctly three consecutive instructions by the end of this age period, however. And keep in mind that your child can remember more familiar instructions than he can ones he's never heard before.

[2] See "Shop and Learn," Four to Five Years, page 215, for some ideas to make grocery shopping an enjoyable learning experience for your child. Some of the ideas are applicable to children this age, too.

## GETTING DRESSED

**Participants:**   Two- to three-year-old child and an adult. The principles here apply to other age levels as well; the only difference is in the level of the child's skill development.

**Materials:**   Clothes for the child that have simple fasteners and that are easy to put on and take off, e.g., pants with elastic waists; shirts that pull over or which have a very few large front buttons or snaps; jackets, coats, and sweaters with large front buttons or snaps; shoes that the child can slip into herself.

**Explanation:**   Getting dressed is an activity which takes up a part of every day in your and your child's life together. It can be a time of arguments and power struggles between you, or it can be a time you enjoy together and learn. Below are some ideas to make dressing a positive learning experience for your child, now and in the future.

1. Select clothes for your child which are sturdy, functional, and easy enough to get on and off that she can begin to do much of the job herself. Avoid, particularly, clothes that are easily wrinkled, easily soiled, and hard to clean, and which have lots of little buttons, hooks and eyes, or other fasteners like sashes that your child cannot see to manipulate and which are beyond her motor skills at this time.

2. Choose clothes for your little girl as well as for your little boy that permit and encourage active play and which will not be a source of conflict between you because you're constantly worrying about her getting her clothes messed up. The way you dress your child can be inhibiting to her full human growth when it limits the kinds of activities and behaviors that are possible, acceptable, or expected in such clothes.

3. Let your child begin to participate in the purchase of her own clothes, at first just letting her choose between two items or decide which color she prefers. As she gets older and better able to understand the importance of function and durability as well as appearance, let her take more responsibility. Teach her about these things now by involving her in the selection process, pointing out to her in words and by letting her look and touch and test, why some things are more practical and durable than others.

4. Always keep in mind when you're shopping that children are not dolls; dress them for their own comfort and ease of movement, not just

because a particular piece of clothing will look cute. Good, sturdy, functional clothes can also look good, but their appearance should not be your primary criterion for selection.

5. Set up your child's closet so that she can use it. Build shelves low enough that she can take out and put back folded articles of clothing. Put up several low hooks for her to hang a jacket, a hat, a scarf, and so on. Hang a bar across the closet that is low enough that she can take her clothes off their hangers and learn to put them back on. Hang a shoebag on the door low enough that she can take out her own shoes and put them back. Hang a laundry bag on a hook for her to put her dirty clothes in.

6. Help your child learn increasing amounts of responsibility for dressing, undressing, and putting her clothes away. Follow your child's lead on how much she is capable of and interested in doing. Responsibility is a learned skill that children pursue as long as it's done at a pace that's comfortable for them. By now your child is probably quite proficient at taking off her clothes as long as she doesn't have to grapple with difficult fasteners.

7. Show her how to turn her clothes right side out, fold them, and put them on a shelf, or hang them up. Give her as much help as she needs, but encourage her to try it on her own, and don't demand perfection. If most of her clothes are no-iron, they don't need to be folded just so. It takes practice to get it right, and if you do it for her because you don't like the way she does it, you're not giving her the chance to learn.[3]

8. You can help your child learn to dress herself by handing her each piece of clothing the right way and starting her off, then letting her finish. For example, put her sock on her toe so that the heel part is below her heel, and let her pull it on. Hand her a T-shirt so that she can stick her hands and head in, and then let her pull the shirt on from there. When she can do this with no trouble, just hand her the article and let her do it herself. Offer help if needed, but let her try to do as much as she chooses. Button two of the buttons on her jacket and leave the other two for her.

9. As you're helping her get dressed, use the time for language practice: Use the names of articles of clothing. Practice counting to two as you're putting socks on feet or mittens on hands. Talk about the front and back, inside and outside, top and bottom of clothes. Point out the colors and textures and weights of different items. Play a matching

[3] However, do remember to be understanding, at this age and when they're older, that children have high and low days, and some days they won't be willing or able to do what they take joy in doing on others. Be patient and helpful when your child needs it.

game with socks and shoes, finding the ones that go together, the ones that are the same color or kind. In general, accompany dressing and undressing time with language to describe what's going on.

10. Selecting clothes from the closet to put on and putting clothes away can be times for getting practice in what things go together. Storage on the shelves, for example, should have pants in one place, T-shirts in another, underpants together, socks together next to them, and so on. This will help your child in taking clothes out and putting them back again. Getting dressed can be an opportunity for matching colors too: "Elisabeth, get the red socks and your red pants." "What color shirt do you want to wear?"

11. Let your child begin to choose what clothes she wants to wear and put together her own combinations. Set aside a time before she goes to sleep at night for the two of you to lay out her clothes for the following day. As she gets better at dressing herself, she'll be able to put on her clothes mostly by herself.

**Purpose:**  To help your child take increasing responsibility for her own care as she develops the skill to do so; to give her practice in the fine motor skills required to put on socks, button buttons, fasten snaps, and so on; to promote the development of thinking skills related to concepts involved in dressing [e.g., spatial concepts such as back and front, up and down, *over* the head, feet *in* the socks, shoes *on* the feet, and so on of clothes in relation to the child's body; number and size concepts related to matching socks to feet, armholes to arms, pant legs to legs, mittens to hands, and so on, and in terms of how things fit (too big, too small, just right); temporal relationships: what goes on first, next, last (putting on socks *before* shoes, shoes *after* pants, and so on)]; and to give the child practice in learning to understand and use words to label these concepts.

Finally, as the child is able to do more for herself, it increases her feelings of competence and self-worth, helping her to feel autonomous in certain areas of her life. It will be a while before your child can be totally responsible for her own dressing. Until that time, if you are responsive to her efforts at self-help and you try to help her assume responsibility as she is able, then she will be capable of taking total responsibility when her skills match the task. If you wait until she has fully developed her motor skills, you may have trouble motivating her emotionally suddenly to assume responsibility.

**Variation:**

1. A game you can play to help your child learn the fine motor skills for fastening and unfastening clothes, getting arms in armholes, and so on is to dress a doll or stuffed animal in some of her clothes. Any saved

from when she was a baby might fit the doll better.) Dressing someone else is easier, because she can see and work at the same time, straight ahead rather than down or to the side. Let her help you get dressed too, buttoning, pulling up zippers, snapping snaps, and so on.

2. In addition, you can make a book out of pieces of cloth with different fasteners attached to the pages in such a way that they resemble their location on clothing.

## LAUNDER AND LEARN

**Participants:** Two- to three-year-old child and an adult. Older children may enjoy a variation of this activity, and even one- to two-year-olds can help hand you things.

**Materials:** Family laundry

**Explanation:** Many educational programs for children include games which require the children to sort objects and pictures into groups, putting the ones that are alike together into piles. Although such games can be fun and serve a purpose (and we've included a few in this book), the basic skill being learned, that of classification, can be learned as well or better at this age through involving children in routine housekeeping activities as through more abstract learning activities. The activity that follows explains how doing the laundry with you can provide your child with an invaluable opportunity to gain experience using classification skills.

1. When you're sorting the laundry into piles (e.g., the whites together; dark things together; bright-colored things together), invite your child to join you. Talk to him about what you're doing and why, and let him help you. Ask him to hand you anything he sees that's white, for example, or ask him to put his socks in the pile with other colored things. Let him help you fill the measuring cup with powder or liquid detergent, pointing out to him that you need just one cup (or whatever the amount is) for each wash.

2. Show your child how to put the detergent in the machine, shut the door, and push the buttons or turn the dials. Talk to him all the while about what the two of you are doing. Use this opportunity to expand vocabulary: Use color words to describe different colored articles. Use words to describe the size of the load you're washing ("We have a big

load; we have a lot of clothes to wash today. Last time we didn't have so many."). Use time words to describe how long it's going to take. Use the names of things you're using (items being laundered, detergent, washing machine, water, hot, cold, dryer and so on).

3. When you're taking things out of the washing machine and either hanging them up to dry or putting them in the dryer, let your child help you sort the things, and talk to him about it: "We're going to let your tights dry on the line. They might shrink if we put them in the dryer. They'd get very, very small, and then you couldn't wear them any more."

4. Then let your child help you put the clothes into the dryer, set the buttons, and turn the dials. Even though he won't be able to read them, you can point out which button is for what, and he might be able to remember them after a while by their color or position.

5. When the laundry's done and ready to be folded and put away, let your child help with some of that too. He can put things into piles for Mommy, Daddy, and himself. He can fold some easy things like dishcloths, washcloths, and his own underpants. And he can help you put things away on low shelves.

**Purpose:** To give your child practice in sorting, a skill requiring grouping things that are alike together and separate from things that are different from them. Much of what we do in life requires classifying objects, events, and ideas into groups. Doing laundry, like other household routines, requires sorting on various dimensions such as color, the response of different materials to different washing and drying conditions, who things belong to, and what they are used for.

In addition, helping you in this kind of task makes your child feel important and useful, thus contributing to his development of a positive self-concept. And it teaches other useful cognitive and socio-emotional skills such as pushing a button or turning a knob[4] to make the machine go, giving the child a feeling of making something happen by his action. Further, it is a very valuable source of language learning for your child as he learns to connect words you use as you're working to the objects and actions involved in the process.

Most important, the laundry game—like the grocery store activity and others based on routine household tasks—gives you a way to turn a time that can be trying for parents and children into an opportunity for learning and enjoying each other's company. This is important in terms of adult modeling.

---

[4] For parents who are concerned about their baby's learning from this to try out every knob he sees, teach him another classification skill—discriminating between those knobs that are okay for him to use and those that he should not touch. In either case, he should be taught to touch buttons and knobs only under supervision.

You are showing your children that you can combine work and play. And, rather than giving them a negative behavioral interaction pattern to model, you are engaging them in a positive, cooperative interaction which will help them be better parents years later.

## FEED THE BEAR

**Participants:** Two- to three-year-old child and adult. Parts of the activity will be enjoyed by older children also.[5]

**Materials:** Large box and large piece of cardboard to attach to the back of the box; beach ball; small rubber ball; balloon; bean bag.

**Explanation:** The following throwing games will give your child practice in motor and cognitive skills as she learns how different objects react to her actions and about spatial relationships between her, the objects, and the area to which she's throwing.

1. Draw a picture of a teddy bear or some other character on the large piece of cardboard and attach it with tape to the inside of one end of the box as shown in the picture.

2. Make a few bean bags: Sew together two squares of cloth, leaving just enough of an opening to fill the bag with dried peas or beans, then sew up the opening. You might want to sew pieces of felt onto the bean bags to make them resemble little creatures.

3. Place the box so that the back of the bear picture is against a wall. Mark a line on the floor with chalk or a piece of tape about five feet away from the box. Stand behind the line and throw the bean bag into the box. Tell your child, "Pretend the box is the bear's tummy, and we're throwing it some food." Give her a beanbag and let her try to throw it into the box. If she has any trouble, move the line closer to the box until she is successful. Then, as she practices and improves, move the tape further back again.

4. Next, move closer to the box again and try to aim at the bear's stomach to bounce the beanbag off the cardboard backing and into the box in that way. If, over a period of time playing the game this way, the child gets good at hitting the bear's belly, encourage her to try to hit other

[5] See "Play Ball," One to Two Years, page 101, for ball play with younger children.

parts. For example, play "catch" and "kickball" with the bear by throwing the beanbag to its hands or feet.

5. Repeat the game using different kinds of balls and a balloon so the child can see how she has to change the way she throws when throwing with the different things. Talk to her as she uses each one, pointing out so that she takes note of it the different ways she handles each one.

**Purpose:** To give your child practice in the large and fine motor coordination required to throw a ball or other object. This kind of activity helps develop coordination of the entire body. It also helps develop skill in using the arm separately from the rest of the body and in using the hand to grasp and release with control. In addition, it helps the child learn to match her actions to her intentions by learning to aim correctly and to reach the area she aims for.

**Variations:**

1. Use a wastebasket, laundry basket, or a large coffee can to throw into instead of a box.

2. Let the child try throwing different objects such as a rolled-up sock, a piece of paper or foil crumpled into a ball, a block, an empty box, and so on. Help her take note of differences in the way each thing must be thrown and its reaction to her action on it. See if she notices any

patterns (e.g., the difference between throwing something very light and throwing something heavier).

3. Show her how to play bouncing and rolling games with the balls and all the other things, helping her, by asking her questions when she's experimenting with them, to note which ones bounce and roll and which ones don't.

## READ ME A PICTURE

**Participants:**   Two- to three-year-old child and an adult.

**Materials:**   Books with bright, colorful, realistic pictures of objects and activities familiar to the child and with simple printed captions to describe the pictures; lightweight oaktag or cardboard, a hole punch, string or yarn, pictures cut from magazines, photographs, white paste, a crayon, or magic marker.

**Explanation:**   Reading to your child should be a regular activity in your life. Read with him sitting on your lap, curled up beside you in a comfortable chair or on the floor, or resting up against the pillows in his bed before he goes to sleep.

1. Let your child lead the way in reading his books. Hold the book so you can look at the pictures together. Let him turn the pages and decide which pictures he wants to look at and for how long. Let your child set the pace. Spend as much time on the activity as he is involved with it.

2. When your child stops on a page, look at the pictures and talk with him about them: "What's that?" "That's right. It's a ball." "Where's your ball?" "What is the little girl doing with the ball?" "Remember yesterday when we played catch with your ball?" and so on. Encourage your child to talk about the pictures himself. If he doesn't do so spontaneously or in response to your questions, then just talk to him about what you're looking at, and relate the pictures as much as possible to things and events in his own life.

3. Show your child the words in his books, and tell him what they say, e.g., "Look, Thom, this says 'The girl is bouncing a ball,'" or "This word says 'ball.'" If he gets impatient with this part of the activity, skip it and try again another time. The primary focus of the activity should be to "read" the pictures, not the words. Unless your child shows a

particular interest in the words, their main function, at this point, is simply to get him accustomed to seeing words in books.

4. Select books for your child this age that have pictures of objects and activities with some relation to his own life experience. The pictures should be simple, realistic, and colorful. Many children this age prefer pictures with people to ones with humanized animals engaged in human-type activities. They may enjoy pictures of animals such as those they are acquainted with—dogs, cats, squirrels, birds, and others children would recognize from their experience. There should be pictures of both girls and boys in your child's books. Check to see that the boys in the pictures don't outnumber the girls and that they are both portrayed in a variety of activities, not just girls with baby dolls and boys with trucks, for example.

5. Look for books with beautiful and simple drawings. Uncomplicated line drawings, for example, are easier for children to understand than drawings that are very "busy." Books that have one good-sized, attractive drawing to a page are best for this age. Colors should be bright, and they should have some logical relation to the picture. Children this age tend to lose interest quickly in the multicolor, "psychedelic" splashes of form and fantasy that have been produced in great quantity in recent years.

6. Always let your child be the final judge of what *he* likes, however. Take him with you when you buy him a book, and show him a couple to see which he responds to more enthusiastically. Note which of the books he already owns he chooses over and over to read, and look for others that have similar characteristics.

7. Pictures should predominate in your child's books at this age. Verbal text should be kept to a short description of what's in the pictures. Print should be fairly large and well spaced.

8. Your best chance of getting books that will be just right for your child still is to make them yourself. Save your old magazines with pictures, and ask your friends for theirs. Go through them with your child and find pictures that he responds to positively. Paste them to big pieces of lightweight oaktag or shirt cardboard, one picture on each side. Write a caption below the picture describing the object or activity, using large capital letters. Punch holes in one side of each piece of cardboard, and tie them together with pieces of string or yarn. Tie the string loosely enough that your child can turn the pages easily.

9. If you own or can borrow a camera, take a series of pictures of your child engaged in typical activities of the day: sleeping, getting out of bed, brushing his teeth and washing his face, eating breakfast, playing indoors and out, eating lunch, and so on. Get them developed in a

fairly large size (e.g., 5″ × 7″), and paste them, in sequence, on oaktag pages for your child's very own activities book. Write captions underneath each picture, being sure to use your child's name: "Here's Thom sound asleep." "Now it's time for Thom to get out of bed." "Thom is eating his breakfast. He's having toast, an egg, and orange juice." "After breakfast, Thom goes outside. Here he is putting on his coat."

**Purpose:** To stimulate your child's continuing interest in books as a form of entertainment and a source of enjoyment; to give him practice associating pictures with the objects they represent; and to introduce him to the printed word as another way of representing objects and actions. Further, reading together provides you and your child with important time in a shared activity.

**Variations:**

1. Using material from your child's book (see "The Baby Book, Birth to One Year, page 62), make up a storybook about your child from his birth to his present age.

2. In books with simple stories about children like him, substitute your child's name and activities that relate to his life for the child in the book.

3. Other kinds of books your child might enjoy at this age include: ones with rhythm, rhyme, and repetition; ones with simple information, for example, about transportation or animals; nursery rhymes; simple stories. Whatever the nature of the content, children this age like the same book repeated over and over again, and they like best those books that relate to them and their life.


## A SPACE OF MY OWN

**Participants:** Two- to three-year-old child. The principle is applicable to children any age, though it is particularly important at this time.

**Materials:** A place in her living environment where your child can go when she wants to be alone; some kind of container, piece of furniture, or space in each room of the child's environment which belongs to her, in which she can keep her things, e.g., a plastic laundry basket and some shelves in the room in which she sleeps for stuffed animals, blocks, and other toys; a bookcase in the living room for her books, records, and puzzles; a plastic silverware tray, styrofoam egg carton, or some other small container in the kitchen for her to keep her very small toys.

**Explanation:**   As important as it is for children to learn to relate well to other human beings, in order to be able to do so, it is also essential that they be able to have and enjoy some personal privacy, some time and space to themselves which they can structure in their own way.

1. If you have the space to do it, set aside a corner of each room (and more, if possible, in the room the child sleeps in) that is your child's own special area.

2. If you have more than one child, set aside separate areas for each one. Even if you have a very large family, try to find some corner somewhere in your living space that can be each child's own place.

3. You can make a bookcase from wooden cartons gotten from the grocery store. Or perhaps you can pick up a bookcase or a small chest of drawers inexpensively at a garage or house sale. Even a plain cardboard box will do.

4. Put your child's name and perhaps her picture or some symbol to represent her on her special place(s). Explain to her that this place is for her to keep some of her things, and that you would like her to clean it up at the end of each day since it's in a place where everybody else spends time. Otherwise, let the child take responsibility for what she puts in her area and how she uses it.

5. In addition to one or more spaces in your living quarters where your child can keep her own things and not have them bothered by anyone else, there also should be a space somewhere that your child can go to get away from everybody else and not be bothered. You might make or buy a screen to enclose a small space with a cushion on the floor, a box to keep some things, and so on, or you could hang a piece of material from the ceiling.[6]

6. The point is to give your child a place that is accepted by everyone else in the family as her own private space which they will respect. It provides her not only with the physical space which she can feel is hers. It also gives her a way to signal to people that she's in need of some psychological space to herself for a little while.

**Purpose:**   To give your child "a space of her own"—if you have lots of room, in each room in which she spends time; and if not, then at least in one

---

[6] If you have more than one child, hang a hook or a library card holder on the screen. Make up name-and-picture badges for each child which they can hang on the screen to indicate the area is in use and they don't want to be disturbed.

area of your living environment. This will help her to establish her own sense of identity through having her own private spaces. It will also, better than any amount of lecturing about it you could do, help her learn to respect other people's property. She will be more likely to leave your books and records alone, for example, if she has her own in her own little area, than if everything that's in the living room belongs to you.

In addition, you will teach her through your example of respecting her property that she should respect yours. In every family, there will be some things which are shared by everyone, and your child should be beginning to understand this toward the end of the year. Meanwhile, it is important for her to have some things she doesn't have to share, some things she can call her very own. It is not the things that are important; it is what they represent—a little bit of life-space that is hers alone.

As we explained in "Self-concept: The Script for the Play," page 32, this is a period of transition for children, from a time when (because they were babies, dependent on others for all their needs) they had a sort of pseudo-power that enabled them to "command" others to do their bidding, to a time when they are expected to begin to assume increasing responsibility for themselves and to conform to others' needs. A space of their own is particularly important at this time to give them some small area of their lives in which they don't have to conform to others' wishes and demands, which they can structure themselves, in their own way.

**Variation:** For children who are in a day care or nursery situation for all or part of the day, it is even more important to make sure there is a special space for each child to keep a few things and to go to to be alone if she chooses. Group situations are sometimes hard for children this age, just because they are still learning how to share time, attention, activities, space, and possessions with others. Having some private space and some possessions all her own can help the child be willing to share in other areas of her life.

## LIKE ONES TOGETHER

**Participants:**   Two- to three-year-old child and an adult. Older children will continue to enjoy the more complex forms of this activity, especially as a game to play on their own.

**Materials:**   Two boxes with tops; two groups of objects, about five to a group, e.g., pennies and clothespins. Start off with common objects that would be familiar to your child and that are fairly different from one another.

**Explanation:**   Here's a game to give your child practice with classification, sorting objects into groups of items that are the same or that resemble one another along specified dimensions.[7]

1. Put all the objects together in a pile on the floor or a table. Show the child that there are two kinds of objects: Pick one up and say, "Look, Joseph, this one's just like these (pointing to the others that are the same). They're all the same." Put it in one of the boxes as you tell the child: "I'm going to put the penny in this box." Then pick up one of the other objects and, pointing to the others like it, say: "Look at this one, Joseph. It's just like these other clothespins." Then tell the child: "I'm going to put the clothespin in this box," and do so. Ask him: "Can you put all the pennies in this box (pointing to the box with the penny in it) and all the clothespins in this box (pointing to the box with the clothespin)?"

2. Let the child sort the objects into the boxes. If he does them all correctly, respond with praise and enthusiasm: "Very good, Joseph! You put all the pennies in the same box and all the clothespins together in the other box." Encourage him to dump them all out and do it again if he wants. If he makes any mistakes as he's sorting, don't correct him

---

[7] See Launder and Learn," page 138, "Cleaning Up," page 158, and "Shop and Learn," page 215, for examples of activities which use routine occupations as sources for practice with classification.

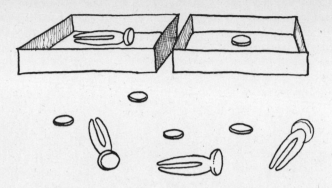

or tell him he's wrong. Instead, ask him if the one he put in is the same as the others in the box, showing them all to him.[8]

3. As your child engages in this activity, watch his problem-solving approach. Does he pick up an object and then look for the box to put it in? If he does it this way, does he pick up speed as he goes along, apparently remembering which box holds which objects without having to look each time? Or does he fill one of the boxes completely first and then the other? There's really no right or wrong approach. In some situations, one way of approaching the problem will be more efficient and effective than another, and it is therefore most important that over the years your child develop a flexible and self-monitoring approach to problem-solving rather than one particular way of doing it. When your child is working on an activity, observe how he goes about it so that you can be more informed in the future in your guidance of his learning.

4. After a while, your child will accomplish this activity with such ease that it becomes boring to him. You'll know this by his attitude toward it; if he shows no interest in it any more, then it's probably lost its challenge for him. When this occurs, expand the game: Include more groups of objects for him to sort. Or change the dimensions according to which the objects can be grouped. For example, you could make cardboard cutouts of groups of circles, squares, and triangles; of red, yellow, and blue circles; of three different sizes of the same thing; of happy and sad faces; of smooth and rough squares (covering one set with sand sprinkled on top of glue); and so on.

---

[8] If your child doesn't seem to get the point, at all, of sorting the objects into two piles, or if he's resistant to such a structured game, just offer him the materials to play with in any way he chooses, and play his game with him. In this activity, as in all others, be flexible in your approach; always be ready to adapt your plans to fit your child's response rather than insisting that his responses fit your requirements.

5. A more difficult way to play the game, but one you might want to try out with your child as he gets older and more skilled with some of the easier versions of the activity, is to have objects or pictures for the child to group according to conceptual classes, e.g., things to eat vs. things to wear; animals vs. people; and so on.

6. Once your child understands the activity, you can prepare materials for him to play with on his own without your direction. This will make an excellent game for solitary play. Put the objects to be sorted into a large plastic bag with a rubber band tied loosely enough that your child can get it off without help. Put the bag of objects together with the sorting boxes, perhaps in a large bag or box. On top of each of the sorting boxes, tape one of the objects or pictures to be sorted. Let your child put the entire set of game materials away somewhere so that he can get them when he wants to play with them.

**Purpose:** To give your child experience sorting objects and pictures into groups of things that are alike, first along the dimension of like identities (i.e., pennies vs. clothespins; marbles vs. pencils), then according to one variable characteristic (e.g., red circles vs. blue circles; small squares vs. large squares), and finally according to conceptual classes (e.g., food vs. clothing).

Much of what we know and do in life requires that we classify objects, events, and ideas along various dimensions such as what their function is, how they appear, what usefulness they have, what kind of action they require, and so on. This kind of activity, combined with everyday life experiences in which you include your child in figuring out what things go together and how various things are alike and different, will help your child gain competence in this important thinking skill.

**Variation:** Using similar rationale for your choice of objects in the succeeding stages of this activity, you can vary it by giving your child a pile of objects which contain a number of matched pairs, e.g., two pennies, two clothespins, two pencils, two erasers, for him to sort, matching up the ones that are the same. Use pairs of different kinds of empty food boxes and cans for such matching games, too.

It's important for you to understand that young children, in a relatively unstructured situation, will not group things in the same ways adults do. For example, if you gave a large group of pictures or objects, containing things to eat, things to wear, people, animals, things to ride in, and so on, to a child as old as six to eight years, and asked him to put the ones that are alike together, you could not necessarily expect him to group them according to these categories. He might, for example, put a boy with a coat because "The boy wears the coat." A younger child might put a number of things together because they were all the same color. By about eleven years, most children group things in the same way adults do.

It is only in a very structured task such as this one in which there are only two choices that a young child will, for example, group things to eat together and separate from things you can't eat; even in this case, you may find some unusual grouping procedures and rationale. Try different procedures for presenting grouping games to your preschool age children (three to six years) and observe the different responses you get. You can learn a great deal in this way about the way they think and look at the world. Don't try to change the way a child groups things. Through his own developmental changes and life experiences, he will learn new ways, at his own pace.

## WHO WAS THAT?

**Participants:** Two- to three-year-old child and other family members. Older children may enjoy this game as a group activity.

**Explanation:** Children spend their first years processing different kinds of information about things. Gradually, they learn to combine all their previously separate ways of knowing people and objects (e.g., by the way they look, feel, etc.) in order to really know the whole entity. Having done this, they must then learn to analyze things, consciously, according to their separate elements and attributes. This is important in order to understand the difference between those attributes of a thing that are essential to its identity and those which are only incidental (e.g., red is not an essential attribute of an apple). The following activity contributes to this process by testing your child's ability to recognize something she knows as an entity when she is given only one element of it.

1. Sit or stand in a circle around the child. Explain to her that you're going to play a game to see if she can tell without looking who's talking. Tell her to close her eyes and listen carefully.

2. One by one, have each participant say something to the child, using her name, e.g., "I love you, Mary." "Mary is *so* smart." and so on. After each person speaks, stop and ask the child: "Who was that?" "Who said that?"

3. When she guesses correctly, the person who did the talking should respond, saying something like: "That's right. It *was* Daddy." "I said 'I love you, Mary.' "

4. When the child guesses wrong, the person speaking should respond "No, I'm not Robert. Try again." and repeat what he said before. If she still

doesn't get it, tell her to open her eyes and look while the person talks. Then have her close her eyes again and play some more. Slip the one she got wrong in again later, and see if she gets it right then.

5. Change everyone's positions in the circle regularly relative to the child so that she doesn't guess based on where she saw them standing.

**Purpose:** To give the child practice in problem-solving—learning to recognize something she knows through various characteristics when she's only given partial information, in this case to guess familiar persons' identities by hearing their voices alone. In addition, it's a fun activity for a child this age because it allows her to be the center of everyone's attention. Taking the opportunity when speaking to say something that lets her know how special she is to you also contributes to her development of a positive self-concept.

**Variation:**

1. If you have more than one child at home, let them take turns being the one inside the circle. Try it yourself, too.

2. This game can be played also as a group game with a number of small children in this age range or older who are in a play group, nursery school, or day care center together. It can help them get to know each other better and give each one a chance to be the center of attention.

## WHICH HAND HAS THE TOY?

**Participants:** Two- to three-year-old child and an adult. Older children will enjoy playing and figuring out the system.

**Materials:** A toy small enough to be held in your fist.

**Explanation:** The following game is one you've probably played yourself at some time in your own childhood. A learning game by any name, you can increase its teaching potential by knowing *why* and injecting a system into it.

1. Hold the toy in one hand and make a fist. Put your hands behind your back, and ask the child to tell you which hand has the toy.

2. If your child chooses the correct hand, bring it in front of you and open it up so he can see the toy. Then put your hand behind your back again and change the toy to the other hand. Tell the child, "Now I'm going to hide the toy again. See if you can find it this time."

3. If the child chooses the wrong hand, say "No, not that one." If he needs to look to be sure, show him your empty hand, then let him try again. Whenever he gets it right, get very excited and say to him: "That's right. The ball (or whatever it is) was in my right (or left) hand."

4. Once the child understands how to play the game, introduce a system. The easiest system is to keep holding the toy in the same hand. A harder system is to alternate, right, then left, then right. Another is to keep it in one hand twice, then change it to the other hand twice, then back to the first hand twice, and so on.

5. Whatever system you choose, stick with it until the child has figured it out and picks the correct hand consistently. If he's still having fun at this point, switch your system and see if he can figure out the new one.

6. Give your child a chance to be the one who hides the toy while you try to guess which hand it's in.

**Purpose:** To give your child an opportunity to enjoy his fairly recently acquired understanding that hidden objects still exist and can be found; and to give the child the experience of figuring out patterns, an early step in problem-solving. This requires that he figure out what system you are using, remember it, and act upon it. Shifting from one system to another is even harder, requiring a flexibility in problem-solving that many adults lack.

**Variation:** Play a hiding game with cups: Have your child close his eyes while you hide the toy under one of three cups; then, ask him to open his eyes and find it. Choose a pattern (e.g., always in the middle, or alternating between one end and the other). Stick with it until your child figures out and remembers the pattern and can find the toy consistently on the first try. Then, switch to another pattern.

## MODIFIED MUSICAL CHAIRS

**Participants:** One or more two- to three-year-old children and adults.

**Materials:** Small, child-sized chairs equal to the number of participants, record player and marching record, radio, drum, or voice.

**Explanation:** The following activity modifies the rules of an old favorite so that younger children can enjoy it and practice some valuable motor and cognitive skills.

1. Set up the chairs as you would for regular musical chairs, with chairs back to back, but provide enough chairs for all the players including yourself. If you have more than one child participant, then you can take turns being responsible for the music when you use something that requires your complete attention such as a record player, radio, or piano.

2. Explain to the children that you are going to play some music and that while it's on, they should march around the chairs, and that when the music stops, they are supposed to sit down as quickly as they can. Tell them not to watch you, but to pay attention to the music. Once the children understand how the game works, you can trade places with you one at a time so that they can each get a chance to work the music while you join the others.

3. If you and your child are the only participants or if you'd just rather not be excluded from the game, then use a drum, some other instrument you can carry around with you, or sing a song (e.g., You can make up a simple song to describe what you're doing: "Walking 'round the chairs; Walking 'round the chairs; Walking 'round the chairs while the music's on. When the music stops; When the music stops; When the music stops; We all sit down."). It probably will be too much for your child to concentrate on at one time for her to take a turn with the music while she's marching, but if she wants to, you can let her try.

4. Begin the game by keeping the music going a while before you stop it, and stop it at a fairly predictable point. Once the children have the point of the game, you can stop and start the music more abruptly and at irregular, unpredictable intervals.

**Purpose:**   To give your child practice seating herself in a chair with speed and ease; to give her practice matching her movements to music; and to provide her with exercise in paying attention. Most children have just become competent at about age two at seating themselves in a child-sized chair smoothly and without having to look behind them or between their legs to adjust their movements to get their bodies seated. Once any skill is learned, children enjoy games which push that skill to its limits, testing it and adding new variations. This is a fun game which gives the child a chance to practice the motor skill in a context where she must pay attention to the music rather than to her motor performance.

**Variations:**   If this becomes a game that your child enjoys over an extended period of time, and she gets to a point that it is no longer challenging, then introduce her to the rules and procedures of the real musical chairs. The only problem with playing it the traditional way with very young children, however, is that once they lose their seat, they're out of the game, and that's no fun. If you have some older children, you might ask them to join and not to be so competitive that they force the little one out of the game early.

## POURING, FILLING, WASHING, SPLASHING

**Participants:** Two- to three-year-old child and an adult. This activity continues to be appropriate after three years also.

**Materials:** Kitchen sink; chair or stepstool; kitchen utensils and equipment such as metal or plastic bowls, small unbreakable pitcher, paper cups, a strainer, different-size plastic or metal measuring cups and spoons, foil pie tins, unbreakable plastic dishes, a couple of pots, a big stirring spoon with holes in it, a ladle, dishwashing liquid, a sponge.

**Explanation:** Water play is an age-old favorite of children, an activity which is loads of fun for them as well as being an almost unlimited source of different kinds of learning. Below are some of the ways your child can learn from "pouring, filling, washing, and splashing" with water.

1. Set out a small number of materials to begin with. Start off, for example, with two different-size bowls, a pitcher, and some paper cups. Leave a couple of cups as is, and punch holes in the others: one big hole in the middle of one, two medium-sized holes in another, three small holes in a third. If you have a double sink, put all the materials in one of the sinks. Otherwise, put them in the dishrack or on the counter next to the sink.

2. Have your child carry a chair or a stepstool over to the sink and stand up on it so that he can reach the faucet. Let him turn the water on, showing him how to adjust the hot and cold to get the temperature he wants. Talk to him all the while about how the water feels, how to adjust it for force and temperature, and so on, accompanying your words with actions and experiences:

   "Turn this handle. It's for the hot water." "Feel it getting hotter?" "Better take your hand away. You might get burned."

   "Now, turn that one all the way off, and let's try the cold water." "Turn this handle for cold water." "Put your hand under the water. Does it feel cold?"

   "Let's make the water warm. Leave this one, and turn the hot handle." "Feel the water while you turn. The more you turn, the hotter the water gets."

"Now turn the cold handle more." "Feel what happens? The water got colder again."

"Turn both handles as much as you can." "Oh, my! Look how much water's coming out. Better turn them back the other way." "Now look. There's just a little bit of water coming out."

"Okay. How do you want the water? You turn the handles so it's just right for you. Not too hot and not too cold; not too much and not too little." [9]

3. Show your child the various materials you have collected for his water play. Talk to him about each one as you guide his activity: "Look, Sean. Here's a cup. Let's see what happens when you put some water in it." Hand it to him to hold under the faucet. Then give him the one with the big hole, and comment on what happens when he holds that one under the water. Guide him in pouring, dumping, filling from the faucet, filling one container from another, comparing how fast the water goes through each of the cups with holes, and so on, talking with him all the while about what's going on as he manipulates the materials.

4. Whenever your child gets tired of your chattering—when he starts just playing with the materials on his own, paying little attention to what you're doing or saying—then leave him to enjoy the water play by himself. Put some newspapers on the floor in case he gets a little carried away, and put an apron or some kind of covering or just an old pair of pants on him (so that you won't worry about his getting himself messed up). Check up on him regularly to make sure he's okay and hasn't done anything destructive, but otherwise leave him to entertain himself for as long as he finds the activity interesting. Pour a little dishwashing liquid into a cup for your child to use to "wash" the dishes with a sponge or dishmop.

5. Let your child engage in water play often. Even though it can get a little messy sometimes, it's worth the trouble for the fun and learning it affords. Each time you do it, introduce one or two materials, and talk with your child as he plays with each one about what's happening as he uses it. Always be alert to his cues of when he's had enough of your talking and participation, and bow out gracefully leaving him to his own devices for as long as he wishes.

**Purpose:** To give your child the opportunity to experiment with the

---

[9] How you talk to your child and help him to work the faucet will vary according to the particular kind you have in your kitchen sink as well as how much language he understands. But since you're accompanying *his* actions with words to fit them, you can increase his vocabulary by using unfamiliar words and expressions in this way. Give him a chance to participate in the talking, too, answering questions and initiating his own comments.

properties of water, finding out through his play about quantity and volume; temperature; container and contained; what happens when the container has holes; what difference it makes how many, how big, or where the holes are; what happens when you mix soap and water; and so on.

At the same time, it provides you with an opportunity to feed your child's language and expand his learning by helping him to note similarities and differences in results from different actions and helping him connect his own actions, the responses of the water to the materials, and the materials with words which represent them.

Finally, water play is a very relaxing and enjoyable activity for young children that gives them feelings of mastery, stimulates their curiosity, and is emotionally satisfying because it allows them to make a mess in an acceptable context. This is especially important at this time in their lives when, in many areas (e.g., toileting, feeding), they're expected not to make a mess.

**Variations:**

1. Put a stopper in the sink, fill it half full of water, and give your child a supply of different kinds of materials with which to play "sink or float."
2. Let your child take some of his water-play materials into the bathtub with him, to try out some of his experiments there.

*KICKBALL*

**Participants:**   Two- to three-year-old child and an adult.

**Materials:**   Large rubber ball or beach ball, wastebasket, chair, two long pieces of wood or substitute (e.g., a broom and a mop), several empty cans.

**Explanation:**   The following ideas for ball play are good examples of activities in which your primary function is as a model and a companion to your child in play. Once you have demonstrated to her how to do each activity and joined her in her play for as long as she wishes, she still has much work to do. She has to practice by herself (or with you again on other occasions if she asks), until she "makes the skill her own."

1. Practice kicking the ball at the wall with your child. If she has any trouble kicking, hold her hand to help her balance on one foot while you help guide her other foot to kick the ball. Keep practicing kicking with her as long as she's enjoying it until she can kick the ball with

some control. If she gets tired of it, quit and come back to it another day.

2. Put the chair between you and the wall. Show the child how to kick the ball through the legs of the chair to the wall, and then let her try. Have her stand close to the chair at first and gradually move further from it. Take turns kicking the ball through the chair legs, and leave her to practice on her own if she's enjoying herself. If more than one child is playing, have them take turns.

3. Make an "alley" by putting the two pieces of wood or the mop and broom on the floor parallel to one another and about eighteen inches apart. Show your child how to kick the ball down the alley, and then take turns practicing doing it. Let her have more turns, and leave her to practice on her own if she'd like.

4. At the end of your "alley," lay a wastebasket on its side so that the opening faces you. Show the child how to kick the ball into the wastebasket, and then let her try to do it herself. Encourage her to practice until she can get the ball in the wastebasket, and help her by noting if she's kicking too hard or not hard enough, and so on: "Oh, it didn't go in. Try kicking the ball a little harder." Let her try also without the alley and standing closer to the wastebasket. Practice for a while with her, then leave her to play by herself.

5. Set the empty cans up in a pyramid and show the child how to kick the ball and knock them down. Set them up again and have the child try to knock them down. Encourage her to practice until she can do it. Once she's gotten the knack of it, she'll probably enjoy doing it over and over and finding other things to substitute for the cans too (a doll or stuffed animal that can be sat upright; some paper towel or toilet paper cardboard rolls set upright). Show the child how to set the objects back up so that she can continue to play the game on her own.

6. Kick the ball back and forth between you. This is hard for younger children because they must deal with a moving ball, getting themselves in the right position relative to the ball to stop it and then kick it back. Start off fairly close to each other, and show the child how to kick it very lightly. Even if your child isn't successful at accomplishing a smooth to-and-fro kicking game with you, it will be fun and good exercise for her to run around after the ball when she misses. Just don't put too much emphasis on "learning how to do it the right way," and you'll both have a good time. For older and more skilled children, kicking the ball from person to person in a circle can be fun too.

**Purpose:** To give your child opportunities to develop the balance and large motor coordination necessary in order to kick a ball with ease and accuracy.

In addition, kicking activities such as the above stimulate the child's thinking skills. She must figure out how hard or how softly to hit the ball in order to perform the various actions, and she must evaluate where to stand in order to receive a kick from another. Aiming the ball and getting it to go where she wants it to go requires the development of a sophisticated understanding of spatial relationships: the relationship between the ball and the object or area to be hit and the relationship of both of those to her own movements.

**Variation:** Try doing the same activities *rolling* the ball instead of kicking it, and try using different sizes and weights of balls to do so.

## CLEANING UP

**Participants:** Two- to three-year-old child and an adult. The principles involved in this activity apply to children any age, at home or in a group care situation.

**Materials:** Child's toys and other possessions.

**Explanation:** Except for your child's private spaces (See "A Space of My Own, page 144), which he should be allowed to organize as he chooses, there should be specified places for your child's possessions—a place for everything and (at the end of the day) everything in its place. Most children begin by about eighteen months to know where things belong, to look for them there, and to enjoy putting them back there. This kind of consistency helps them understand the structure of their world; this is particularly important in a time when there are so many other changes in their lives. This is the time, while they are interested in helping, to get them used to keeping their things in an orderly fashion.

1. Your child should be encouraged to put things back where they belong when he's done playing with them rather than pulling out toy after toy and leaving them in piles on the floor. Don't get into fights over it. When he's unable to find something he wants, that's a good way for him to find out why it's important to keep things in their place. Just explain to your child that if he puts things back where they live, then he'll know where to find them when he wants them again. If you do it with him, you can make a game out of cleaning up. It can be a time for sharing and being together that you both enjoy rather than a source of conflict.

2. Set aside a time at the end of each day to get things put away and cleaned up. Use this time to get in a lot of language practice—talking to toys, asking your child to find and hand you things or put them away: "Where's the other red block like this one?" "Put these blocks in the big box." "Where does this doll go?" "Can you fit the big ball under the shelf?" "Hi, Bear. How are you today. Bryant hasn't been playing with you, has he?" [10] "Bryant, hand me the puzzle." "What's this, Bryant?" "Would you please hang up this jacket?" "I'll put away the doll's clothes. You put away his toys. Let's see who can finish first." Talk as you go, accompanying everything you're doing with words to describe the objects and actions you're involved with.

3. In order to make cleaning up easier as well as to give your child practice in classification, you should arrange shelves and drawers so that things that are alike live together: blocks in one place; puzzles in another; paper and crayons, clay, and paints together; dolls and stuffed animals together; and so on. Even within one group of toys, you can have subgroupings: all the square blocks together, all the cylinders together, all the triangle blocks together, and so on.

[10] Fantasy is good for children. It's important to stimulate their imagination. Later this will be reflected in their ability to do divergent thinking, an extremely important cognitive skill and essential in the development of creative expressive abilities.

4. If you can draw or have access to a camera, tape pictures up on shelves or drawers to show what goes there. On the bottom of each shelf, put silhouettes cut from black contact paper in the shape of your child's blocks and other toys and materials. Matching pictures or silhouettes to the objects they represent can be a game you can play just for the fun of it in addition to using them as guides for putting things away in their correct homes. The skills required and methods used are similar to those for "Like Ones Together" (page 147).

5. Most important in this "activity" is your attitude. Many parents and children get into fights over putting away toys. If at any point you sense a fight growing, because your child is tired, in a bad mood, or wants to do it *his* way (a typical source of problems with children this age), then just relax your expectations, be flexible, and relieve the child of the responsibility for the day before a conflict begins and a tantrum results.

6. If you don't get into win-lose battles with your child, you insisting he do what you tell him, and he demanding to do it his way, you'll avoid countless problems and hurt feelings in addition to stopping bad patterns from developing. Most of the time, if you approach cleaning up as an enjoyable activity—a time to be together and to help your child learn a whole range of skills involved in the process—then it will be just that.

**Purpose:** To help your child learn organizational skills—putting things that are alike away together—as well as the value of taking care of his things so that they will last and so he can find them when he wants them. If these things are taught in a relaxed, enjoyable way as part of an expected routine that is conducted in a game-like manner, then they will become habits rather than remaining an ongoing source of conflict as they are in many families. This is also an important part of a child's beginning to understand his responsibilities as a family member—to take care of his own possessions to the extent that he is able to do so, in addition to contributing his part to other areas of household management.[11]

[11] Don't forget the importance of your model to your child in influencing his behavior. It will be much more difficult for you to convince him of the importance of keeping his own things in good order if the rest of the family keeps things in disorder. As we've said before, expecting to keep a home perfectly neat and clean with a young child is unreasonable. But by this age, he can begin to contribute to your keeping things in a recognizable order.

## TOUCH AND KNOW

**Participants:**  Two- to three-year-old child and an adult. By increasing the number of objects used and their similarity to each other, as well as asking the children to identify the objects themselves rather than simply locating ones named by the adult, this activity can be used with older children, alone, or in groups.

**Materials:**  A paper bag; a few familiar objects such as a toothbrush, a plastic cup, a toy animal, a toy car, a piece of soap, a washcloth, and a clothespin.

**Explanation:**  This is another problem-solving game which gives children practice recognizing and identifying familiar objects when given only partial information, in this case, touch alone.

1. Choose two objects that are very different in configuration from each other, e.g., a toothbrush and a toy car. Show them to the child and make sure she can either name or identify both of them (i.e., when asked "What is this?" she should be able to give the correct name or, if not, when asked "Show me the toothbrush," and so on, she should be able to do so). Put the two objects in a paper bag.

2. Hand the bag to the child and show her how to put her hand inside and feel the objects without looking into the bag. Then explain to her that you want her to give you the object you ask for by feeling the two and deciding by touching only which one is the right one.

3. Then, ask her to feel the objects and hand you the toothbrush. If she does, take it from her with great enthusiasm, and say, "That's right, Diane. You found the toothbrush with your fingers. You knew how it felt," or something similar. Put the object back in the bag, and ask the child for the other one.

4. If the child fails to produce the object you asked for, show her how to feel it at the same time as she looks at it, and talk about the way it feels, e.g., "Feel the soft bristles. Now feel the smooth plastic part. Feel how long it is." Compare the way it feels to the other object. Then, put them both back, and give her another try.

5. When the child consistently is able to locate the object you request, make the game more challenging by using new objects, this time three of them. Still make sure they're familiar to the child and that they're very different from each other.

6. Over time, as the child plays this game repeatedly and continues to improve her skill at it, add more objects to the bag at one time and put in some that are more alike, e.g., an apple and an orange.

7. Switch roles with your child, and let her direct while you "look with your hand" for the object she requests. This would make a good small-group activity, too, with you and the children taking turns being director and finder.

**Purpose:** To give your child practice using her sense of touch alone to derive meaning from an object—to identify, solely through feeling it, an object that she has known before principally by the way it looks. Although young children are very used to using their sense of touch to learn about the world, they usually combine that way of knowing with the information they receive through the other senses, particularly through sight. This kind of activity lets the child play a kind of guessing game, teaching her to use only partial information to find out about an object.

**Variations:**

1. Put several pairs of objects in the bag, and ask your child to find the ones that are the same through touch alone.

2. Put duplicate objects to the ones in the bag on a table in front of your child (in this case, you can use unfamiliar objects). The task then is for the child to try, through feeling the objects in the bag, to find one by one the mate of each object that's displayed on the table.

3. Let your child try to name each of several objects in the bag through feeling it, then take it out after naming it to see if she's right (as opposed to your asking her for a particular object).

4. This also can be played as a group game for older children, using a big bag full of objects. Let the children find objects around the room to include in the bag. As they gain experience with the game, try it with a "surprise bag," so they have to identify its contents through touch alone without seeing what went into it.

## A WORLD FOR A CHILD[12]

**Participants:** Two- to three-year-old child. Older children also will enjoy this type of activity.

[12] After Lois Barclay Murphy, *Personality in Young Children* (New York: Basic Books, Inc., 1956).

**Materials:** Toys which are miniature representations of people and things in the child's environment and within the child's experience through books, televisions, and other sources. The collection should include the following kinds of things:

one small doll to represent the child himself and one for each member of his family, as well as a few to represent other people who are important in his life;

furniture to represent each room of his living environment, including especially pieces that are suggestive of ones that are, or were in the past, particularly meaningful in the child's life, e.g., a toilet and potty seat or potty chair; a highchair or baby-tender similar to what the child was fed at; a crib, and so on;

some farm, zoo, and domestic animals, and props for them;

a few transportation toys—car, bus, truck; and

any other objects that are particularly relevant to the way of life the child leads within his family and subculture.

The people-dolls should be bendable plastic or rubber so the child can change their positions, and the rest of the toys should be plastic, wood, or metal, of a size that is in correct proportion to the dolls. You should be able to get such toys at a dime store or through a distributor of toys and materials for preschool and kindergarten children. You shouldn't spend a lot of money on them since children this age give their toys a lot of wear and tear.[13]

**Explanation:** Small children usually have not developed their language skills enough to communicate in words what they're thinking or feeling about their life experiences. But they do communicate quite clearly through nonverbal means. This activity gives your child a way to act out and work through some of his reactions to his real life experiences on a child-sized level in a fantasy (and thus, safe) context. At the same time, it can provide you with some valuable insights into the ways your child's experiences are affecting him, how he's interpreting them, what kinds of concerns he has, and how you could change your behavior toward him to increase his comfort and happiness with his life.

1. Set the toys out in boxes on the floor in a room with an open area where the child can spread out. Let him play on his own, selecting which ones he wants to play with and in what way.

---

[13] An alternative to buying miniature toys is to make them: Paste pictures of people, furniture, and so on, each on a piece of thin cardboard (e.g., shirt cardboard or from shoeboxes); cut around the picture, making a straight cut at the bottom and a slit in the middle. Make a stand for each figure by cutting a trapezoid-shaped piece of cardboard, making a slit in the middle of it and attaching it at a right angle to the figure.

2. Stay out of your child's way sufficiently that you neither disturb him nor intrude on his play, but keep your eyes and ears open to observe his play.

3. Watch which toys your child seems to choose with some regularity. Notice how he organizes the toys in his play. Listen to his verbalizations as he plays. Observe his "style" of playing, how long he spends doing the same thing, whether there's a theme to his play or whether it's just random manipulation of materials, how absorbed he becomes in his play, and so on.

4. Does your child spend a lot of time playing in ways that seem to reproduce his own home situation or recent experiences he's had? Can you observe in his play any particular problems, worries, or sources of anger that he's working out in his play? If you can, make a note of them, and see if there are any ways you can change your treatment of your child or make adjustments in the demands on him that will relieve these anxieties.

5. Is he overly orderly and precise in his play for such a small child? If so, perhaps you're being so yourself in the model you present him and in your expectations of him.

6. Is he random and disorganized in his play, not seeming able to focus on any kind of meaningful activity with the toys? Perhaps there's not enough structure and consistency in his life.

7. Are there toys that he systematically and consistently excludes from his play even though they have some relation to people and events in his life? He may be developing too constricted a definition of what is appropriate and acceptable for him.

8. Children reflect many of the aspects of their own life and their feelings about it in their play. How your child uses these toys and what particular meaning his play has will depend on him and his unique life experience. You won't have to look for interpretations to "read into" your child's play; the meaning of children's behavior tends to be more transparent and less disguised than adults'.

9. Through giving your child these kinds of "life toys" to play with, you provide him with the opportunity to work through some of the things that may be bothering him. Through observing him sometimes you can pick up on things that can help you structure his existence in such a way to make it happier and more productive for him.

10. Sometimes, at his invitation, you may enjoy joining your child in his play. Let him take the lead and tell you what role he wants you to play and in what way. This, too, may teach you a great deal about how he thinks and feels.

**Purpose:** To give your child materials and the opportunity to use them on his own, in his own way, through which he can construct and act out his own little world; to give you a chance to observe how your child sees his world and what his feelings about it are.

## WALKING THE LINE[14]

**Participants:** One or more children, two to three years and older, and an adult. The first parts of the activity are appropriate for children at the lower end of the age range. Toward the end of the year, most children should be able to participate in the more difficult rhythm-related movements.

**Materials:** Bright-colored masking tape, several building blocks, a drum or something else to beat out a rhythm, a record player and records.

**Explanation:** When children first learn to walk, they make many exaggerated and superfluous movements. As they grow older and accumulate practice, they increase the control and coordination of their movements. They gradually eliminate unnecessary and inefficient movements and learn to vary and control their movement at will. The following series of activities offers practice that will help your child achieve greater economy of movement, improved balance, and increased ability to vary her movement, changing speeds, stopping and starting, moving in time to rhythm, and the like.

1. Cut two strips of tape, each about five feet long. Tape them to the floor, parallel to each other, about six inches apart.

2. Show your child how to walk between the two lines without stepping on or outside either one. The eventual aim is to have the child walk heel to toe, and you should show her how to do this. At first, however, it will be okay for her to walk any way she can, watching her feet to make sure she keeps them within the two lines.

3. When she can walk the line forward, show your child how to walk it backwards, still concentrating on keeping her feet within the lines. Let her try, and then practice with her as long as she enjoys the game.

[14] This, like many of the activities covering an age span of an entire year, is intended to be done in small steps over that period of time. You may stay at the same step for many sessions of playing the game. Let your child be your guide of how long to spend on each session and when to move on to a new stage of the activity.

4. Put rectangular building blocks (or some other similar-sized obstacle) at regular intervals along the path for the child to step over as she walks the line. Encourage her to practice with you until she can walk the line smoothly without having to change her pace when she comes to the obstacles.

5. When your child has mastered the procedure of walking between the lines, explain to her that you are going to beat time on the drum, and you want her to try to walk to the beat. If you don't have any kind of toy drum to use, you can make one from a coffee can, using a spoon to beat on the can with, or you can clap your hands instead.

6. Begin by beating out a simple, steady rhythm, about one beat per second (You can estimate the timing of one-second intervals by saying to yourself: one kangaroo, two kangaroos, and so on). Show the child how to walk to the end of the line, stop, turn around, and walk back as you beat the drum, and then do it with her.

7. When your child has gotten used to walking to the beat of the drum, you can introduce a new element. Tell her that now you're going to change speeds: sometimes you will make the drum beat faster, and sometimes you will make it go slower. You want her to listen very carefully and see if she can make her walking fast or slow like the drum. Show her what you mean by walking in time to changes in the drum beat yourself. Give her a chance to be the rhythm-maker too.

8. When the child has learned to monitor the speed of her walking to match the pace of her own and your drum beats, add the further dimension of stopping and starting. At first, introduce the stops when your child is walking slowly; later, you can try it from a fast pace too. Demonstrate to her what you're going to do now, and let her try it.

9. Try the game with music too. Put different-paced musical selections on the record player (or use a radio), and let the child practice walking to the music. You can do the stop and start procedure with records too, like musical chairs without the chairs.

**Purpose:** To give your child practice in balance and coordination—walking between two lines without stepping on or over them; in rhythm-related movement—making her movements match the beat of the drum or music, learning to speed up, slow down, stop, and start according to the pace set by the music.

In addition, this kind of activity is excellent for giving the child practice in focusing her attention: She must pay attention to her own movements to make sure she stays within the lines and follows the rhythm, and she must pay attention to the music and drum beat to respond appropriately to changes in them. You may find the attention-focusing aspects helpful and calming yourself. See "Attending Exercises," Five to Six Years, page 258, for more focusing activities.

**Variations:**

1. When the child gets very good at the various ways of playing this game, try substituting one wide strip of masking tape for the two strips and see if she can do the same activity walking heel to toe on the wide line. This requires greater balance and coordination and will take a bit longer to accomplish.

2. If you have a group of children, give each of them a turn as leader and beater of the drum. The game can be played with several children walking the line in a row as well as with one; if there are too many children for this line, lengthen it.

3. For older and more skilled children, make the line into a circle or a figure eight.

## MORE MEMORY GAMES

**Participants:**    Two- to three-year-old child and adult. Some of these activities will continue to be interesting to older children. See, also, "What's Not There?" Three to Four Years, page 180 for a slightly more complex memory game than the ones included here.

**Materials:**

1. Three paper cups and a toy small enough to fit under them.

2. Several boxes that fit inside each other (e.g., a matchbox, an empty food container, and a shoe box), and a small toy that fits in the smallest one.

3. 3″ × 5″ cards with drawings, magazine pictures, or photographs of familiar objects pasted on them.

4. Six 5″ × 7″ cards, four with a single swatch of different-textured material on each one, and two with two swatches of different-textured material on each.

5. Several objects that are familiar to the child (e.g., a pencil, crayon, ball, small toy).

**Explanation:**    There are as many kinds of memory as there are different things to know and ways to learn. Intelligence tests generally assess a child's memory by asking him to repeat numbers (or sometimes, words), and they generalize about his total memory processes from that. It is not an adequate test of a child's total memory skills to test only one, rather abstract kind of memory. Nor is it correct to assume that by giving a child practice using one kind of memory that there will be a transfer of the skill learned in that instance to other different kinds of memory tasks. On the following pages are just a few different kinds of memory games to give you some ideas of the various kinds of memory and of ways to exercise them. Based on these, you probably can think up more games yourself. Just remember not to make them too complex at this age.

1. *Memory of Location:* "Find the hidden toy," two variations. Both these games require the child to remember where you put something when a short period of time and some other actions occur between the time you hide the toy and the time he looks for it.

   a. Turn the three paper cups upside down on a table or the floor. While your child is watching, put the toy under one of the cups, and put a cardboard screen between him and the cups for about 10 seconds. Remove the screen, and tell your child to "Find the toy." Repeat this, hiding the toy in different positions each time.

   b. While your child watches, hide a small toy in the matchbox. Then put the matchbox inside the middle-sized box, and put that inside the shoebox. Take the shoebox and hide it under a towel. Then ask your child to "Find the toy." Repeat this as often as he enjoys playing it. You could also wrap the toy first in a piece of tissue and add an extra box to make it harder when the first version gets to be old hat.

2. *Memory of Pictures.*

   a. Go through some magazines with your child and find some small pictures of things that are familiar to him (that he can identify when you ask him to point to them, or that he can name himself). Paste them onto $3'' \times 5''$ cards, one to each card. If you can draw, or if you have access to a camera, include drawings or photographs of objects from the child's environment.

   b. Show your child one picture card, then take it away. Then, show him two cards including the first one he saw. Ask him to show you the one he saw before. Don't use the name of the picture in this game. Just say something like "Look at this," when you show him the first card, then, "Now where is it?" when you show him the two. Continue this procedure with different pictures as long as your child enjoys the activity.

   c. If your child can easily identify the first card he saw from a choice of two, see if it makes any difference if you increase the number of choices to three or four. Also, try showing him two cards the first time, then showing him four to choose from. As your child gets practice with the activity, and as he gets more skilled, increase the number of cards you show him at first and the number of cards you hide the first ones among.

d. If you're using drawings, you can also increase the difficulty level by giving your child choices in the second stage that look similar to each other. For example, you might present a single picture, in the first stage, of a smiling face, and in the second stage, present two faces, one like the first, and the second with a turned-down mouth.

3. *Memory for Faces.* This can be played in the same way as the picture game, but using pictures of family members and other people rather than pictures of objects. Try playing it when family members are home, too, combining people and their pictures. Check first to see that the child can do this as a straight matching task (i.e., that he can look at a picture and point to the person pictured) before you ask him to look at a picture, remember it, and then point out the person from among a group of people.

4. *Memory for Objects.* Play this like the picture game too.
   a. For example, show the child a crayon. Take it away, and bring it back along with a pencil. Say, "Look at this," when you present the crayon, and "Now find it," or "Where is it now?" when you present the pencil and crayon.

b. Try it with unfamiliar objects too, and see what difference familiarity makes in the child's ability to remember correctly. As in the picture game, increase the number of choices to three or four and see if it makes a difference. Try presenting two objects to be remembered, then three or four to choose among.

c. Try using some objects that you have picture cards of. Is there any difference in how your child does with the objects as compared to the pictures? Can he do as well if you use the pictures and objects together, e.g., presenting a ball, taking it away, then showing the child a picture of a ball and a picture of a pot to choose between?

5. *Memory of Texture:* touch memory.

a. Mount a different-textured material on each of four 5″ × 7″ cards, e.g., a ball of cotton on one, a piece of silver foil on another, a piece of sandpaper on another, and a small piece of wood on another. On two other cards, mount two kinds of material each, duplicates of the materials on the cards with the single material.

b. Give your child one of the single-material cards, and show him how to feel the material. Take it away, and give him the card that has the same material as the first plus another kind of material. When you give him the first, say "Feel this." When you give him the second card, tell him "Feel these. Now where is it?"

c. Try having your child close his eyes to play the game so that he has to use his touch memory alone.

  d. If your child has any trouble with the activity, check to make sure he can match the duplicate material swatches when he's allowed to feel them together.

  e. If your child enjoys this game and becomes skilled at it, expand it by making up some more cards and increasing the number he has to remember as well as the number from which he has to choose in the second stage.

6. *Auditory Memory:* memory of nonsense syllables, words, and phrases, requiring a vocal response.

  a. Say to your child "Say 'la.' " "Now, say 'la la.' " "Say 'ba.' " "Now say 'ba ba.' " "Say 'me.' " "Now, say 'me me.' " and so on. Then try combining different nonsense syllables that he's been able to say singly or in double syllables, e.g., "Say 'ba la la.' "

  b. Say to your child "Say '(name).' " "Now, say 'my name.' " "Say 'My name is. . . .' " and so on. Use words and phrases you know your child is able to say since the point here is attention and memory, not speech production. Extend the length of the utterance you ask your child to repeat until he reaches his limit.

  c. You can make this activity more fun by using silly or rhythmic sounds and word combinations, e.g., "Pat the cat." Keep in mind, however, that your child's memory will be better for familiar and meaningful words and phrases than for unfamiliar words and phrases or meaningless syllables.

7. *Auditory Memory for Rhythm.* Using a drum or just the table top, beat out simple rhythms for your child to copy. Start with just two beats, e.g., a strong beat, followed by a soft one. Increase the length and complexity in accord with your child's skill.

**Purpose:**  To give your child practice using different kinds of memory; to enable him to develop his memory skills in a variety of areas. In addition, all these games require the child to pay attention, a very important component of memory. If you think of the things you forget in your day-to-day life, they're usually things you didn't pay sufficient attention to in the first place for them to register.

Children's attention spans increase as they grow older. They learn to pay attention for a longer period of time and to a greater number of "bits" of information. The number of bits of information most adults can attend to, remember, and reproduce is from five to nine, usually about seven.[15] Children

[15] The absolute number of bits adults and children can recall is increased by combining them into "chunks." For example, 1900191019201930 is much easier to recall than 25184790 even though the first series is twice as long, since it can be "chunked" into four units: 1900, 1910, 1920, and 1930. Learning to organize information in this way is a valuable tool for using your mind more effectively. You should practice it yourself as well as help your child develop this skill.

this age usually can handle a maximum of three, but there is some variance depending on the nature of the material (e.g., whether or not it's meaningful or familiar) and the task requirements (e.g., whether the child has to produce an answer or just point to something).

The kinds of activities we've presented are not intended to increase your child's memory span; that's got a ceiling on it imposed by his level of maturation. Rather, they are intended to help him learn to pay attention and practice using his memory at its maximum capacity for his present level of development.

# 5

# Three to Four Years: Enter into Consciousness

Three begins the "age of reason." To three- to four-year-olds, everything is simple and logical and has a reason for being. And if they don't know the reason, they will ask. They are discovering (if their experience so far supports it) that adults are resources to them; adults' advice, help, or knowledge can be sought when the child has determined that the task is beyond him or that he cannot answer for himself a question he has. At three, many children ask questions to which they may already have an answer. This probably is a way to check themselves and, perhaps, the adult too. By four, if their questions have been answered, children will pose them now more to seek information.

Three- to four-year-olds join human society. They no longer always try to bend people to their whims. They are willing to bend themselves. They learn to share, to take turns, to play cooperatively with other children. As they become more aware of other people, they also become more aware of themselves. Children at this age are very interested in what they were like "when they were little." They learn to tell what sex they and other people are (although because this knowledge is based on superficial characteristics such as clothes, hair, jobs, and mannerisms, it may be quite fluid for children at this age; they may think it possible to switch sexes if they'd like).

Children from three to four are very interested in sociodramatic play. This is a way they have (1) to act out relationships they're involved in, often taking

**173**

other roles than their own, and (2) later, to try out different role behaviors they've seen in other people, including roles they've never had any personal experience with. In addition to allowing children the opportunity to work out some of their own role relationships through play, sociodramatic play is an avenue for them to expand their thinking skills. It helps them, through sharing ideas about role definitions with other children, to see things from other points of view and to broaden their own scope. In addition, it is a way that they can manipulate the order of things in their own way, to fit their own point of view.

Children's endeavors both to learn the existing organization of things and to apply their own is seen also in their manipulations of objects. In this age period, children are very interested in taking things apart to see how they work and in putting things together. Most children are still interested in the process involved in an activity more than they are in the product. But in the year from three to four, they may become more concerned with using materials to make something (e.g., a picture, the letters of their name, a prop for dramatic play).

The child's motor skills are becoming so good by this age that he can begin to use them in his new learning priorities; they have become a part of his behavioral repertoire. By four most children have good balance and coordination. Walking is automatic, and running is accomplished with ease, with quick stops and starts, changing speeds, turning corners, and so on. They can jump, and they can skip with one foot. Fine motor coordination is being used effectively in the manipulation of tools in this age period. For example, by four many children are beginning to use crayons, pencils, and scissors to make something, whereas before, they were learning how to use them.

From three to four, language begins to be used as a tool to help children find out about things in their world, through questioning, labeling, and thus classifying not only things but groups of things (e.g., animals, fruit) and as part of their sociodramatic play. Vocabulary is expanded, and various complex sentence constructions are added to the child's repertoire. In addition, the child's speech becomes more articulate, more easily understood.

Self-help skills improve in the year from three to four, making children increasingly able to care for some of their own needs, including feeding themselves except for cutting; dressing and undressing themselves; toileting themselves; washing their own face and hands; and brushing their own teeth. Supervision is needed, but most children learn to do these things for themselves. These and other developing skills help to make children more independent and more responsible to themselves for their own actions. And the reciprocal outcome of their growing independence from others to meet all their needs is that children become more aware of and concerned about others.

## YOU BE ME AND I'LL BE YOU

**Participants:**   Two people—an adult and a child, or two children, three to four years or older.

**Explanation:**   In Chapter 1, one of the first things we discussed was the importance to human development of being able to put yourself in another's place, to see things from their perspective in addition to your own (see "If I Were You and You were Me," page 3). The following activity can help you and your child do just that.

1. For part of a day or just for a short period, "trade" identities with your child or have two of your children (your own or ones in your care) trade identities with each other. Each person should pretend to be the other, taking on her point of view and behaviors, "playing" the other as if he really were that person.

2. When the game is over, talk about how each of you felt about the other's portrayal of you: Did you think it was accurate, fair, funny? What did you learn about how someone else "sees" you? If the game is being played by two children, set a time limit on it, and sit down with them when the game is over to talk about these questions.

**Purpose:**   To give you and the children an opportunity to "try on" each other's roles—to attempt to understand how it might feel to be the other person and to try to look at the world through her eyes; to see "yourself" through the other person's eyes by observing how she portrays you.

This is an essential part of socio-emotional development that enables human beings to learn better self-evaluative abilities—to see themselves in perspective, "one step back" from themselves, as well as to become more perceptive about the needs and perspectives of others than themselves. Unfortunately, there are many adults who have never learned the art of "putting themselves in another's shoes" or, in other words, behaving according to the Golden Rule.

Children at this age are just beginning to learn about sharing and cooperating, to become aware that others have feelings like them, and to sympathize with others. It is, therefore, an excellent time to begin giving them opportunities to refine these emerging social skills further through learning to take the role of another.

**Variations:**

1. Give children in a preschool situation many opportunities to play this

game, taking on each other's and the adults' identities for short periods. Let the children choose whom they want to trade with sometimes, and sometimes assign them each a different identity. Maybe, if they enjoy this activity, set aside a period of time each week or even every day to play the game.

2. As they gain practice and skill, try it as a small group activity with one child as "actor" and several others as audience. The actor must choose someone from the group to be but not tell anyone whom she has chosen. The child who guesses correctly first then becomes actor.

*Note:* The one rule that must be followed in this game is a variation on the Golden Rule—the children may, in their portrayal of someone else, do whatever they choose, *as long as it is not at anyone else's expense.* In particular, this means that nothing they do should, in any way, hurt the feelings of the person they're playing.

If a child breaks this rule and does hurt another person's feelings, use the opportunity, not to reprimand her, but rather to help her "put herself in that person's shoes," to imagine how she might have felt if the other person had done to her what she did. Remember, always, to be compassionate and understanding, not accusatory. We all make mistakes; that's how we learn not to repeat them.

## SINGING AND DANCING

**Participants:** Three- to four-year-old children and an adult. Some children younger than three may be able to participate in this activity also,[1] and children over four will enjoy similar activities, but will be able to add more complex movements.

**Materials:** Record player and records; piano, guitar, or other musical instruments if you can play them; a drum; records should include ones for children with simple actions to accompany songs, e.g., "Here We Go 'Round the Mulberry Bush," "Farmer in the Dell," "Looby Loo," and others with simple, repetitive words directing actions set to a simple rhythmic melody; and other "adult" selections from rock to marches to gentle waltzes to old and new popular tunes.

**Explanation:** The following activity describes different kinds of singing and dancing experiences for preschool children. They range from conventional

[1] See "Sing Me a Song," page 117, and "Dance with Me," page 124, both One to Two Years, for ideas for singing and dancing with younger children.

singing activities (i.e., songs with words that instruct them how to move) to free-form, nonstructured, self-directed use of their bodies and voices for creative self-expression. Both are important. The first contributes to children's continuing to develop control and coordination of their body. The second provides a valuable outlet for their practicing using their bodies to express their own individual inner feelings and ways of responding to a musical stimulus.

1. Children this age enjoy learning to sing songs with simple accompanying movements (e.g., clapping hands, stamping feet, standing up, sitting down, turning around, putting one foot in, out, and so on). Deliberate, specific "instruction" is neither necessary nor recommended. Rather, the combination of your model, the opportunity for repeated practice, and a systematic presentation of each new singing activity will enable the children to learn the words and movements "from the inside out" instead of being taught "from the outside in." [2]

   a. Start out with a simple singing and doing activity such as "Here We Go 'Round the Mulberry Bush," which involves a small number of very repetitive words and movements. As the children gain experiences, you can introduce more complex activities such as "Looby Loo," which, although still very repetitive, includes more different words and accompanying movements.

   b. The first time you play a new record, let it play all the way through while you and the children listen. If the children feel like trying some of the movements, they can, but you shouldn't try to organize them for action the first time around. Encourage them, instead, to listen to the words and to join in with song or movement where it's easy to do so.

   c. Then, play the record again while you and the children form a circle and try to follow as much as you can of the music with your own singing and accompanying movements. The children will naturally look to you as a model, so if it's a complex activity, you should try to rehearse the words and actions ahead of time. You don't have to draw specific attention to yourself and insist they do it just as you do. They'll try to copy you without any coaching, and that way they can do it at their own pace.

[2] Both methods ultimately will result in the children's learning the activity, but they have different potential "incidental" consequences. The first has the advantage of enabling each child to learn the generalizable skill of gradually matching his own movements, in his own way, at his own pace, to an internalized model (which, in this case, you provide). On the other hand, when you teach each movement and each lyric, step by step, all the children are forced to conform to an arbitrary pace, learning to make their movements match an external model, never having time to match themselves up against the task and practice on their own until they can "make the movements their own." Further, you risk undercutting the self-concepts of children who are slower to learn than others.

d. Watch the children to see which parts or refrains they pick up on most easily, and emphasize those in your own singing and actions until they seem to have the idea. Then, leave them to practice on their own. Each time you join them in a particular singing activity, you can emphasize a new part, using your observations of their behavior as a guide to when, how much, and what to specially emphasize (remember, not by stopping them and saying "Now, we're going to do this," but only by paying particular attention to that part in your singing and movement, perhaps raising your voice and emphasizing your movements).

e. If you notice a child having trouble with a particular part, go over and do the activity with him. Watch to see which parts he can do, and emphasize those; then, build from there to the harder parts. There may be some activities for which it will be necessary to stop and go over a particular part. But in general, there's enough repetition that it's better to just let the whole record play through rather than break the pace. If you respect each child's pace, then a child who is slower to learn won't feel uncomfortable about it.

f. There are many good children's records with singing activities. In addition, you can make some up with the children's help, using repetitive lyrics of actions you know the children can do, set to a familiar tune.

g. After the children have participated in the activity with you for a while, they will internalize the general idea of how they are supposed to move. But they still need practice before they will be able to do so smoothly and with skill. Encourage them to put on records themselves and practice when they feel like it. In addition, after experiencing a number of different records plus the activities and songs you've made up and done with them, the children should begin to build up a large enough repertoire of movements and tunes that they'll enjoy making up their own.[3]

2. In addition to this kind of structured "song-and-dance routine," children will enjoy the opportunity for free-form movement and singing to music of different types and tempos. Your role in this kind of activity should be as a sort of "indirect model." That is, you should join the children and, through your model, communicate to them that each person should move and sing as the music makes him feel, not copy anyone else. If anything, you should look to the children in this one and try copying them. Most important is that you be relaxed and fluid in your movements. Your "singing" should simply be using your voice to imitate the rhythm of the music at whatever pitch is comfortable for you.

---

[3] Make a tape recording of any singing and dancing activities the children make up so they can use them when they wish.

3. As a general rule, children do not need to be taught to sing any more than they need to be "taught" to speak. But, as with talking, they *do* need a model—you, the radio, and records. If your children hear you singing as a normal part of living, singing popular songs, spiritual hymns, or tunes you make up yourself, they'll want to sing themselves and will practice doing so. And it's practice most of all that's needed—learning to make their own voices match the music they can hear inside their heads.

4. Another excellent model for children's development of the use of movement and voice for creative expression is nature. Take the children on watching and listening walks. Watch the movement of a bird, and listen to its song. Observe the way a tree moves when the wind blows through its branches. Look at the squirrels, and listen; can you hear them make a sound? What you can find to observe will depend on where you live, but whatever it is, then go back to the classroom, clear the floor, and let the children be their choices of things they saw and heard.

**Purpose:**  To provide children with experiences which will help them develop their capacity for the use of their bodies and voices as tools for creative expression. In the first type of activity, the children's goal is to integrate their movement and singing together in accompaniment to a record. It requires concentration, focus, and practice for the children to gradually match their movements to their intentions. And it teaches them to use their bodies and voices in a specified, conventional goal-oriented manner.

The second type of activity, in contrast, requires the children to use their bodies and voices in a spontaneous manner in response to a nondirective musical stimulus. There are no instructions; there is no *right* way of responding. Rather, the children are asked to respond on an emotional, visceral level—as the music makes them *feel* like moving.

The third type of activity, in a sense, represents an integration of the first two; it requires each child to use his imagination to make his movements and voice match his conception (based on observation) of an animal or some other thing in nature.

These three different ways of responding to music are all important in enabling children to enjoy a balance of disciplined, free-form, and imaginative kinds of activities; life-requirements include these different elements, and so should children's experiences.

## WHAT'S NOT THERE?

**Participants:** One or more children and an adult. It is most appropriate for three- to four-year-olds, though a simpler version could be used with slightly younger children or a more difficult version with older children.

**Materials:** A bag of small toys and other objects that are familiar to the participants in the game, e.g., a toothbrush, a crayon, a cup, a toy, a ball, a block, an orange, an apple, a banana. Any objects that the children can name are fine, and they don't have to be related to one another in any way. A piece of cardboard large enough to serve as a screen for a row of three objects.

**Explanation:** Here's another memory game. This one requires the child to remember what objects are put in front of her so that when one of them is removed, she can tell which one is not there any more. This is harder than most of the other memory games we've proposed for younger children, because the child has to *recall* the missing object, not just *recognize* an object or picture she's seen before.

1. Show the child each toy in your bag, and ask her to name it. If there are any she doesn't know, don't use them in the game. Put three objects on the table in front of the child. Select ones to begin with that look very different from each other. Call the child's attention to the objects, and let her know that you're going to take one away, and you'll want her to tell you which one is gone: "Look, Carla. Here's a ball, a toothbrush, and a car. Say their names." "I want you to remember what's here, because I'm going to hide them and take one away. Then I'll ask you which one isn't here any more."

2. Have the child close her eyes. Then, hold the cardboard up between the child and the objects, and remove one. Drop it into the bag. Take the cardboard screen away and ask the child, "What's not there?" "What's missing?" If she answers correctly, say "That's right. I took away the ball. The ball is missing." Put the ball back, and repeat the process, this time removing a different object.

3. If your child can't tell you which object you removed, try to refresh her memory by saying, "Remember, there was a toothbrush, a car, and one more thing. Can you remember what it was?" If she still doesn't remember, give her a hint: "It's round and red, and you can bounce it." If she still doesn't recall, give her a choice: "Was it an apple or a ball?" Then let her try the game again with just two objects, and play the game that way until she can do so successfully enough to try with three.

4. Repeat the game as long as the child enjoys it, changing the objects and adding additional ones as she gets better at it. Choosing objects that are more similar to each other in appearance will also increase the difficulty level of the task, as will shuffling them around so that the child can't use the position of the object as a hint in remembering.

5. You can play this with a small group of children, letting them take turns answering. Or two children can play it together, taking turns being "teacher." You should take a turn, yourself, as the rememberer while a child plays your role as teacher.

**Purpose:** To help develop children's attention and short-term memory for meaningful objects. As we have discussed before, memory underlies all learning, and memory requires attention. This kind of game gives children an opportunity to practice using these cognitive skills.

**Variation:** Use picture cards as a substitute for the objects. Otherwise play the game in the same way.

## HOW DO YOU FEEL?

**Participants:** One or more children, three to four years or older, and an adult.

**Explanation:** A large proportion of human beings' messages to one another come not through words, but through nonverbal signals—facial expression, body stance, and so on. Understanding and using nonverbal communication consciously and effectively is an important socio-emotional skill that is not well developed in most adults. This is chiefly because they never have been given a chance to practice it, deliberately and openly, in a context that provided feedback. The following activity can give you and your children some of the experience you need to become more consciously aware of and skilled at nonverbal communication.

1. Have one person choose an emotion to communicate nonverbally to another person or to a small group. With children this young, it is best to begin with a choice of two very different emotions. Happy and sad, loving and angry, pleased and annoyed, or afraid and calm are pairs that would be good to start with.

2. Tell the children that you are going to try to tell them how you feel

without using any words, and you want them to watch you and tell you which feeling you are expressing. Tell them which two it might be (e.g., happy or sad). Demonstrate several pairs, having the children guess your feeling each time.

3. Pick a child from the group to be the first to try being the "actor," and join the audience yourself. Let the child choose an emotion to express, and direct him to give the group the choices. If he has any problem understanding how to play the game, give him some choices. Let him whisper to you what feeling he's going to express, and you tell the group what the choice is. The child who guesses correctly first then gets to be the next actor. Continue playing until every child has had at least one turn for as long as they're enjoying it.

4. Once the children understand the game and can correctly distinguish between such obviously different emotional expressions as the examples given above, you can suggest that they make the game harder by (1) using, as pairs, emotions that are more alike, e.g., anger and annoyance; (2) adding more choices to the number of different emotions they might be expressing (e.g., happy, sad, or afraid; love, anger, or surprise), or (3) not giving any verbal hints of what emotion they are going to express, i.e., not telling their audience which emotions it might be.

5. Take this opportunity to talk to the children about feelings—what things make them happy, sad, angry, afraid, surprised, lonely, and so on; when was the last time they felt really happy, sad, etc.; how they can tell when somebody loves them, is angry with them, is sad, and so on, and how it makes them feel.

**Purpose:**   To enable the participants to become more skilled and precise in sending and receiving nonverbal, emotional (behavioral) messages. We all are aware of other people's nonverbal behavior. In fact, our communications to one another are characterized by a significant nonverbal overlay. Body stance, the amount of physical tension in our faces and in the way we hold our bodies and move, the distance we place between us, eye contact or the lack of it, our use of touch, the tone of voice we use, and other nonverbal factors tell each other as much or more than our words.

The problem is that the nonverbal messages many people send to others are disguised and unconscious. And most people are not sure how to interpret the nonverbal messages they receive. Few of us have a level of trust with others sufficient to make it "safe" to check out what communications we feel we're getting from another's nonverbal behavior toward us or to make sure they're receiving from us the message we are intending to deliver.

Thus, this kind of activity with children is good practice for adults as well as for children. Through the opportunity for feedback that it provides, this activity can help you both learn to communicate more effectively and to understand others' communications more accurately.

## Variations:

1. Another way to play the game is with partners, using touch only. One person takes the other's hands in his and concentrates on sending an emotional message to the other, who must guess on the basis of the feeling he receives what the emotional message is. The same beginning ground rules apply to this variation. The sender should give the receiver two distinct choices to begin with. Then gradually he should expand the number of choices, include emotions that are more closely related to each other, and work toward trying it without verbal cues.

2. Try acting out a feeling using voice but no words. Follow the same guidelines as for the other approaches to the activity, starting with a choice of two emotions announced to the audience before beginning and eventually presenting an emotion without any prior clues to the audience.

3. Try the following variation with older children and adults who have achieved a level of competence and comfort with this activity. Have two people act out, in front of a small group, interactions that typically lead to misunderstandings in communications because the people's words say one thing while their behavior says something else.

   a. One example might be an adult telling a child to choose whichever food he wants at a restaurant, but then growing tense when the child asks for anything other than what the adult really wants him to choose. Or you can use any other example in which an adult gives a child a choice and then acts in a way that communicates that he really isn't giving him one.

   b. Choose two children or a child and an adult to be the actors. Tell them and the audience the scene, and tell the actors to decide whether to play it so their words and their behavior are consistent with each other or so that they contradict each other. Let them whisper to you their choice and then enact the scene. When they are done, have the audience discuss it with them, (1) giving their ideas of what the actors were communicating, and then (2) after hearing the actors' intentions, giving them feedback on the clarity of their communication.

   c. This is a good opportunity to discuss such situations in the children's own lives and how they feel about them. Give everyone a chance to be both actor and audience, and encourage all the children to contribute to the discussion.

## MORE MIRROR GAMES

**Participants:** Small group of children, three to four years and older, and an adult. See "Mirror Games," Birth to One Year, page 74, and "Happy Face, Sad Face," One to Two Years, page 121, for examples of mirror games for younger children and babies.

**Materials:** Full-length mirror attached to wall or door at the children's height.

**Explanation:** Here are some more mirror games. The mirror provides feedback which can help children become more conscious of their own movement, appearance, and so on.

1. Have one child at a time stand in front of the mirror.
   a. Ask her to point to her nose, touch her toes, clap her hands, stamp her feet, jump up and down, balance on one foot, and so on, while watching herself in the mirror.
   b. Ask her to describe what she sees in the mirror besides herself (i.e., other people, the things in the room behind her, and the like).
   c. Stand behind the child and make different movements—raise your hands over your head, make a face, smile, stick out your tongue, put your hands behind your back and bring them back in front of you, turn around, stick one leg and one arm out to the side, and so on. Ask the child to watch you in the mirror and mimic your movements, trying to "mirror" you with her actions.

2. Facing the mirror enough to see yourselves, play variations of "How Do You Feel?" (page 181). In particular, whoever is sending the emotional message should observe her own emotional expression and body stance to assess whether she looks to herself the way she feels, and try to make her appearance match her intentions. Let the child choose the feeling she wants to portray to "the audience," in this case, her mirror self. Or, you can suggest to her "Make a happy face," "Now, look like you're really sad," and so on.

3. Try giving the children a little vignette instead of the name of an emotion, e.g., "You're playing quietly, and another child comes over and grabs your toy. How do you feel?" "School is over, and it's time to go home. There's no one here to pick you up. How do you feel?" and so on. Try enacting such a vignette with the child in front of the mirror or having two children do so. It may be too distracting for them at first, to interact, pretend, and watch both persons' facial expressions, body stance, and movement all at the same time, but you can give it a try.

4. When the children have had some practice with mirror games, play "mirror" without a mirror, i.e., let a child engage in movements that you try to follow as if you were her mirror image, then trade and have her try to follow your movements. Have a mirror handy to check out how to be a mirror, especially for movements such as putting your hand right up to the mirror or moving it back from your body. Have children pair off, too, to play the game. (But, do participate yourself; you'll learn something and have fun). Sit facing each other, and mirror each other's facial expressions, too. If either of you thinks the other isn't accurately mirroring her, use a real mirror as "referee."

**Purpose:**   To give the participants practice in (1) observing themselves; (2) matching their actions to a model; and (3) matching their actions to their own intentions, given the visual feedback of seeing their mirrored image.

In addition, these games contribute to a child's development of her body image through making her more aware of her own body configuration and how she looks standing, sitting, in movement, in the midst of an interaction with another, and so on. This, in turn, has a relationship to the child's development of her self-concept. How she appears to herself—her image of herself—is informed through the feedback the mirror provides.

Finally, the practice in matching her movements to a model and to her own intentions contributes to the child's development of coordinated movement and, in the case of the "What Do You Feel?" mirror game, to the improvement of her capacity for sending and receiving emotional messages with some degree of accuracy. Playing her own audience is particularly good feedback for a child's development of this skill as well as for showing her how she looks to others in such situations.

**Variation:**   If you are fortunate enough, in an educational setting, to have sufficient funds to purchase videotape equipment (for your own center or to be shared among a number of centers), all these activities are readily adapted to that medium. Videotape lends the additional advantage of enabling the children to put all their energy into unself-consciously participating in an activity and then getting the feedback afterwards, rather than trying to watch themselves at the same time they're doing something. An inexpensive movie camera can serve this same function if your funds, like most, are limited.

## WHAT DO YOU DO WITH A CHAIR?

**Participants:**   One or more children, three to four years or older, and an adult.

**Materials:** Common objects that can be found around the house or classroom, e.g., pots and pans, a watering can, a cup, a toothbrush, soap, a washcloth, a comb, a chair, a broom, a vacuum cleaner, a wastebasket, a sponge, a crayon, paper, blocks, and a ball. Anything at all can be used.

**Explanation:** The following game will help children expand and extend their language to include more specific and descriptive words for communicating what they know with others. It can be played, as outlined, as a special sit-down learning activity, and it can be incorporated into your daily routines with your child and played anytime, on the run, riding in the car, in the grocery store, in a restaurant, as an attention-getter or a distracting device.

1. Form a circle of chairs with space enough in the middle for one child to sit or stand. (If you are playing this game at home, alone with your child, then sit facing your child.) Put a collection of objects with which the children are likely to be familiar on a table or the floor outside the circle.

2. Explain to the children that you want them each to pick an object from the pile to bring into the circle and tell everyone about it and show them what you do with it. Ask for volunteers, or choose a child to go first. Tell him to pretend that he's a visitor to a strange world where they've never seen any of these things before. So, he has to show and tell you about his object *as if only he knew what it was.*

3. Continue the game until each child and you have had a turn. If a child is too shy to feel comfortable "performing" from the center of the circle, let him sit in his chair for his turn. Encourage the children sitting in the circle to ask the child presenting his object questions. Tell them to pretend they've never seen the object before, and that they don't know anything about it. Show them, through your own questions, what you mean.

4. Accept whatever response each child gives. Encourage him to expand his explanation and demonstration, but don't make him feel uncomfortable. Some children this age are very verbal and will give detailed and imaginative descriptions; others will do well to say something like "This is a toothbrush. You do this (demonstrating)." Accept each child on his own level, and do not compare his performance with another's.

5. In general, for this kind of activity it's best to include helpful, cooperative, verbal children who will encourage and not intimidate the less verbal ones. Remember, in your responses to individual children's performances, that you are a model to the children, and that it is more impressive for a usually nonverbal child to say one word than for a usually verbal child to talk for five minutes.

**Purpose:** To give the children practice connecting words with their own actions, describing what they're doing; to give them practice communicating with others, learning to use specific terms that do not assume the listener already knows what they're talking about; and in this way, and through playing both speaker and listener, giving each child practice in exchanging places with another, putting himself in another's shoes. These are all skills that will require extensive experience and time before they're mastered, but this kind of game can be helpful in beginning the process.

## LETTER DAY

**Participation:** A whole class of children, three to six years old, and adults.

**Materials:** An experience chart; pictures from magazines; large felt letters; old shirts; lightweight cardboard; envelopes; scotch tape; $8\frac{1}{2}'' \times 11''$ sheets of white paper.

**Explanation:** Studies of reading in young children have found that one of the predictors of children's success in learning to read is their knowing the alphabet (letter names) and letter sounds.[4] In addition to letting children watch *Sesame Street* and *Electric Company* to learn about letters, you can expose them in other ways to the letter and sound systems underlying all reading skills. Following are a few examples of fun ways to do that which "teach" through the children's involvement, not as a rote lesson in which the children are little more than passive receptacles for meaningless information.

1. Make one day each week "Letter Day." Write on a big calendar that the children can see, and tell them ahead of time, what the letter of the week will be. Then they can bring in things and wear clothes that start with that letter. On "Letter Day," have the children *be* that letter.

2. Give everyone an envelope of paper letters of the day, and have them go around the room during the day and tape letters to objects they think begin with that letter. Encourage the older and more skilled children to serve as advisors to the younger and less skilled ones, and be available yourself for questions about objects' names and spellings.

3. Help the children begin to put together a "picture dictionary." As a

[4] See, especially, Jeanne Chall, *Learning to Read: the Great Debate*, Chapter 5: "The ABC's of Reading: Is the Alphabet Necessary?" pp. 140–59 (New York: McGraw-Hill Book Co., 1967).

special organized group activity, or just something you do in the course of the day, ask the children to suggest words they think start with the letter of the day. Whatever the word is, write it down on a list on the blackboard. Later, when the list has grown, you can have the children look at it and evaluate which words do begin with the letter of the day. Those can become part of the picture dictionary. Do the same with the objects in the room that the children have labeled with their paper labels.

4. Give the children a pile of old magazines (ask parents to save ones with pictures for this activity) to go through and look for pictures to go with the words you and they have determined do belong in the picture dictionary under this day's letter. Put some of the duplicates on the experience chart, and write the names underneath. Let the children help to write the words on the experience chart and on the sheets for their picture dictionary (see "I Can Write," Five to Six Years, page 264, for guidelines).

5. Use $8\frac{1}{2}'' \times 11''$ sheets of paper for the picture dictionary. Show the children how much room to leave on the sides for binding, and help them as they need it and ask for it, to paste the pictures in and write the words. (But, let them do it as much as possible on their own.) Have them write the letter of the day, in capital and small letters, at the top of each page. They can either bind each letter-book separately or wait and bind the whole thing together at the end when you've gone through the entire alphabet.

6. Write a story with the children, and put it on the experience chart, stressing words which begin with the letter of the day, e.g., a story about "Bertha the Bear, who didn't like bees, but whose best buddy was a boy named Bobby who liked bread with butter, berries, and bananas." Ask the children to think of names of toys, objects, people, activities, and so on which start with the letter of the day, and then see if, together, you can put them all into a story.

7. Sew a big felt capital "letter of the day" on the back of an old shirt, sort of like an athlete's "letter jacket." Let the children whose name begins with that letter take turns wearing the letter shirt of the day.

8. Some children might enjoy trying to talk using only words that have the letter of the day in them. Some might enjoy making their own alphabet book with pictures and words and a story as on the experience chart.

9. Have the children play-act the letter, trying to form the shape of it with their body, moving in a way the sound of the letter makes them feel while they repeat the letter sound, playing a variation of charades in which one child pretends to be someone or something whose name begins with the letter of the day.

**Purpose:** To give the children "living experience" with letter names and sounds, with the ultimate goal of enabling them to learn both systems in preparation for learning other reading skills that require knowledge of these underlying systems.

The alphabet and the phonetic (i.e., basic sound) system are helpful for children to learn before attempting to learn to read (more than just recognizing signs, cereal boxes, and the like) because they are closed systems, and having learned the basic elements of the system, the children can then learn to combine and analyze those elements to decode the printed word.

## PUT THE BALL IN THE BOX

**Participants:** One child or a small group of children, three to six years old, and an adult. Some of the prepositions will be difficult for the younger children in this age range.

**Materials:** A small ball and a box large enough to hold the ball, or any other object and container; another couple of objects small enough to fit in the box.

**Explanation:** Prepositions are among the last of the little connecting and qualifying words of the child's language for him to learn. They are learned through day-to-day experiences as well as through activities such as this. This activity gives children a chance to "see" a preposition's meaning, to hear it used in conjunction with the action and position in space it represents.

1. Set out the materials on a table in front of the children. Turn to one child and say, "Peter, put the ball *in* the box."

2. If he does it wrong, don't correct him. Rather, describe what he did do, and ask someone else to do what you had asked him to do, e.g., "Peter put the ball on the box. Vivien, can you put the ball *in* the box?" He'll get the message just as well this way without having to deal with being corrected in front of his peers.

3. If the child does follow your direction correctly, respond similarly: "Peter put the ball *in* the box. Vivien, will you put the ball *beside* the box?" In each case, return the materials to their original position before giving the next instruction.

4. Continue the game, giving each child multiple opportunities to respond.

Sometimes, let one child do several, one after another, and sometimes go from one child to the next, giving each one a turn.

5. Use the prepositions on, on top of, over, in, into, inside, beside, next to, under, beneath, behind, in back of, in front of, in between, and so on. Use ones that mean the same thing one right after the other, and explain to the children that they are different ways of saying the same thing.

6. If there are prepositions that none of the children know, show them as you say the words: "Look, I am putting the ball *beneath* the box." "Who knows another way to say that the ball is beneath the box?" "Right, the ball is *under* the box."

7. Point out to the children, through giving the directions right after each other so that they can see it, that some of the prepositions are the reverse of each other. So, for example, you can say "Put the ball *behind* the box," and it implies the same action as if you say "Put the box *in front of* the ball." But if you tell a child to "Put the box *behind* the ball," that requires a reverse of the position in the previous instructions but is the same as saying "Put the ball *in front of* the box." It sounds very complex when trying to explain it in words, but if you use the instructions one right after another, the children will begin to get the idea.

8. Alternate between the different objects so the children get an opportunity to practice using the same preposition, with different objects. For example, you might tell a child to "Put the box *next to* the ball." "Now put the box *next to* the doll." "Put the doll *next to* the ball," and so on. Use three objects to teach the preposition *between*. Be sure to give children who were unable to follow a direction correctly another chance with that same preposition and a different set of objects, after they've had a chance to see it done correctly a few times.

**Purpose:** To give children practice learning to connect prepositions with the positions in space they refer to—to learn to understand and follow directions correctly that use these words. Some prepositions are easily confused with each other, and a small change in word order can totally alter the meaning of a direction (e.g., "Put the ball over the box," vs. "Put the box over the ball."). Therefore, practice such as this game provides can help children prepare for kindergarten or first grade. A child can experience a lot of difficulty in school if he doesn't understand prepositions, since they form an essential part of many of the directions he'll be expected to follow there.

**Variations:**

1. Ask the children to verbalize what they did, e.g., "I put the ball in the

box," after following your direction. This gives them a chance to practice saying the words in conjunction with the action in addition to matching their actions to words spoken by another person.

2. Have the children "act out" instructions using prepositions, e.g., "Tammie, stand *behind* Michelle." "Susan, sit *beside* Nancy." "Angie, hold the block *in* your hand, . . . *behind* your back, . . . *over* your head, etc."

3. Set up an obstacle course with a tunnel to crawl *through,* a chair to crawl *under,* a barrier to step or jump *over,* another to walk *around,* a ladder laid on its side for the children to step *between* the rungs, a large tire to step *inside* and then *over* and *out of,* and so on. Direct the children, one by one, through the obstacles, using the words as they perform each action.

## LET ME ENTERTAIN YOU

**Participants:** One child three years and older as performer, any number in addition as "audience," and an adult. Younger children also might enjoy this activity; the content of their performance would differ, but the process is the same.

**Explanation:** The following activity gives children an avenue for self-expression and a socially approved forum in which to "show off" in any way they choose.

1. In a preschool setting, start off each day by letting a different child present the morning entertainment of her choice. She can do a dance, sing a song, tell a story, "read" a book to the other children, teach them something, tell them about something interesting that's happened to her, bring something in to show them—whatever she wishes. Have all the other children sit on the floor in a circle around the child who is performing.

2. Suggest the idea to the children, and start off by taking volunteers. Mark their names on a large calendar that's used to record important events in their lives. Once it becomes a routine, others probably will volunteer too. You and other adults in the classroom or at home should also take turns being the entertainer. Though, in a sense, you take that role every time you lead the children in any activity, in this one, you'll be more specifically conscious that it is your purpose to entertain the children.

3. Keep an eye on the shy children who are unlikely to take the initiative of volunteering to entertain, who may feel that they wouldn't know what to do. Note what kinds of things they do well and that spark their interest. Then ask them, individually, if they'd like to do that for the class as their entertainment. Some children might even feel more comfortable if joined by a friend. Don't force any child to participate. If you don't push her, sooner or later, she'll choose to do it herself.

4. The one rule that should apply here as to all interactions in which the children are involved together is: *Respect for the rights and feelings of others.* In practical terms for three- to four-year-olds, this can be translated into "fair play." Explain to all the children that when it is *their* morning, they'll be very excited about what they're doing. They'll want everybody else to be interested and pay attention to them. That wish, shared by all, can be fulfilled for all, *if* everybody remembers when it's *not* her turn, to act the way she'll want others to act when it *is* her turn.

5. Don't say this to the children in a moralizing, preaching, or lecturing tone. They'll understand just what you mean if you explain it to them simply and straightforwardly. In fact, many children understand and follow this basic human rule better than adults. Even more important than your *telling* them is your *showing,* through your example, that each child is an important person who deserves the respect of your attention and appreciation of her efforts.

6. At home, set aside regular times for your children to "entertain" you as they choose. Younger children can participate too. Particularly for them, express your appreciation and enthusiasm for their performance, whatever it is. Being the center of attention, receiving applause and praise, feels great now and then to everyone. If you provide an acceptable forum such as this, your children may be less likely to seek attention in other, unacceptable ways.

**Purpose:** To provide children with an opportunity to "show off" in an acceptable way, guaranteed to win them the attention, approval, and acceptance they need. Attention is as vital a psychological need for human beings as hunger is a physical need. It is people—children and adults—whose need for attention is not met in socially acceptable ways who resort to antisocial means to get that need met.

In all your interactions with children, try to be alert to their need for attention and provide it when their behavior "asks" for it. In particular, look for cooperative and productive behaviors which you can reward with positive attention, and ignore any maladaptive ways some children may have learned to seek attention (usually because it was the only way they found they could get it).

In addition to providing an acceptable forum for behavior which adults often term "showing-off," this activity gives children a chance to practice whatever skills are involved in the particular form of entertainment they choose. It enables them to do so publicly where they can receive feedback from others as well as "observe" themselves. Further, by being both performer and audience at different times, the children can learn more about how it feels to be in someone else's shoes and, ultimately, to look at things through others' eyes as if they were their own.

## GETTING READY TO READ

**Participants:** Three- to six-year-old children and an adult. Children should not be forced into reading activities at any age, but games to develop reading skills should be available to those children who evidence interest and readiness. Many of the suggested games also can be adapted for older children with specific learning disabilities in the area of reading.

**Materials:** Casette tape recorder, food packages, oaktag, magazine pictures, magic markers, paste, scissors.

**Explanation:** Although some children may learn to read with ease in the preschool years, others still may not be ready to read in first grade. There should not be such an emphasis on reading in the preschool that it interferes with other important learnings or contributes to feelings of insecurity in children for whom the skills of reading don't come easily. But there are many activities which are fun and developmentally appropriate for most preschool age children that can help prepare them to read whenever they're ready, whether in preschool or grade school. A number of the activities in this book are of this nature, and more will be offered on the following pages.

1. Many children begin "reading" advertisements and food packages at an early age. This is a good signal that they're ready for some simple reading activities based on this developing skill. The skill involved, one of several necessary to learn to read, is the *ability to recognize the general visual configuration of a word and distinguish it from others.* In the case of food packages and advertising, the task is much easier than with isolated words because there are a variety of distinguishing cues including color and package design. Advertisers work hard to find a logo for their products which will make them distinctive. This makes them good material for beginning reading activities.

Save empty boxes, labels from cans and bottles, and magazine ads. Ask others to do the same. Cut out enough of the name and logo of each product that it's easily identifiable. Mount each one on an index card or on cards made by cutting up large pieces of oaktag. Try to get at least five of each name so you can use them in different games. Save some labels, also, for making larger cards for lotto and bingo and for making a wall chart. Following are a few of the nearly unlimited number of games you can play with these materials; you probably will be able to invent many more yourself.

a. **Card games.** Give each child several product-name cards, and keep a set yourself containing duplicates of all their cards. For this game, none of the children's cards should be duplicates of each other.

  (1) Hold up one of your cards, and ask, "Who has Campbell's Tomato Soup?" The child who has it (or whatever name card you are holding up) takes your card. When you have no more cards, choose a child to become "teacher."

  (2) Continue playing as long as they are enjoying the game. Give all the children who want it a chance to be teacher. As the children get better at this game, you can increase the number of cards you give each of them at the start of the game. And you can try out various kinds of more formal card games.

  (3) This game involves another reading skill: *associating the visual symbol with the spoken name.* Later, you can play it using letter sounds and names, and words. Your master set should have pictures and words to give the children an additional clue to use in matching their cards to yours.

b. **Pocket wall chart.** Make a large wall chart from oaktag. Paste small pieces of oaktag on the large piece to form pockets big enough to hold the product-name cards. On the outside of each pocket, paste one of the product names. In an envelope attached to the chart, put product-name cards which are duplicates of all the names on the pockets.

  (1) The goal of the activity is to put each of the cards in the envelope inside the correct pocket on the chart. It can be played by one child or as a group game.

  (2) This same kind of chart also can be made to give children practice matching letters and words. When making a word chart, include pictures on the pockets to help the children associate the visual configuration of the written word with the thing or action the word represents.

c. **Lotto.** Make your first lotto cards with only four squares, one product name per square. Each square should be the same size as the product-name cards you made earlier so you can use them in the lotto games. As the children gain practice and skill, make some lotto cards with more squares.

(1) Show the children how to match each product-name card to the space on the lotto card containing its mate. Then let them play by themselves, alone or with a partner.

(2) Vary the game by having one partner hold the product name cards while the other asks for a card by name to match to a square on his lotto card.

d. **Bingo.** Each card will need eight product names, with the center square "free." This game, like the card game, requires its players to identify the visual symbol upon hearing its spoken name. But this one is harder, because the visual clue included when matching the cards is not available in bingo.

(1) The children have to find the name on their bingo cards that corresponds to the name you call out, then cover it with a blank marker. At first, you should check the children's cards after you call out each name to make sure they're "reading" their cards correctly.

(2) The child who wins the bingo game then takes over as caller. Continue until everyone who wants one has had a turn. If there are children who are slower at catching on to the game, pair them with children who are skilled at the game who can help them. Or play the game just with the children who need more practice, at a pace that's comfortable for them.

e. **Grocery store.** Probably the most interesting and involving activity you can create with packages and labels is a grocery store game. See "Shop and Learn," Four to Five Years, page 215 for a few ideas. In addition to these, you can set up a mock supermarket with shelves filled by empty boxes, cans, and bottles with labels.

(1) Make up cards with shopping lists. At first, use cut-out labels for the shopping lists; later try just printing the names. This will be harder because the printed names will not contain color, style, and other visual clues as the actual product logos do. Give each child (or a pair of children) a shopping list and a box or basket to serve as a grocery cart, and let the children "go shopping." When you check them out, check to see that their groceries match the names on their shopping list.

(2) Make up labels for the shelves that identify only the general category of food (e.g., soups, canned fruit, vegetables). Remove all the packages from the shelves, and then let the children work in pairs to restock the shelves according to the category labels you put up.

(3) Try verbally directing children to "buy" different items, e.g., "Joey, go to the store, and get some tuna fish."

2. Another skill children need in order to read is the *ability to distinguish small differences between words' visual configuration.* For example, *and* vs. *end, fan* vs. *fun, lap* vs. *lad,* and *on* vs. *no* each represent one of the different kinds of discriminations children need to learn to make.
   a. They need to be able to tell the difference between letters that have the same shape, but are upside down or backwards from each other, e.g., *b* and *d, p* and *d.*
   b. They have to pay attention to the details of each word, not just to the general configuration, in order to notice, for example, that *fun* and *fan* are not the same.
   c. They also have to pay attention to the order of the letters in a word, both to tell the difference between words such as *on* and *no* and to learn to write words correctly themselves.

3. All these skills outlined in #2 are difficult for young children, because up to this point they've been learning to discount such small differences in the way things look in order to develop consistent ideas of an object's identity. They've learned, for example, that a chair is still a chair whether it's small and made of wood or large, stuffed, and covered with material. And they've learned that a table is a table whether you look at it from underneath or on top, whether it's round, square, rectangular, and so on.

   Now for reading, they have to learn a whole new set of rules for identifying elements within words that can change the word's identity. Following are some ideas for helping children learn these skills.
   a. When planning activities to help children learn to notice and detect small differences in the way things look, it's best to start out with objects and pictures of objects and then move on later to letters and words.
   b. Make up collections with two to five things to a set of objects or pictures. Keep in mind the following guidelines to level of difficulty when making up collections.
      (1) The greater the difference between objects, the easier it will be for a child to detect the difference. For example, it's easier to tell the difference between a face with a smile and one with a frown than between two faces that differ only in that one has eyelashes.
      (2) The smaller the number of items in a set, the easier the task of noticing differences between them. For example, it's easier to tell whether two pictures of a dog are the same than to identify the differences, if any, among five pictures of a dog. (Differences might be in whether it's sitting, standing, lying down, etc. or in what kinds of markings it has.)
      (3) Telling simply whether two items are the same or different is an easier task than finding the differences between items, and the

more items there are, the more difficult the task becomes, especially if the differences among them are very slight.

Therefore, keep the sets very simple at first, and give children more difficult sets as they practice and gain skill with the easier ones.

c. Start children off with two objects that are the same or that have fairly obvious differences (e.g., a doll with a blouse and an identical doll without a blouse), and ask them whether these two things are just the same. If a child says they're different, ask him to explain how. Try the same technique with many different pairs of objects, then pictures, and finally letters and words. Make the differences between the items increasingly smaller as the child gains skill at the task.

d. Next, show the children an object and then two others, either both different, both the same, or one the same and one different from the first. Ask one of the children if they're all the same, and then (if he says no) to show you how they're different. Continue this procedure with more objects, pictures, letters, and words.

e. As children gain skill, increase the difficulty level of the task, always keeping it just hard enough that it's challenging, but not so hard that it's frustrating. Teach a small group of children at a time, and encourage the children to help each other while always giving each child the opportunity to do his own work and offer his own answers to the extent that he can.

f. When making cards for playing the game with pictures, letters, and words, use the format illustrated below (the number of squares you include will depend on the difficulty level that is appropriate for your children.) It is easier for children to see similarities and differences in items that are close together like this than in ones that are separated in space.

| pot | top | dot | pot | pet |
|-----|-----|-----|-----|-----|

g. When making materials with letters and words, be sure to incorporate all the possible differences in visual details described on page 196, #2. At first, include only one of the kinds of possible confusions, e.g., $p$ vs. $q$, with the other choices (when there are more than two) being obviously different. Only later, when the children have gained skill in differentiating among the various similarly formed letters, should you include as many potentially confusing forms as in the above example.

4. Another set of skills children need in order to learn to read are those related to *hearing the similarities and differences of the various sounds in words.* In order to learn to sound out words phonetically, children have to know the sounds that correspond to the different letters, and be able to both "take apart" words and "put them together" in terms of their sound components. Following are a few activities to help children learn the skills that go into being able to recognize and analyze the sounds in words.

In a similar way as with the visual aspects of pre-reading skills, it is easier for children to learn the necessary auditory skills in relation to familiar sounds first before trying to transfer those skills to hearing similarities and differences in speech sounds. "Be Very Quiet" and "What's That Sound?", Four to Five Years, pages 231 and 237, are two activities which you can use to help children learn to listen. Here are a few more.

a. Choose a sound, such as blowing a whistle or clapping your hands, and explain to the children that any time they hear that sound, they should call "stop." Then play them a tape recording you've made ahead of time which has a different sound about every five seconds, with the target sound repeated at irregular intervals. You can play the game "live," but you may become very tired from repeatedly switching sounds, and the children will be able to see you make the sound unless you have them turn away from you.

b. When the children become skilled at recognizing various sounds this way, try the same game using speech sounds. In this case, you don't need to record the presentation, but it's a good idea to practice ahead of time and write down the sounds you will present. Go slowly, and be careful not to give any nonverbal cues to the fact that you've just said or are going to say the target sound.

c. When the children can do this activity well using sounds in isolation, try it using words. Very slowly, giving the children time to listen and respond, repeat a series of words, some of which begin with the sound you've chosen (one the children can recognize with ease by itself). When the children hear a word with that sound, they should call out "stop." If this technique doesn't seem to work well with a small group of children responding at the same time, try it having each child listen and respond in turn while the others listen quietly.

d. Play a game in which you present two consecutive sounds, sometimes the same and sometimes different, and ask the children to tell you whether they're the same. Start with sounds that are very different from each other (e.g., someone coughing and a dog barking) and work toward presenting pairs which differ only slightly (e.g., two similarly pitched musical notes).

e. When the children can play the game easily with environmental and musical sounds, try it with letter sounds and words. When presenting two different sounds, start with ones that are very different from each other (e.g., m and r, shoe and car) and proceed to ones that are very similar (e.g., m and n, s and z, wash and watch, cap and cat). When they become skilled at this, try presenting word pairs such as moon and milk, car and cat, etc. and asking the children to say whether they start with (end with, or have in the middle) the same sound.

f. Present a word to the children and ask them to listen to a list of words and tell you to stop when they hear one that starts with the same sound as the first word. When they can do that successfully, ask them to think of other words that start with that sound. Do the same thing for sounds at the end of words and ones in the middle. (In the latter case, they'll be listening for or thinking of rhyming words).

g. With the children's help, try to think of as many words as you can that contain a particular sound, and make up a silly story or a song using those words, e.g., The magic mountain made of marble mostly melted into mushy marshmallows. Also, ask the children to help you think of sounds we make that remind them of some of the letter sounds they're learning, e.g., When we eat something we like, we sometimes say "mmmm."

h. Play a game in which you see if the children can identify words you say when you leave parts of each word out. For example, you might say "oor-ell" for doorbell or "el-e-one" for telephone. Try, also, simply splitting words up into syllables to see if the children can tell you what the word is, e.g., tel-e-vi-sion, or breaking up one syllable words into their component sounds, e.g., b-e-l (bell). Remember to use letter sounds, not letter names (e.g., the letter sound for the e in bell is "eh," not "ee"). Help the children learn to break the words into their component sounds as well as blend them back together into words, encouraging them to take turns being "teacher."

5. In addition to refining their looking and listening skills separately, children need to learn to transform information they hear into information they can see, and vice versa, in order to read. We've already mentioned a few activities which provide practice in this skill (bingo, finding grocery items they've been told in words to get). "Letter Day" and "Send a Letter to a Friend," Three to Four Years, pages 187 and 203, and "I Can Write," Five to Six Years, page 264, all contain ideas. The Variation of "Read Me a Story," Three to Four Years, page

207, which suggests taping children's favorite stories for them to listen to while they "read" along with them is another example. Following are a few more such activities.

a. One of the best ways to teach this skill is through children's own stories that you have written from their dictation. Transcribe children's stories exactly as they tell them to you, then print this transcription neatly on sheets of $8\frac{1}{2}'' \times 11''$ paper folded in half to make a "book." Leave every other page blank so children can decorate or illustrate their books as they wish. Use half a manila file folder, folded in half, for a cover. Punch holes in the side where the paper is creased, and tie the book with colored yarn or use brass fasteners. On the front of each child's book, help him print his name. Read his story back to him as many times as he asks, and help him learn to read it himself. Put it on tape so he can listen to it when he wants while he reads along with it.

b. Another way children can strengthen their understanding of written language as spoken language written down and learn connections between words they know and the written symbols used to represent them is through the use of labels.

(1) Ask for volunteers of children who would like to help you put "name tags" on all the things in the classroom. Tell them to come to you whenever they find an object everybody can see that doesn't already have a name tag, and you'll make one for them to put on it. Cut some oaktag, ahead of time, into strips large enough to write a name in large, easily read letters. When a child comes to you with the name of an object, write its name on one of the pieces of oaktag, and give it to him with a piece of tape to put it up.

(2) Explain to the children that you're going to leave the name tags up around the room for a while, until everybody gets a chance to get to know each object's name. Advise them to look very carefully at the names, because one day, without telling them when, you'll take them down. Then they can play a game to see how many of the name tags they can put back up in the right place without any coaching. Leave the labels up for about a week; if you leave them much longer, they begin to be ignored. If the children ask, you can repeat the game.

(3) When you've played this game through as many times as it interests the children, then ask them to help you think of signs to put up different places in the building to help people find people and places, to give instructions, to send messages, and so on. Some of the kinds of signs you might suggest to get their thinking started if no one offers any ideas include name lists on the doors of classrooms to show who's in each room, instructions

in the reading corner to "Please put books on the shelves when you're through," and a "Quiet Please" sign to hang in the quiet nook.

c. Another good activity for helping children learn the value of reading to gain information as well as make the connection between spoken and written language is cooking. A recipe is, essentially, a written message from one person to another about how to cook something.

(1) Print a recipe in large, neat letters on an experience chart and tape it up on the wall by the area where the children will be cooking. Include pictures where they will help clarify, Help the children with the reading if necessary, but encourage them to consult the recipe for instructions of how to proceed rather than ask you questions.

(2) You can make things with them such as cookies, Jello, pudding, cornbread, and egg salad. The only real limitations you have are those related to what kinds of cooking facilities are available to you. Supervise the children closely on anything involving cooking, but let them do as much as possible themselves on the non-cooking procedures. Make sure you think of some practical work-sharing strategies so everyone gets a turn to participate.

6. In spite of the length of the activity, these are just a small number of the many possible games you can use to help children learn the skills they need to read. These ideas plus the explanation of the kinds of subskills that contribute to being able to read should enable you to think of others as well as adapt these to the particular needs, interests, and skills of your children.

7. Whatever games you play, please remember to go as slowly as is necessary to keep it fun, lively, and interesting while respecting each child's individual rate of learning. Don't make it competitive or make children who are slower and need more repetition feel uncomfortable. The most important part of reading is motivation—wanting to read because it's fun, informative, and expanding. Keep your reading activities so involving and exciting that your children will be highly motivated now, and in the future, to read.

**Purpose:** To provide children with opportunities for practice in the various skills necessary to learn to read: motivation to read; understanding of the purposes and functions of reading; ability both to recognize general configurations of words and to detect the kinds of visual details related to spatial orientation of letters that are necessary to identify a word and distinguish it from other, similar-looking ones; ability to hear similarities and differences in sounds and sound-combinations, to blend sounds together into words and to break words into their component sounds; and recognition of the connection between spoken names of words (and their component sounds) and the written words (and letters making up those words) that represent them.

The skills just summarized, and explained in greater detail within the activity, are the building blocks of reading. When a child cannot read, whether because he's never had any practice or because he has a specific learning disability in relation to reading skills, it's essential to analyze what his level of skills is in all these areas. Then, you can start the process of teaching him prereading and reading skills *where he is* rather than risk getting him involved in reading activities that are way beyond his present level of skills.

Thus, you should use the information included in this activity not only to prepare materials and games to stimulate children's development of these building blocks of reading, but also to determine just where in the developmental sequence of reading skills each child is. This is particularly important for children with any kind of special learning problem that might interfere with his learning to read, so you can devise a special program for him that emphasizes and works through his areas of skill while trying to increase his skill in areas of deficit.

## WHAT I LIKE BEST ABOUT YOU IS . . .

**Participants:** A small to medium-sized group of children, three to four years or older, and an adult. This is also appropriate for a family to play together, with members of all ages participating; even smaller children will enjoy the receiving part though they may not have the words to express to others.

**Explanation:** This activity is the opposite of "roasting," a process in which a number of people "honor" another by saying terrible things about him. In this activity, the children honor another child by telling her what a special person she is and describing all the things they like best about her.

1. Choose a special day each week or the children's birthdays as "their day." On any child's day, have her stand or sit in a circle with the other children. Then give each child in the group a chance to come up and address the "child of the day." He should say whatever he chooses that he particularly likes about her and show her in any other way he chooses (e.g., giving her a hug or kiss, singing her a song) that he cares about her.

2. The "child of the day" should then be given a chance to respond in terms of how she feels about the things being expressed to and about her.

3. Teachers and parents should participate, too, both in telling the child what you like about her and in being the person of the day.

**Purpose:** For the child receiving the compliments, "her day" is an opportunity to feel very special and to receive feedback on what others like about her. It is also good practice in learning to receive compliments graciously, a skill many adults lack. For the other children, the activity helps them learn to focus on the positive aspects of their peers' behavior. Doing so tends to make both people feel good and to reinforce and increase those positive behaviors. A person's attitude toward other people as well as toward things and events has a powerful influence on her behavior and consequently on the feedback she receives from the world of people and things.

Like many other aspects of living, attitudes are learned habits that have a built-in self-reinforcing feedback mechanism. People who habitually focus on the negative aspects of situations tend to receive negative feedback from them, thus reinforcing their original attitudes. The same is true of positive expectations. If we can help our children early in their lives to learn to focus on the positive aspects of people and situations, we will be enabling them to develop a skill that will serve them well throughout their lives, making them much more satisfied and happy than many adults we all know.

## SEND A LETTER TO A FRIEND

**Participants:** Three- to four-year-old child and an adult. Older children will enjoy this activity too and will be able to take an increasingly more active role as their skill increases.

**Explanation:** Sending mail to someone can be fun, a learning experience, and a motivator to children this age and older to learn to write. It's especially fun if children send letters to each other so that each child both sends and receives a piece of mail.

1. Let the child decide what he wants to send his friend. He may want to draw or paint her a picture, cut out and paste a pretty picture on a piece of paper, dictate a message for you to write, or "write" something himself with your help.

2. If he wants to write something simple, such as his initials or name, draw it out in dot-to-dot fashion in large capital letters for him to trace. Or help guide his hand as he forms the letters.

3. Or, if he isn't concerned about the legibility of his "writing," just let the child form his own message in his own way. Follow his lead and his desires, giving help if he asks and otherwise letting him do it himself.

4. Using an envelope received through the mail as a model, explain to the child that he'll need to put on a stamp if he wants the postperson to deliver the letter. Let him lick and place the stamp.

5. Then show him where he'll need to put his friend's name, street address, city, state, and zip code so that the mail deliverer will know where to take the letter and so that his friend will know who it's for.[5] For this part, and for the return address, since it must be legible, you'll need to use the dot-to-dot technique and help guide the child's hand to make the letters.

6. Younger children who haven't had much practice writing may prefer that you do most of this part. Follow your child's lead. Explain why it's important to have a return address—in case they can't deliver the letter to his friend, they'll know where and to whom to return it.

7. Take your child to the post office to mail his letter. Point out to him any mailboxes you see on the way, and explain that, usually, you can just drop your letter in one of those, and it will get where you want it to go as long as you remember to . . . "What?" Remind him, if he has forgotten, by pointing to the stamp, name, and address.

8. But, explain to him, this time you want him to go to the post office so that the people who work there can show and talk with him about what happens to his letter after he mails it. Pick a time that you know won't be too busy and a small post office where you know they'll be friendly and responsive to him.

**Purpose:** To give the child experience in a practical activity, writing and sending a letter. This experience, in addition to providing practice in long-distance communication and a chance to learn about the requirements of the activity, is also a motivator to the child to want to learn to write for herself. (See "I Can Write," Five to Six Years, page 264, for ideas.)

**Variations:** In a preschool setting, keep a calendar of children's birthdates, and have each child send the birthday child a card. Use holidays and children, parents, and teachers' illnesses as other opportunities to send letters.

---

[5] Your child will learn these things better by your directing him to the answers through leading questions (e.g., "What do you think would happen if we sent this letter without a stamp?") than if you just tell him.

This is good, not only for practice in the procedure of writing and sending the letter, but also in developing thoughtful habits of remembering people on special days or letting them know you hope they feel better when they're sick.

## ACTING IT OUT

**Participants:**  Small group of children, three to six years, and a teacher.

**Explanation:**  This activity involves a specialized, structured form of sociodramatic play and will be most successful with children who have experience with the more informal, conventional type of sociodrama described below.

Sociodramatic play is, simply, pretend play in which two or more children each take on the role of somebody other than themselves (e.g., a Mommy, a Daddy, a teacher, a mail deliverer, a doctor). This form of play is a vehicle for children to learn many important language, social, and cognitive skills. For example, in sociodramatic play, children use language to describe make-believe situations, as a substitute for action, to designate the pretend identity of an object, and so on: "Let's pretend I'm a doctor, and I just operated on you." "This is a hospital, and you're the patient." They learn to see things from various points of view as they simultaneously take the roles of actor, observer, and interactor. They learn to incorporate real-life occurrences and relationships into their play and to create new situations based on their experiences in combination with their imagination. Sociodramatic play enables children to try out various roles, relationships, social rules and actions in a safe context.[6]

You should encourage this form of play when you observe it and stimulate its development where it's absent. You can do this by providing props for children to use (e.g., different kinds of clothing and accessories, and props for recreating home, work, and recreational activities), joining them in their play, and initiating sociodramas yourself (e.g., going on a pretend airplane trip with some of the children, making up a pretend TV quiz show, going on a pretend visit to a zoo).

The more structured form of sociodramatic play described in this activity is a good way to work out classroom issues and problems as well as strengthen language, cognitive, and socioemotional skills.

[6] For further explanation of the content, process, and function of sociodramatic play, see Sara Smilansky, "The Effects of Sociodramatic Play on Disadvantaged Preschool Children" (New York: John Wiley & Sons, Inc., 1968).

1. You can choose situations to act out that have occurred in the classroom, or make up ones similar to typical issues that come up with regularity. Several examples are: One child is playing with a toy and another comes up and grabs her toy from her; two children are building with blocks and a third kicks over their blocks; a child is drawing with crayons and another child takes some of the first child's crayons without asking.

2. Choose children to play the parts in the sociodrama you have selected. Have a small group of other children (up to about five) form a semicircle in front of the "actors." Explain the sociodrama to the audience and to the actors, and assign parts to the actors. Don't tell them how to play the parts. Just describe the situation to them, and let them determine how to play it.

3. Explain to all the children that at some time during the sociodrama, you may call out "Switch parts!" and that when you do, you want the two "actors" to trade parts with each other, each taking over the other one's role. Do this, so that each child has a turn in each part.

4. After the sociodrama has run long enough to get a good idea of how each of the children has chosen to play each of the parts, stop the action and open it up for discussion. Encourage the children to talk about their reactions to the way the sociodrama was played: "Was it close to a real-life situation?" "Who has been in a situation like that?" "What did you do?" "What did the other person do?" "What do you think you should do if someone takes something you're playing with?" "Is there another way to deal with it besides hitting?" "Why do you think somebody would take someone else's toy?" "Have you ever done that?" "How would you feel if someone took your toy?" "Do you think people do things like that sometimes just to get someone to pay some attention to them?" and so on.

5. The particular questions you ask will depend on the sociodrama as well as on your knowledge of your children. Don't moralize or tell them through your words or behavioral reactions to their responses what you want to hear. Just ask questions that will get them thinking about how it might feel to be in either position.

6. When the discussion begins to drag, ask for volunteers from the "audience" to enact the same sociodrama in their way. Also, explain to all the children that after each of the actors has had a chance to play both parts, anyone from the audience can trade places with one of them by calling out "Freeze!" and then asking the actor to step down. Continue the activity until all the children have had a chance to take the part of the actors or until the children get tired. You should take a turn at being in the sociodrama too.

7. Some other examples of situations that would adapt well to this kind of sociodramatic play would include: two children squabbling and a teacher; several children playing together and a strange child approaching them, wanting to play; several children refusing to play with another because they don't like the way he looks (he's too fat, dresses funny, talks strangely); a child telling her mother she broke something; or parents bringing home a new baby.

8. Look to your classroom and your children's own personal lives for material. This is often an excellent vehicle to help children work out things that have been bothering them. Once they've got the idea, ask them also if they have situations they'd like to play or see acted out.

**Purpose:**    To give children opportunities to play-act situations similar to ones they encounter in their real lives, taking on, in turn, each of the different roles of the people in the sociodrama and thus experiencing how each might feel. In addition, getting a chance to see other children's portrayal of the same roles and hearing their thoughts and feelings about the situation gives children opportunities to see that different people view things in different ways, according to their particular experiences. Finally, all these elements of the sociodrama experience plus the experience of having her actions and beliefs questioned in the discussions can help a child develop more sympathetic attitudes toward others, learning to treat them as she'd like to be treated in such a situation.

Children this age generally are able to feel empathy for others who share the same or a similar experience as one they've had. More difficult than being empathetic, however, is being sympathetic—not projecting your own feelings onto someone else, but trying, instead, to see the situation from his point of view. This requires understanding that he has a point of view that's different from your own, a thing most preschoolers are only just beginning to learn and which many adults still don't really understand. This kind of activity can help teach this skill.

## READ ME A STORY[7]

**Participants:**    A small group of children, three to four years and older, and an adult.

[7] For ideas relating to reading to younger children, see "Baby's First Book," Birth to One Year, page 76; This Is Me," One to Two Years, page 109; and "Read Me a Picture," Two to Three Years, page 142.

**Materials:**   Books, commercially available or homemade, that tell stories about people, animals, objects, and events, providing information in story form. Pictures still should be bright and colorful, or simple line drawings, clear, and illustrative of the story. Print should be large and easy to read.

**Explanation:**   Books serve a different function for children in this age range than they did for younger children. Children learn new information about the world around them, now, through spoken language (e.g., asking questions and talking about things). They are beginning to enjoy books for the same purpose.

1. Children this age usually enjoy books that tell stories about people, activities, and objects which are similar to their own experiences, but which broaden their understanding through the addition of new information. For example, children who have spent most of their lives in the city might enjoy a story about some city children taking a trip to the country (especially if you can then arrange to take them on such a trip).

2. Information books are excellent resources to precede or follow-up activities related to subjects covered in the books. For example, children engaged in a sociodrama about moving to a new place might enjoy a story afterward dealing with that subject. An activity in which the children plant some seeds in hopes of growing a plant could be preceded by a story such as *Johnny Appleseed*. Field trips can be followed up by making individual books or one for the whole group that has pictures and descriptions of what the children saw and did. In all these ways, children begin to see books as valuable sources of information.

3. In selecting books for the children, be sure to monitor them for sexism and racism. Check to see that there is a fair balance of children portrayed in the stories from each sex and different races and cultures and that there is not a stereotyping of any of them. If you do decide to use a book that, for example, has all white male characters, because it's an excellent book in other ways, include as part of your discussion about the book questions about whether the story could just as well have had a female character or one of another race. Alert the children, themselves, through your discussions, to do their own monitoring of books for ideas, plots, and portrayals of characters which discriminate against some groups.

4. Fantasy tales such as *The Three Bears* and *Little Red Riding Hood* also will be enjoyed by children this age. The repetitive quality of the words

encourages the children's learning of the story so they can join in the reading of it. These are the sort of books that children ask to hear over and over again, usually with absolute insistence that you neither skip nor change a single word. This, again, enables them, in time, to "memorize" the story so they can repeat it right along with you or "read" the book to you or to other children.

5. When reading to children this age, a small group of no more than five is best. Sit with them in a semicircle, with you in the middle holding the book so everyone can see the pictures as you read. Go slowly, and read in an animated voice, taking on different voices for different characters in the story.

6. When introducing a new story, always read it all the way through without interruption the first time. Children get restless and understandably impatient with stops and starts when they're waiting to find out what's going to happen next. As they become familiar with a story, then they'll enjoy answering questions about it, e.g., "What is going to happen when the wolf tries to blow down the straw house?" "Why couldn't Peter Rabbit crawl under the fence?" Also, when the children begin to know a book well, let them take turns being "teacher" and reading the story to the group.

**Purpose:**    Reading to children serves many purposes. First of all, it is an enjoyable, quiet activity that is both a source of new information and a stimulus for children's imagination. A good book for children, like a good book for adults, absorbs the attention of its readers and pulls them into the story, allowing them for a short time to enter the world of the book. It widens children's horizons, giving them a view of things they might not otherwise know anything about and enabling them to see things from still another point of view different from those of the people they know. It is an obvious stimulus in motivating them to want to learn to read for themselves, showing them that reading can be fun and informative as well as being an activity which adults value and are skilled at.

**Variations:**
1. Make tape recordings on a casette recorder of you reading the children's favorite stories. Include, in your story, instructions on when to turn the page, so a child can "read" along with you as he listens to the tape. Tape a picture on the casette to identify it, and number the sides 1 and 2 if the story takes more than one side. Keep a collection of such tapes on a shelf with a casette tape recorder near the book corner so the children can read and listen when they wish. Show them how to use the recorder and, if possible, have ear plugs so that a child can listen without disturbing anyone else.

2. Make up picture cards from children's favorite stories for them to practice putting in sequence. You can do it with them at first, until they understand the task, and then leave sets of cards in rubber bands on shelves where the children can use them when they choose. You might be able, with some of the books, to find inexpensive editions that you can cut the pictures out of, mount on cardboard, and cover with clear contact paper. The other alternatives are either to photostat the pictures in the book you use to read to the children, color the photostats, and mount them on cardboard, or—if you have the skill—to draw duplicate pictures yourself.

3. Make up cards on necklaces of string, long enough that they'll hang chest- or waist-length on the children, with the names of each of the characters of their favorite stories. Then, have them take turns being different characters, wearing their name tags, and telling the story by acting it out, with you reading the narration in between their lines. You also can make other special props such as ears (making a band big enough for a child's head from lightweight cardboard, and pasting onto it bear, rabbit, or cat ears) to get the children more into the spirit of the story.

## SALT AND SUGAR[8]

**Participants:** One to five children, three years and older, and an adult.

**Materials:** Two shallow bowls, one with sugar, the other with salt; an empty salt shaker; an empty sugar bowl; a funnel; a spoon; a small pitcher or cup with a pouring spout; two paper cups with water; plastic spoons; a cucumber.

**Explanation:** In the following activity, you call the children's attention to some aspects of one of their everyday experiences (in this case, eating) that they probably would not think of otherwise. This kind of activity can help awaken their minds to the fact that there are many interesting ways of

---

[8] This activity can be extended over several sessions or done in one, depending on the children's interest and attention. Don't be rigid about following this procedure. The direction the activity goes in will depend very much on the children, and you should be flexible enough to follow their lead, offering them these ideas but not demanding they follow this particular sequence.

examining common objects and events in our lives that we can discover only if we're awake, alert, and inquisitive.

1. Set the bowls of salt and sugar on a table in front of the children. Tell them the bowls contain mystery substances, and you want them to try to figure out what they are. Ask if anyone can guess what's in the bowls and encourage each child to offer his idea. Don't tell them if they're right or wrong, regardless of their answers. Rather, after all of the children have made a guess, ask them how they could check out their ideas.

2. Encourage them to use any "tests" they suggest. If no one makes any suggestions, ask if they can tell by looking? By smelling? By feeling? In each case, have them try it and see if that means of investigation helps them identify the substance. If it has not yet been suggested by the children that they try tasting what's in the bowls, give them a hint—"They're things you can eat." Then let each child stick his finger in each bowl and taste the substances.[9] Can anyone guess now?

3. Up to the point of tasting, the children have not known whether the two bowls contained the same substance or two different kinds. After tasting, if they're able to identify that one is salt and the other sugar, ask them how they can tell the difference between the two. If the only answer you get is "tasting," ask if when their mommy or daddy cooks, they have to stop and taste to see whether they're using salt or sugar. Have them repeat the look-feel-smell tests to see if they can tell the difference in any of those ways. If no one mentions it, ask the children what kind of containers salt and sugar are usually kept in.

4. Bring out the empty salt shaker and sugar bowl. See if the children know what they're for. If necessary, explain that these are the kinds of containers in which people usually keep salt and sugar. Then ask them to see if they can figure out how to get the salt into the salt shaker and the sugar into the sugar bowl. Give them the funnel, spoon, and pitcher or cup with the pouring spout, and explain that these are possible tools that could be used.

5. Suggest, if there are more than two children, that they work together to solve the problem. If there are only two, they can each take care of one job, or they can do both as a team effort. Don't coach them or tell them how to do it. Put some newspaper on the floor under the table if you're worried about a mess, or just let the children use a broom, dustpan, and sponge to clean up afterwards.

[9] Explain to the children that they shouldn't ordinarily go around tasting strange substances to find out what they are because they could be things that would make you sick, but that this one you know is okay.

6. Have the children put some salt in one of the cups of water and sugar in the other.[10] Suggest that they watch to see what happens with each. Do they mix with the water in the same way? What if you use hot water or very cold water?

7. Suggest to the children that they experiment with different amounts of salt and sugar in each cup of water.
   a. Have them mark the cups, each in the same place, and fill them to that level with water. Direct them to put a sprinkle of salt in one cup and a sprinkle of sugar in the other and mix up each one. Then give them plastic spoons to take a tiny taste of each, noting how salty or sweet it is.
   b. Have them empty the cups, refill them to the mark with more water, and try adding an even teaspoon of each substance to their respective cups. Suggest they taste the flavored water again. This time, direct their attention not only to how much saltier and sweeter each is than before, but also to any difference they notice between the relative saltiness or sweetness of the two—that is, is one "stronger" than the other, even though they used the same amount of each?
   c. Talk about this in terms of how much salt we usually use on food versus how much sugar we use on things we sweeten.

8. Cut up the cucumber so that each child gets three small pieces. Talk to the children as you're cutting and handing out the pieces: "Let's see. One, two, three, four. There are four of us. I'll cut the cucumber into four big pieces." "Look. First, I'm going to cut it in half this way. That makes two pieces. Now I'll cut each of these pieces in half again. Now we have four pieces." "I'm going to cut each of these big pieces up so that each of us can have three little pieces." "One, two cuts to make three pieces." "Here, Megan, one, two, three pieces of cucumber for you," and so on.[11]

9. When all the children have their pieces of cucumber (with napkins or paper plates to put them on), tell them to taste one piece. Then give them some salt to put on one of their remaining pieces and some sugar for the other, and tell them to taste the cucumber with those seasonings. Which one tastes better—the plain one, the one with salt, or the one with sugar? Talk about what cucumbers are used for (e.g., in salads, as a snack), and how they are usually seasoned (e.g., with salt, mayonnaise, vinegar and oil).

---

[10] For a group of children, have enough multiple sets that everyone can be involved.

[11] This could also provide a good opportunity to let the children practice using a blunt-edge knife to cut. After cutting the cucumber into big pieces for each child, you could let each one cut her own piece into three small pieces.

10. Talk with the children about what kinds of foods we season with salt and which we use sugar for, encouraging the children to name foods they eat and then tell which seasoning it takes. You can suggest other foods and let the children say whether they need or contain salt or sugar; you can also talk about foods that are naturally salty (e.g., bacon, anchovies) or naturally sweet (e.g., fruit).

11. At another time, you could make cream of wheat or another hot cereal with the children which, though eaten with sugar, is seasoned with a little salt when cooking. Make a batch with the salt and one without, and let the children taste the difference salt can make in cooking even something that doesn't taste salty and in fact is sweetened to eat.

12. Talk with the children about other uses they can think of for salt or sugar, serious or silly.

**Purpose:** This activity is primarily an exercise in problem-solving—guiding the children to apply search techniques on the basis of available information and their past experience in order to identify two mystery substances and, later, in order to figure out how to get them from one container into another. The latter part also provides good practice for the children's small motor skill and spatial judgment.

There are further instances of learning rudimentary scientific procedures, e.g., as in putting equal amounts of each substance in equal amounts of liquid—controlling some variables while studying others. Mathematical concepts are involved in this part as they are in the division of the cucumber, but if the latter is done by the adult rather than by the children, there will be less real learning, other than hearing numbers applied to a concrete situation they can see and hearing some vocabulary words that will have more meaning later.

In general, the activity helps the children learn to focus on the characteristics of different things that identify what they are. In addition, it provides an opportunity for them to learn new vocabulary to apply to the objects, actions, and concepts involved in the activity.

**Variation:** This same type of activity can be done with many different "mystery substances," e.g., mustard and ketchup; flour, powdered sugar, and baby powder; vinegar and water. You can probably think of many more food and nonfood substances to use. When the substance is something that would not be good for the children to taste, tell them it's not something to eat.

# 6

# Four to Five Years:
# I Can Be Anything You Can Be

From four to five, most children become more organized, focused, and conventional in their thinking. They learn to follow an idea, problem, or task to its conclusion, staying with it even from one day to the next until it is successfully completed. Five-year-olds are concerned about order and completion. They can think of an idea and then carry it out, whereas at the beginning of the year they might flow quickly from one idea to the next. Their thinking is becoming more defined, and their memory for events, situations, strategies in problem-solving, and so on is improving.

Their growth in independence increases from four to five. The things they did at four to care for themselves, children do more easily and with less supervision at five. By five, many children are very helpful around the house, washing or drying dishes, setting the table, and the like. From four to five, children should be beginning to internalize social rules and to rely on their own judgment of their behavior. They are becoming more aware of themselves in relation to others, and will pursue learning tasks because the task makes them more like an admired person who possesses attributes similar to and valued by them. They continue to participate in sociodramatic play as a way to define their own self-concept through exploring a range of different roles.

Four- to five-year-olds' large motor skills are sufficiently advanced that their play can include a variety of stunts and simple gymnastics as well as some simple organized games such as "Mother May I?", "Simon Says," and "Statues." By five, they can hop, jump, skip, run, climb, twist, and so on. These games are a way to practice motor skills as well as learn to cooperate with others, fit actions to verbal instructions, and retain and follow a simple set of rules.

Fine motor skills become more refined and in control. Some children may be interested in learning to write. Most children's drawing is more controlled and adapted to a mental plan or image. Their pencil grasp is improving, and scissors are used effectively for cutting out things.

Language is used in this period increasingly as a substitute for action. Children can "pretend" to do something just by verbally saying they did it; e.g., "Let's pretend I'm the mother and you're the baby and I just gave you a spanking." Children are learning to seek verbal solutions to problems to which they used to react bodily and with heightened emotions. From four to five, children continue to expand their vocabulary, extend the length of their sentences, increase the complexity of their sentence structure, and use language more and more as a way to learn about things in their world. Questions are becoming more information-seeking, and interest in books and stories more reality-based. Finally, language is not only a part of their play, but it can serve as the basis of play itself. Playing with rhyming and silly words can be a fun game for the child of this age.

Four-year-olds already understand that the things in their world have an order, that they can put them back in that order once they have taken them apart, and that many things can be compared or related to each other in an orderly way. Between four and five years they are free to explore more complicated ways of ordering more and more objects in their world, according to their physical attributes (including how they look, taste, smell, sound, and feel and what you can do to them or with them), their positions in time and space, and/or how they are defined or described by other people.

## SHOP AND LEARN

**Participants:**    Four- to five-year-old or older child and an adult. Some of the beginning parts of the activity, such as having your child hand you things from the shelves, are appropriate for children as young as two years. And even your year-old baby riding in the grocery cart can take packages from you and put them into the back of the carriage as well as learn from your talking to her about the things you hand her.

**Explanation:** Grocery stores are an endless source of learning for preschool children. The organization of the merchandise into sections containing similar items provides practice in classification. The labels on the cans and boxes are great pre-reading and reading material. Size, color, and shape concepts and vocabulary can be learned in relation to grocery packages. The following activity contains some ideas of how to make shopping with your child a pleasure and a learning experience instead of a problem.

1. Let your child help you shop, handing you things off the shelves as you ask for them. Getting one loaf of bread, two cans of tomato soup, and so on, in itself is a learning activity. At first, you'll have to point out which kind of bread you want or which canned soup says tomato. In time she'll learn to recognize the packages of the brands you buy as well as the names on the labels of things you get regularly—an easy, painless lesson in reading. She'll learn beginning math skills through practice getting you "just one," "two," a "six-pack," the "big" bottle, the "small" can, and so on.

2. As your child becomes practiced at handing grocery items to you, and as she gains familiarity with the stores you shop in, you can begin to let her go get things for you on another aisle.[1] Give her one instruction at a time at first, and keep it to things that are close by. Increase the number of items you ask her to get at a pace she can handle. Have her go get the item(s) and then come right back so that she doesn't get lost.

3. Tell your child exactly what you want and where it is. Until she becomes very skilled at this, stick to things she's used to getting for you when you're on the same aisle together. "Chrisy, please get me a small box of Cream of Wheat. It's in the middle of the next aisle with all the cereals."

4. By taking a little time to make up a special kind of shopping list for your child, you can make shopping into a pre-reading activity.
   a. Whenever you use up the contents of cans, boxes, and bottles, save the labels. Cut out the printed name of the product and a picture, trademark, or some other identifying feature so that your child will be able to recognize it.
   b. Then, before going shopping, paste onto a sheet of paper all the labels of things you need to buy. Organize them so that things that can be found together in the store are grouped together on your child's "shopping list."
   c. When you get to the store, give the list to your child, and let her get

---

[1] You can really do this only when the store is fairly quiet. Ask the cashiers what times the market is not very busy. If your working hours prevent you from shopping except at busy times, it's probably best to have your child stay on the same aisle with you or within your sight.

the things. Bring along a magic marker, too, so she can make a mark next to each label as she's gotten the item.[2]

5. By this time, you're ready to play "the classification game."

   a. As you shop, point out to your child that like things are shelved together, e.g., "Chrisy, we need some lettuce. It's over here with the other fresh vegetables." "Here is all the canned fruit. Can you find the peaches?"

   b. Sometimes, when you have the time and energy, play a "Where can you find it?" guessing game: "We need some milk, Chrisy. Where would it be?" Start the game by giving choices— "Would you find milk with frozen packages or with cheese and sour cream?"

   c. Once you've established where an item can be found, then, through asking questions and offering information, help your child understand why the things in that section are put together, e.g., "Why do you think milk and butter and cheese and sour cream are all together?" "I'll give you a hint. They're all called 'dairy products.' Do you know what kind of animal they have at a dairy farm?" "That's right. All these things are made from milk; and milk, as you know, comes from cows," and so on.

6. You can make up a grocery store game to play at home which will reinforce the things your child learns at the market and increase her shopping skill.

   a. Take a notebook with you to your local market on a quiet day. Copy down the labeling system they use above the aisles or at the rear of the store, i.e., the food and other categories they list on signs to help you find where things are.

   b. Later, at home, make signs like the ones at the market out of oaktag or cardboard. Have your child help with the lettering to the extent that she is able. (See "I Can Write," Five to Six Years, page 264, for materials and activities for learning to write.)

   c. The two of you then can go through old magazines looking for ads of foods and other items that can be found at grocery stores. Cut them out together, and mount them on posterboard, oaktag, or shirt-cardboard. When you've amassed a representative collection of pictures, you're ready for the first stage of the game—setting up your store.

   d. Stick your signs up on the wall with scotch tape, and then look through your picture collection together for items that go with each sign. For example, if one of your signs says "Relishes, mustard, ketchup, etc.," find those pictures and put them side by side under that sign. As this is a good game for a group, recruit other family

---

[2] Have your child stay with or close to you for this. In general, it's best to have her stay within your visual range or at most, one aisle away. This precaution is necessary primarily because other people in the store, less attuned to children than you, may give your child a hard time if they see her walking around, unaccompanied, taking items off the shelves.

members too.[3] At first, you'll have to do most of the reading, but with repeated experience, your child will begin to recognize the words herself.

e. Once you've got your grocery store set up, you're ready to go shopping. First, you'll need to make up a list. Let your child compose it and dictate it to you. Print the words in neat, large letters like those they use at the store. Then give the list to your child and let her look for the sign that has each item on it.

f. In some cases, the words on her list will have no duplicate on the grocery signs; instead, the signs may have broader categories into which a particular item would fit. In the first case, all she has to do is look for matching words and then go to the area of that sign to find the grocery item on her list. In the second instance, you may have to help her find the category name that her item would fit into. Give her a box that can serve as a shopping cart to put her picture cards in.

g. When your child's all done shopping, you can pretend to be the cashier and check her out and bag her "groceries." You can get some arithmetic skills in by marking the grocery items on the back

[3] This game also can be adapted for use with a small group of children in a preschool setting.

with prices and making some play money for her to pay for it. Your child probably won't be able to really understand and handle all the details of the money transactions. But she can get the general concepts through this activity, and the details can be filled in later when she acquires those skills.

7. After playing the grocery-store game at home, your child will be able to begin using the signs in the store as guides to find things. You can begin to ask her, for example, to look for the aisle where the mustard would be, or to look at a sign to see if canned vegetables are on that aisle.

8. Having tried some of these "shop and learn" games, you probably will be able to think of many other ways to use the grocery store as a learning resource. Let your own child be your guide to what's interesting and what she's ready to do. Remember that responsibility, like any other skill, requires practice; give your child only as much at one time as she can comfortably handle.

9. For example, whatever your child's age, don't suddenly turn her loose in the grocery store to help you shop if she's never even participated in the simplest act of taking an item off the shelf and handing it to you or putting it in the basket. Start where your child is, and move slowly from there, gradually giving her more freedom and responsibility as she shows she's ready to handle it.

**Purpose:**   To transform a routine activity parents and children engage in together from one often marked by conflict (between the adults' wish to get a job done and their children's natural tendency to explore, experiment, and generally check out their environment) to one in which parents and children can function effectively and happily together, satisfying each one's needs simultaneously.

Initially, it takes a little more effort and attention to give your child opportunities to practice being helpful than to do the job yourself. But if you're willing to invest some time and energy in the beginning, your patience will be rewarded by your child beginning to really be a help instead of a hindrance to your task.

Even more important, she will learn the immeasurably important skill of responsibility. Being able to be useful in the adult-oriented world of the grocery store will give her feelings of competence and self-worth. Learning to do things on her own that previously she was excluded from even participating in will contribute to her self-reliance and self-confidence.

Further, the grocery store is a rich source of learning opportunities related to reading, classification, arithmetical, quantitative, and language skills.

If you take this opportunity to turn an often boring and frustrating job into an interesting and entertaining learning experience, your child will become a much happier, more competent, and better-behaved shopping companion.

**Variation:** If you have more than one child to take shopping with you, your initial efforts will be more demanding. But as each of them acquires skill at her own level (e.g., A baby seated in the carriage can be handed items by an older sibling which the baby can then put in the carriage behind her.), your job will get even easier as your children learn to cooperate with each other in their learning games and in helping you.

## HOW CAN YOU MOVE?

**Participants:** Four- to six-year-old children and an adult. Some younger children also may enjoy a simple version of this activity.

**Materials:** A refrigerator carton or something else to make a tunnel; blocks of different lengths and shapes; several different-sized boxes ranging from a shoebox to a large carton; heavy string of different lengths; a drum, bells, tambourine, and other rhythm-band instruments.

**Explanation:** With any skill that a child learns, there comes a time when that skill is well enough developed that the child enjoys extending and expanding it, integrating it with other skills, adding variations, and so on. By this age, most children can walk and run with ease, balance heel-to-toe on a walking beam and on one foot, jump, hop, gallop, tiptoe, and by six, skip. They are ready to put these skills to use in developing more varied, controlled, and refined ways of moving. The following activities will help your children develop more coordinated, graceful, and efficient movement.

1. *Moving in Space.*
   a. Set up an area for you and the children to move in that includes a variety of different kinds of spaces such as:

   *enclosed spaces,* e.g., a tunnel made from a refrigerator carton with both top and bottom removed;

   *narrow spaces,* e.g., chairs or a couch set close to the wall so you'll have to squeeze through;

   *small and large spaces* for you and the children to walk within, e.g., using different-sized boxes or enclosures made with blocks to define the spaces;

   *open spaces;* and *spaces defined by obstacles* that must be walked around, e.g., chairs set up like a slalom course.

b. First, just walk through the area with the children. When you're done, ask the children to describe the different ways they were able to move in the different spaces (e.g., "You have to take little tiny steps inside the little box." "You have to lift your feet way up to step into and out of the biggest box.").

c. Then, move through the area again, this time paying conscious attention to the kinds of movement that each space defines through its structure.

d. Try it at different speeds, jumping, hopping, and so on, noting how different spaces inhibit or permit these different kinds of movement.

2. *Partners.*

a. Have about five children divide into pairs, choosing one child to be your partner. (When they've done this a few times, you can expand the size of the group.) Tell the children to hold hands with their partner and try moving different ways together:

walking regularly; matching each other's strides as they walk; walking so that one person moves his right foot forward while the other moves his left foot forward; stepping on a line or over a block at the same time together; marching; running at different speeds and stopping and starting as they run; hopping; jumping; galloping; trying to skip; and so on.

b. Give each pair, including yourself and your partner, several different lengths of string, ranging from six inches to several feet, and try moving together in different ways while each partner holds one end of a piece of string.

c. Tell the children to make note of how different their movements were when holding hands and when using the different lengths of string, and talk with them afterwards about it.

3. *Statues.*

a. This is a game in which the participants move as they wish until a leader calls out "Freeze!" Then everyone must assume whatever position he was in at that moment until the order is given to move again.

b. It's usually played so that anyone caught moving after the *freeze* order is given is out of the game. Although you can do this, there's more opportunity for learning if you don't eject players from the game in this way.

c. Instead, you be the first leader, calling the *freeze* command, and checking to see if anyone moved. Anyone you catch moving must then take your place as leader until he finds someone moving with whom he can then trade places.

     d. You can modify "Statues" by having the children and yourself see how slowly you can move from the freeze position to another position, the point of the game being to move almost without seeming to move.

5. *Movie Games.*
   a. Tell the children to pretend they're in a slow-motion movie. Perform actions with them, such as sitting down, standing up, walking, talking, lifting a cup to your mouth, and so on, in slow motion.
   b. Then, ask the children to pretend you're all in a speeded-up film, rushing jerkily through your actions. Repeat the same kinds of movements as if in fast motion.
   c. Ask the children to try imitating the appearance of a film being run backwards, at different speeds.
   d. If you have access to a movie camera and projector, take movies of the children playing. Then show the movies forwards and backwards at regular speed, slow motion, and speeded up to demonstrate to the children what you mean.
   e. Then, take a movie of the children trying to imitate themselves in the "silly movies." When it's developed, show the two films one after another to them.

6. *Move to the Music.*
   a. Using rhythm-band instruments such as drums, bells, pieces of wood to knock together, and tambourines, you and the children can make up movements to accompany the different kinds of instruments. Have each child select an instrument to "be"; he should then think up ways of moving to accompany the instrument and represent its sound and rhythm. Also, you and the children can make up tunes and rhythms to accompany different movements, e.g., a "running song," a "hopping rhythm".
   b. Everyone, including you, should have a chance both to compose and to perform his own and others' compositions. You can use different-sized dots on lines to illustrate visually the rhythms and tunes. The size of the dots can indicate the strength of the beat, and their position on the lines can note rise and fall of the pitch.

**Purpose:** To provide children with opportunities to experiment with movement—to become more aware of the ways that different spaces dictate the kinds of movements you can make in them; to learn greater coordination and control of their movement; to practice matching their movements to their intentions; to learn more about the relationships of different objects in space to each other; to learn to move in coordination and cooperation with another person; and to learn to coordinate their movements with music and rhythm. All these things contribute to children's becoming more consciously aware of their own movement in space and thus more capable of using their bodies effectively and efficiently, with coordination and grace.

## "TELL ME A STORY"

**Participants:** Four- to six-year-old children and adults. Younger children enjoy stories too, though of a less complex nature. You'll know from your child's response if you're on target in terms of content and language level.

**Explanation:** Children this age love "made-up" stories, especially at bedtime. Following are a few ideas for material.

1. Tell your child stories about yourself when you were a child. Share with her the special things you remember, the things that made you happiest, your favorite people, activities, toys, places, and so on. Tell her also about times you were sad, disappointed, afraid, angry, or hurt (especially as these relate to her own recent experiences). Talk with her about what her grandparents were like as parents, about what it was like to live when and where you did, about the many things that have changed since then, and so forth.

2. Tell your child stories about how you and her daddy (or mommy) met, about your courtship, why you fell in love, about getting married, about the time you spent together before she was born. Tell her what it was like to be pregnant with her, what your ideas were of what she'd be like, about getting ready for her to be born, and so on. If you were awake during the birth, tell her what that was like, what she looked like at first, what the doctor did, and so on.

3. Tell your child stories about herself. Check in her book for story material (see "The Baby Book," page 62), and let her look at her pictures, listen to her tapes, and so on. Explain to her, especially, about that period of her life that she can't recall, her babyhood. Talk with her about the things she liked and didn't like, about cute things she did, about when she learned to crawl and walk and talk, and how those developments changed her approach to the world.

4. Let your child be the story guide. Be prepared to tell the same story on request over and over. And expect to answer lots of questions, sometimes the same ones again and again. Although you may have a story idea in your mind before bedtime, be flexible enough to change it if that's not the one your child would like to hear. And let her stop and

start you to answer questions or go into a particular aspect of a story in more detail.

**Purpose:** To provide meaningful bedtime entertainment for your child that gives her a sense of history and helps her understand her own roots. For your child to be able to imagine you as a child like her, who had joys and fears and experiences much like her own, helps strengthen her identification with you, an important process in her growth. It begins to give her a sense of perspective, something she won't really understand for a while, but which will stimulate her curious mind for now.

Hearing stories about things she hasn't experienced or doesn't remember gives your child practice using her imagination to visualize these things. This is an often neglected skill in this day of TV, and story-telling can help develop it. Stories also exercise your child's memory capacity for meaningful things and events. Just as making up her own stories helps her organize large amounts of otherwise unrelated and unorganized information, so your telling her stories enables her to learn to store a great deal of information in this form.

This activity will help you, too. Through remembering and sharing with your child how you felt when you were a child and through identifying with your child, you will get back in touch with your own roots. You can pick up again some of your discarded hopes and dreams, and rediscover parts of your essential self that your adult self has been storing away. In addition, talking with your child about your own span of life in relation to hers will help you gain a sense of perspective about your life, perhaps motivating you to live this short life as meaningfully and lovingly as you can.

Finally, talking aloud with your child about your own childhood and hers may help you to realize fully, on a gut level, that however you may feel inside sometimes, from your child's perspective you *are* grown up. And she needs you to be a strong, supportive, and loving adult—to grow beyond the restraints on your growth imposed in your own childhood. Because only if you are continuing to grow can your child continue to grow with you.

**Variation:** In preschool settings, tell children stories about your childhood and invite them to tell you about theirs.

## WHAT CAN YOU DO WHEN YOU'RE FEELING LOW?

**Participants:** Children four years or older and adults.

**Explanation:** Many people suffer occasionally from what seems to them to be unpredictable and uncontrollable mood swings. One day everything seems to be going right. On another, no matter what they do, it seems to be wrong. On such "low" days, things bother them that ordinarily would be taken in stride. They may become unreasonably upset by the slightest change in routine, an unmet expectation, or something someone did or said. And they may be plagued by anxieties about things that might or might not happen.

Following are some ways of dealing with your children's "low moods." They include strategies through which both of you can learn to increase your high moods and decrease the low ones and their effects. In general, they can help you both learn to bring your emotions into a state of balance so that they can work for rather than against you.

1. Help your child learn to recognize when he's in a low mood. Often adults as well as children spend quite a bit of time feeling upset without realizing it's their problem. They may think it's a bad day or that other people are treating them strangely, but be unable to acknowledge that *they* are feeling anxious, upset, or angry.

2. Because of this, it's not a good idea to tell someone he's in a bad mood. Rather, ask your child gently if something is the matter. Or, if you have a pretty good idea of what the problem is, put it into words for him, e.g., "I bet you're mad at Mona because she broke your toy. I'd be upset, too, if I were you. Even though she didn't mean to break it, it was your favorite toy, and she should have been more careful."

3. Sometimes the problem is specific, and your child just needs to "get his feelings off his chest" to an understanding listener. In the preceding case, for example, being able to express his anger to you will enable him to forgive his little sister instead of carrying his negative feelings toward her around with him and take them out on her.

4. Other times, your child's low moods will be more vague, diffuse, and generalized, without a specific focus. In those instances, through giving him a chance to express his feelings, you can help him understand that the reason things are upsetting him which usually don't really bother him is because he's in a low mood.

5. In either case, the first step in dealing with a low mood is to acknowledge that it exists. Next, you should try to help your child identify what's bothering him and whether it's something he can change. If it is, then you can help him work out a plan for changing the situation that's causing him to be upset. If it's something that can't be changed, as with a toy that's been broken, after he's had a chance to express his feelings about it, you should help him to accept and learn from it.

6. Help your child, through the way you respond to him when he's feeling low, to understand that there's nothing "bad" about being sad,

angry, lonely, or frightened. Sometimes we feel that way in response to a particular situation. It is quite normal to feel all those emotions when a person you love has died, for example, or when someone you thought was a friend has done something to hurt your feelings. You should encourage your child to express these feelings, not to avoid them.

7. Emotions *will* find an outlet. It is much better to help your child learn to be aware of his feelings and express them than to force his emotions, through lack of an acceptable outlet, to be submerged and thus emerge in disguised and often personally destructive forms. For example, if your child has lost a favorite pet, he should be permitted and encouraged to cry, get mad, or whatever he feels like. He should *not* be expected to "be a man" and not cry (neither for that matter, should a man).

8. Sometimes people get upset for no apparent reason. This is what we usually hear referred to as being in a "bad mood." You can help your child understand that feeling like this is *not* "bad" by using an analogy of a car whose battery has run down. It isn't a "bad" car because it has no energy, but in order to get going again, the battery's going to need recharging.

9. In a similar way, when people get overtired, when they have too many pressures, when they're hungry, when they're not feeling well, or when their body is just at a low ebb of its cycle, they are susceptible to feeling upset. In order to feel better and "get going" again, they need to "recharge their batteries" by eating, getting some rest, relieving some of the pressures on them, or in some other way satisfying the unmet physical and/or psychological needs that are causing them to feel low.

10. Given this kind of perspective on low moods, you can see that the one thing *not* to do when someone is feeling low is to drain his energy reserves any further. In particular, you should be careful not to make him feel worse by suggesting, through your words or attitude, that he is wrong to feel this way. For example, don't respond to your child's low mood by telling him to snap out of it or that he has no reason to feel the way he does. That kind of response only compounds the problem by causing guilt and self-doubt at not being able to do what you expect.

11. Instead, give your child the opportunity to work through his feelings—by talking, crying, even throwing something or screaming if it helps.[4]

---

[4] As children become older and more skilled at understanding and channeling their emotions, they'll be increasingly able to use words to express their feelings. But there always will be times

Let him know, through your words and your behavior, that you understand and care about how he feels. Be gentle, undemanding, and accepting. Through your model, he'll learn to behave similarly toward himself when he's upset in the future, an important first step in relieving his low mood.

12. As you probably know from your own experience, you can make yourself feel worse by getting upset at yourself for being upset. If you can help your child learn first to recognize when he is feeling low and then to respond to that mood by being gentle with himself, reducing his demands on himself until he feels more comfortable, you'll be going a long way in teaching him coping mechanisms for these times.

13. Having been able to talk about and otherwise express his feelings to you, your child probably will begin to feel better. When you have no outlet for expressing low feelings, it's easy to get caught in the trap of reinforcing your unhappiness by thinking to yourself "I sure am in a terrible mood," "I feel horrible," "I'm so depressed," and so on. Telling yourself how bad you feel only makes you feel worse.

14. But being able to talk with someone else who cares can have the opposite effect. On getting it out and hearing it aloud, you often begin to feel better and to be able to take it less seriously—to see whatever is bothering you in a more realistic perspective. Just sharing your "burden" with another human being usually lightens it, making you feel less alone. If you can do this for your child in his early childhood, you'll be providing him with a behavior pattern that will enable him in his adulthood to help himself and others cope effectively with low moods and life problems.

15. Your child needs a chance to express his feelings and have them received by you with serious concern. Once he has done that and he begins to relax, a little comic relief sometimes helps. If you can, help him learn to find humor in his own fears, in unhappy situations, and in the things that bother him when he's feeling blue. Help him learn to laugh, good-naturedly, at himself and the world, not taking it all too seriously. But remember, this is only possible when you have first considered questions, problems, and fears with seriousness. You can't dismiss them with humor. You can only take away their sting with laughter *after* you have been accepting and understanding of the seriousness with which the child perceives them.

16. After your child has talked and otherwise expressed his low feelings sufficiently that he's ready to move on from there, an enjoyable

---

when the most appropriate and helpful mode of expression is crying or, sometimes, screaming. If the thought of screaming bothers you, give some thought to a culture that has taught us that it's more acceptable to strike out at another person when we're upset than it is just to cry or scream.

activity might help him feel better and get himself back into action. Try such comforting, rewarding, and nondemanding activities as taking a walk, hugging a special stuffed toy, reading or listening to a story, being held and rocked by a loving adult, engaging in a favorite game, or imagining a special place where everything is just the way he wishes the real world could be.

17. If your child is receptive to talking, it may also help to relate the way he's feeling now to his own past experiences. Talk with him about other times and situations similar to this in which he was able to get himself successfully out of his low mood or solve the problem that was upsetting him. Share with him, also, stories of times when you've felt the way he's feeling or had a similar problem. Tell him what you did about it that worked or didn't work.

18. When your child is feeling better, you can help him focus on all the positive things in his life in contrast to the little things that were making him unhappy because he was focusing on them. But, while he's feeling down, don't tell him that he *should* be happy, that he has every reason in the world to be happy, that he has so much more than others, and so on. The fact is that he's not happy *right now*, and you can help him most to regain his sense of balance by allowing him to express the feelings he has.

19. There are some adults who will worry that giving a child so much attention when he's feeling low will encourage him to express those feelings more frequently in the future in order to get that attention. We can only respond to this kind of concern that if you're paying enough attention to your child, routinely, as part of your day-to-day life—showing a consistent concern for his needs, being responsive to him, letting him know through your words and behavior that you respect him and care deeply about him—then you have no worry that he'll "use" claims of low moods to gain attention. And if he does, that should be a sure sign to you that you're *not* satisfying his psychological needs sufficiently in your daily life together.

**Purpose:** To give you and your children practice at working through low moods with the ultimate goal of learning greater control of your emotional states so that they can work for you instead of against you.

Many adults tend to be very hard on themselves when they're in a "bad mood," chastising themselves for taking things too seriously, for being less effective than at other times, or just for being in a low mood. This is partly because we were never taught how to deal with our emotions, especially those considered to be negative.

It is also due to the process of modeling and adopting roles, through which we learn to internalize and reenact all parts of the interactions in which we took part as children. When we, as adults, are impatient with our inability to get ourselves out of a "bad mood," we are reproducing, inside our heads, what was passed down to us through our personal and social culture.

Thus, if we want our children to be able to treat themselves as well as our grandchildren better, we must consciously change our responses to so-called bad moods, recognize what they communicate, and learn to deal with them more constructively.

## WHAT'S THAT FOOD?

**Participants:**   A small group of children, four to six years old, and an adult. Three- to four-year-olds also may enjoy the simpler parts of the activity.

**Materials:**   Some snack foods, e.g., cheese, crackers, popcorn, nuts, fresh fruit, dried fruit.

**Explanation:**   Children (and adults) spend a significant portion of every day of their lives eating. This should be a time for families to be together and share the important things that are happening in their lives. But, in recent years, there has been a growing tendency for people to "eat on the run" even when they are seated and not in a hurry. This is a result of such things as the proliferation of food franchises for curbside eating, the trend toward families not sitting down together for meals or eating while watching television, and the generally rapid pace of life in the United States. The following activity can help you and the children learn to slow down and enjoy what you eat. At the same time, it will teach some important cognitive skills related to classifying and remembering tastes and textures, giving names to the contents and processes of eating, and so on.

1. Put pieces of three or four snack foods, each in a separate "tasting" bowl, on a table. Set some more of each food aside for now. Sit around the table with a small group of children. Have everyone, including you, take one piece of one of the foods, e.g., popcorn.

2. Tell the children (and do so yourself) to close their eyes as they eat the popcorn, and be very quiet except for the sound of their chewing—to concentrate all their attention on the popcorn, the way it tastes, the feel of it in their mouths as they chew, the sound of its crunching, its smell.

3. When the children are done with their pieces of popcorn, give them each a piece of apple. Tell them again, to chew slowly, thinking only of

experiencing the apple, as if this were the first and perhaps, last, time they would ever have an apple. Advise them also to think, as they chew, about the similarities and differences between the popcorn and the apple in terms of taste, texture, crunchiness, smell, and so on.

4. When you all have finished eating your pieces of apple, talk about it, about the popcorn, and about the ways the two of them are the same and different. If the children don't volunteer comments about any of the aspects you have mentioned, ask them some questions such as "How did the apple feel inside your mouth?" "How did the popcorn feel?" "Stacey said the apple was sweet. Was the popcorn sweet, too?"

5. Have the children try a couple more foods in the same way. Keep the total number of foods you have them taste small at first, especially if there are any they've never had before. Each time you play the game, you can add some new kinds of food. Stick with nutritious, healthy foods. You might want to play the game one day with different things to drink too, e.g., milk, water, different kinds of fruit juice.

6. When you and the children have all tasted each food, have everyone take a turn at trying to identify a food without seeing it. Cut up some more pieces of the foods you and the children just tasted. Close your eyes, and ask one of the children to put a piece of food in your mouth. See if you can guess which kind it is. Then, ask a child to close her eyes while you put a piece of food in her mouth. Ask her if she can tell which of the foods she ate before, this one is. Go around the table, giving each child a turn until everyone has gotten a chance to "taste and guess" with each of the different kinds of food.

7. If a child guesses correctly, answer "Yes, it is a piece of cheese. How did you know?" If she can't guess which one it was, ask some questions to help her eliminate alternatives, e.g., "How does it feel when you chew it?" "Is it crunchy?" "Which foods were crunchy?" "Then it must not be an apple or popcorn. What else could it be?" "Yes, it could be cheese or apricot. Is it sweet?" "Then what must it be?" If she guesses wrong, say, "It's not popcorn. Try another piece." Help her, if necessary, with leading questions, and show it to her as a last resort.

8. When the children have some practice playing this game, you can give them food to taste and identify with their eyes closed which they have not pretasted first.

9. For either version of the game (i.e., with or without pretaste), start out with foods that are very different from each other and proceed to ones that are more similar, e.g., an apple and a pear.

**Purpose:** To give children practice tasting, describing, and identifying different kinds of foods through taste alone. This activity gives children the opportunity to try different kinds of foods, to become more attuned to their various qualities and to learn how they are similar to and different from one another; as such it is a kind of classification activity by taste, texture, and so on. In addition, it is a vocabulary expander as the children find new ways of describing the sensory experiences involved in the activity.

The first part, in which the children concentrate on experiencing each food fully, is a good exercise in attending. The second part, requiring the children to identify which food they are tasting with their eyes closed, provides practice in recognition, the initial stage in memory. Identifying foods by taste alone without a pretaste requires recall, a more advanced stage in the memory process.

In addition, this kind of activity with food is excellent preparation for the children's learning to cook creatively in the future. Good cooks are those whose experiences in eating have taught them about flavors and textures so that they know upon thinking, for example, how a food will taste when combined with another or when seasoned in a particular way.

Finally, by using nutritious snack foods that are good for the children and taste good too, you can help them learn to eat better. Eating the right kinds of food is important for children to learn early before they develop such ingrained habits of liking "junk" food that it's hard for them to change their eating habits. They can't afford the empty calories now because of their bodies' need for nutrients to help them grow, and they won't be able to afford them later because of the danger of putting on too much weight. Learning now to eat what they need, at a slow enough pace to both enjoy it and to give their bodies time to give them back a "full" signal, will serve children well throughout their lives.

**Variation:**  As the children become experienced at this game, try making up little snacks containing foods that they've learned to identify from memory, and see if they can learn to identify from memory (with their eyes closed) what the ingredients of the snacks are, e.g., toast, bacon, lettuce, tomato, and mayonnaise, for a bacon, lettuce, and tomato sandwich; peanut butter and crackers for peanut-butter crackers; fruit salad. These are all examples of things the children can learn to prepare themselves, also, thus further reinforcing their learnings about how different foods can be combined.

## BE VERY QUIET

**Participants:**  An entire classroom of children, four to five years old, and an adult. If you have a quiet place away from the classroom, it might be best to start the activity with one small group at a time. Other children in the three-to six-year range may also enjoy it.

**Explanation:** Being "quiet" in mind and body requires concentration and produces relaxation. It is an important skill for children and adults to develop. Its development, in turn, will facilitate your learning to use your energy more efficiently and effectively for any task you choose. Following are some simple exercises in "being quiet." For more advanced ones, see "Attending Exercises," Five to Six Years, page 258.

1. Have the children sit on the floor, facing a window if there is one in the classroom. Ask the children to be very quiet, not to make a sound or move in any way that would make a noise. Tell them to close their eyes and just listen until you tell them to open them again. Do the same yourself. After you and the children have spent a few minutes of quiet listening, tell the children to open their eyes, and talk with them about what kinds of sounds you all heard.

2. Ask the children to be very quiet, close their eyes, and concentrate on listening to the sounds of their own bodies—their breathing, a slight ringing in the head, perhaps a grumbling in the stomach. Ask them to pay attention also to the *feelings* of their bodies—the beating of their heart and pulse, the movement of their chest, ribs, and belly as they breathe slowly in and out. Do the same yourself. After a few minutes, tell the children to open their eyes, and talk about what you all noticed about your bodies that you usually don't pay attention to.

3. Stand at the front of the room. Ask the children to be very quiet, and when they hear their names whispered, to stand up and walk to where you are standing without making any noise or bothering anyone who's still sitting down. Call each child, one by one, waiting each time until the last child called has gotten to the front before calling the next one.[5]

4. Don't try to do all three of these activities at once. Take them at a pace that respects the children's capacity to be quiet and still. Gradually extend the amount of time you ask the children to remain in that state as they gain practice and skill. Proceed to another stage of the activity only when you feel the children are ready for it.

5. If a child starts making noise at any stage, don't reprimand him. Instead, whisper his name and have him come up to you, and ask him to be the "leader" in the quiet activity. His noisemaking is most likely a

---

[5] For further discussion of the procedure and purpose of this and similar "focusing" activities, see Maria Montessori, *The Absorbent Mind* (New York: Dell Publishing Co., Inc., 1967), pp. 261–62. See, also, Gay Hendricks and Russel Wills, *The Centering Book: Awareness Activities for Children, Parents, and Teachers* (Englewood Cliffs, N.J.: Prentice-Hall, Inc., 1975) for more activities to help children relax, attend, and become "centered."

ploy for attention, and in this way he can get attention through participating in the activity rather than through disrupting it. Also, a strong and gentle hand on his shoulder will help to calm a squirmy child.

**Purpose:** To give you and the children practice in focusing your attention at will through concentrating it on quieting your voices and bodies. Children tend to have better capacity than many adults for maintaining absorbed attention to a task that they spontaneously have chosen for themselves. Their ability, like yours, to intentionally focus their attention on something requires practice such as this activity offers in order to develop.

In addition, you can adapt this activity as a technique for getting the children to be quiet and pay attention to you at times when you need to establish immediate order in a busy room. In the Montessori technique, for example, the teacher gets the children to quiet down by writing "Silence" on the blackboard (after having used that many, many times as a prelude in the *Silence Game* described briefly in #3 of this activity).

## WHHHHY?

**Participants:** Four- to six-year-old children and adults. This is the age range in which question-asking predominates. But children do begin asking different kinds of questions before this, and they continue to ask them after this age. The principles stated here apply to children any age when they ask you questions.

**Explanation:** "Mommy, why do birds have wings?" "To fly." "Why do birds fly?" "To travel a long way in a short time." "Why?" and on and on. This is the age of questions. Children want to know all about the world they live in. If they've learned up to this point that adults are a reliable source of information, then they start really using that wonderful tool they've been gaining command of these past years (i.e., language) to find out more about their world. Following are some guidelines to understanding and dealing effectively with your child's question-asking behavior.

1. At first, your child's questions may seem senseless and annoying to you; they may be continuous and repetitive questions to which she already knows the answers. But these are important in her development of a questioning mind that is never satisfied to just accept things as they are.

In fact, children's early questions represent the first stage in the development of the ability to ask questions. And like any other skill, questioning requires practice to become functional and effective.[6]

2. When your children ask you questions, answer them. If occasionally you're preoccupied, try to stop for just long enough to tell your child that you're busy now, but you'll answer her question in a few minutes. Don't leave her hanging, tugging at you and saying "Daddy," "Daddy," "Daddy," repeatedly.

3. Your child's time is important, too, and if she always has to bother you continuously in order to get you to pay attention to her questions, she'll either stop asking them or you'll find yourself in time with a whiner or a child who is a behavior problem.[7] In the long run, it's well worth the time it takes to stop to answer your child's questions.

4. By answering your child's questions, you communicate a respect for her desire to understand the world, thus reinforcing that behavior in her. Further, through really listening to her questions as well as to the answers she proposes when you turn the question back to her, you will come to understand better how her mind works.

5. Answer your child's questions with short, simple answers. As you well know, if your answer isn't satisfying, she'll follow it with another question until she's gotten an answer that makes sense to her at the present time. In your enthusiasm to stimulate your child's curious nature, don't overload her with too much information in any one answer. That will tend to discourage her questioning as much as will not answering her.[8]

6. Answer your child's questions the way your child answers questions herself so that your answers will be consistent with her way of thinking and therefore satisfying to her, e.g., "Why does the sun shine?" "To keep us warm." Children this age generally are not looking for physical explanations when they ask why; they want to know the psychological purpose of a thing's being the way it is.

7. In addition to answering children's questions verbally, when possible and appropriate direct them to a source or activity through which they

---

[6] See Elkind, *Children and Adolescents*, Chapter 2, "Children's Questions," pp. 26–33 (New York: Oxford University Press, 1970), for an excellent discussion of the kinds of questions children ask at different stages, what they mean, and how you can best respond to them.

[7] If you routinely ignore your child until she really starts bothering you, in essence, you are responding to that negative behavior. And, as we've said before, if you want to see a behavior again, pay attention to it.

[8] You may call to mind here the joke about the child who asked his father where he came from, and, after a long explanation of "the birds and the bees," the child answered, "But do I come from Chicago or New York?"

can answer the question themselves. For example, if a child asked something like, "Will this piece fit inside that box?" or "What if I put the ball in water?" say to her, rather than answering with words, "Let's find out," or "Let's see," and guide her to try out the thing she's asking about.

8. This is particularly applicable in preschool settings, where it is not unusual for children to come to the teacher with such questions. Take the opportunity the child gives you through such questions to guide her in problem-solving—in answering for herself questions that she has posed.

**Purpose:**   To encourage children to view question-asking as a valuable tool with which to gain information about the world; and through answering their questions (thus providing them with feedback about the effectiveness of their attempts), to help them become more skilled at question-asking behavior. In addition, of course, through answering children's questions, you provide them with information they are seeking, and thus you help them increase their knowledge and understanding of the world they live in.

Throughout the book, we've stressed the importance of following children's leads in guiding their learning. There is no more unmistakable clue to what a child's learning needs and interests are than the questions *she* asks. Through being responsive to her questions, you will be assured of being an effective facilitator in her learning.

Finally, participation in children's questioning activities can help you grow too. You can relearn to look at the world with unprejudiced eyes through sharing children's questioning minds, through relearning to ask "Why?" of situations and events you have learned to take for granted. Most adults have learned to parcel up the world into nice, neat categories. Joining in children's wonderment and questioning of the obvious can help you open up your own ways of viewing the world and see things in new and different combinations.

## "WHAT IF . . . ?"

**Participants:**   Four- to five-year-old child and an adult.

**Explanation:**   A question that children this age may ask with some frequency is the "What if . . . ?" or "Suppose that . . . ?" variety. Such questions often deal with fears and anxieties such as "What if my dog died?" "What if you and Daddy got divorced?" "Suppose that I got lost and you couldn't find me?" Below are some thoughts to guide you in helping your child work through the anxieties reflected in such questions and, at the same time, give him valuable practice in problem-solving and evaluative skills.

1. When your child asks such a question, take the time to talk about it then or some time soon when the two of you can sit down in a quiet place together where you won't be disturbed. Don't just reassure him that his fears are unreasonable or that what he fears won't happen. Rather, use the opportunity to let him talk about what's bothering him.

2. Turn the question back to your child and ask "What do *you* think would happen if . . . ?" "You're afraid that . . . might happen?" "Do you think you're nervous about this because . . . ?" and so on, leading him, through your questions and responsiveness to his answers, to open up and examine his own feelings. Offer him realistic assurances where they exist.

3. When there are no realistic assurances, such as in relation to questions about death and dying, answer your child honestly. If he asks, for example, explain to him what would happen if you died—who would take care of him, how his life would change, and so on. If you keep your answers simple and straightforward, and you are not afraid, then he won't be. It is unspoken and unanswered questions that cause fear.

4. Be alert to other signals that something's bothering your child in addition to "What if . . . ?" and other kinds of questions (e.g., whining, "talking back," snapping at you or others, sulking, night-mares), and try to find ways of helping him talk about it. For some children, saying in a kind way, "You seem upset" might work; that approach might make others defensive. If you have an idea what's bothering him, sometimes it helps to translate your child's feelings into words for him and then let him confirm or deny your interpretation and take it from there.

5. As a rule, in order to open up lines of communication with your child about things that are bothering him, you should do a maximum of listening and a minimum of talking. Say only as much as is necessary to open up the conversation and then to let your child know you're receiving his messages. Try to be non-judgmental and non-directive. Let him know you understand what's bothering him, and help him work through the problem himself and come up with his own resolution to it. The most important thing is for you to retain a non-defensive, accepting, and receptive attitude that let's your child know it's safe and rewarding to talk with you when he feels like doing so.

6. If you can help your child early in life to deal with his "What if . . . ?" questions, talking them out to their conclusions until he can relax about them, you may save him many anxieties through his life. Too many

adults live their lives entrapped by "What if's," habitually worrying about things that may never happen or wondering what would have happened if something had occurred differently in the past than it did, instead of living life today.

7. By taking your child's questions and the concerns they reflect seriously and spending the time to work through them with him, you'll be teaching him an invaluable life pattern of facing and dealing with anxieties instead of attempting to avoid or escape from them. It is people who have not learned to confront the consequences of those "What if's," who continue to be plagued by such doubts and fears. They keep posing the same questions over and over without ever taking the time to really think them through and consider all the possible alternative outcomes until they no longer seem frightening and threatening. Facing problems and dealing with them, whether they are real or imagined, always helps reduce their anxiety-producing properties.

8. You should also extend the principles of this activity to your own life-questions. Take the time to sit down with your mate, another loved one, or by yourself and work through anxieties and uncertainties that are recurrently bothering you. Be as understanding of your own concerns as we've asked you to be of your children's.

**Purpose:** To help your child deal with issues, problems, concerns, and questions constructively by using them as opportunities to explore and express his feelings and to think through his questions until he has mentally "researched" their possible answers to his satisfaction.

This is not only a useful skill in terms of its emotional components. It also is extremely valuable for general problem-solving to learn to look at the range of possible solutions and different perspectives before coming to a conclusion. Many adults who have not learned this skill still tend to grasp the first solution to a problem that presents itself rather than considering the problem in terms of the alternative outcomes of different strategies.

## WHAT'S THAT SOUND?

**Participants:** Four- to five-year-old children and an adult. This activity will continue to be enjoyed by older children, and some younger ones may like to participate in the simpler parts. As always, let their responses be your guide.

**Materials:** Cassette tape recorder and tape of sounds—household, street, and environmental;

Objects or pictures of objects that produce the recorded sounds (e.g., a toy telephone, old phone, or picture of one to go with the sound of a telephone ringing; picture of a person knocking at a door to go with that sound; picture of rain to go with a sound of rain);

Sound-producing objects including such things as rhythm-band instruments and common household or classroom objects that can be used to make a sound (e.g., pots and pans banging together; the sound of someone painting a picture).

**Explanation:** Of all our senses, sight and hearing are the two most called upon to cope in our day-to-day lives as well as to learn in and outside of school. Following are a few activities that give children practice in using their sense of hearing to make sense of the world around them. Each is a game the children will enjoy and learn from playing many times, since there really is no limit to the number of different sounds you can use or create.

1. *Which One Made the Sound?*
   a. Sit at a table with a small group of children. Set before them three sound-making objects whose sounds are quite different from each other, e.g., a bell, a drum, and a horn. Have each child take a turn making a sound with each of the objects. Tell them to pay close attention to the sounds because you're going to see if they can tell which is which when their eyes are closed. Check to make sure all the children know the names of the objects.
   b. Ask one of the children to close her eyes while you make a noise with one of the objects; then ask her to guess which object made the sound. Go around the table, with you and the children taking turns both at being the "sound-maker" and at guessing which object made the sound while your eyes are closed.
   c. If a child guesses wrong, answer "No, *here's* the sound of the drum (or whatever she said)," and make it. Then, make the other sound again for her, and ask her if it's the bell or the horn. If she still can't get it, have her open her eyes and see. The practice she'll get from being the "sound-maker" and from watching while others have their turn will help her learn to connect the sounds and their sources. When it's her turn again, let her try the one she missed before as well as the other ones.
   d. As the children become practiced at this game, you and they can begin to choose objects whose sounds are more similar to each other (e.g., a bell and a tambourine; three different kinds or sizes of bells) as well as select for your sound-makers classroom objects other than

musical instruments. (E.g., you might contrast the sounds of an eraser, a crayon, and a paintbrush, each being used with paper.)

e. In addition, you and the children can create sounds for your guessing game using your bodies—e.g., clapping hands, snapping fingers, smacking lips, blowing, scratching. When children become very skilled at this game, you can try making a sound they've been able to identify with their eyes closed when they previously had seen it made, this time without their seeing it at all, and see if they know what the sound is.

2. *Match That Sound*

a. If you have access to a tape recorder, take a small group of children on a "sound hunt." Collect on a cassette tape examples of the sounds that surround you and the children in your daily lives—traffic noises (cars, buses, subway trains, honking); animal noises; telephone and doorbell rings; knocking on the door; banging of pots and clanking of dishes and silverware in cooking, serving, eating, and cleaning up; running of water for a bath; washing dishes; rain; wind; people walking; and so on.

b. When making the tape, leave a pause between each sound and the next one. Take a notebook with you to make a written record of what sounds you're recording. Send a note home with the children asking for pictures (photographs, illustrations from magazines) or objects that could be used to represent the sounds you taped. Mount each picture on a piece of cardboard.

c. When you've finished getting the materials prepared, you're ready to play the game. Select three objects or pictures that represent three consecutive sounds on the tape (e.g., a bus, a telephone, and a dog barking), and put them out on a table. Sit down at the table with a small group of children. Make sure all of them can identify the objects or pictures, and ask them if they can imitate the sound each one makes.

d. Then, explain that you're going to play a sound on the tape recorder and you want them to show you the picture (or object) that goes with that sound. Let the children take turns, each getting a chance to match up each sound–picture pair. Keep reversing and replaying until all the children have had their turns.

e. When you've exhausted the first three sounds, proceed to other sounds and pictures, sticking to a choice of three to five. You can make the game harder by including some pictures which do not correspond to any of the recorded sounds, but which might be confused with them (e.g., a picture of a doorbell in a set including the sound of a telephone ringing).

f. As the children become more skilled at the activity, it isn't necessary for every child to identify the source of every sound. Keep your repeat performances mainly to the more difficult ones with which one or more children have problems. Always repeat one that was missed so that the child can find out the right answer and later get another chance on it.

g. When the children have played "match that sound" through the entire tape a number of times (over a period of time), see if they can identify the sounds without the use of the objects or pictures as clues.

h. Try the "match that sound" technique, using recordings of the voices of the children in your class and matching them first to the children themselves, then to pictures of the children, and finally identifying whose voices they are without any visual clues.

i. Try, also, using the technique to have the children match letters of the alphabet and numbers to their names, and in the case of letters, to the sounds as well (e.g., the letter $S$'s name sounds like *ess*; its sound is *sss*).

3. *Mystery Sound.* You and a small group of children can each take a turn making a sound while everyone else closes her eyes. Then, those whose eyes were closed must try to guess what the sound was, using a combination of a "What's My Line?" [9] "Twenty Questions," and "Hot and Cold" technique in which the child who made the sound gives hints and feedback as to how close people's guesses are to being right by answering their questions, e.g., "Did you use your body to make the sound?" Some examples of "mystery sounds" are crumpling paper, blowing your nose, brushing your teeth, and running water.

4. *Where's That Sound?*
   a. One child or adult tries to guess with her eyes closed where a sound (e.g., a bell, a drum beat) is coming from while another person makes the sound from different locations.

   b. You should begin by making the sounds close to the child whose eyes are closed (in front of her, behind her, next to her on either side), and gradually move away to different parts of the room as she gains experience and skill with the game.

   c. When a child guesses incorrectly, have her open her eyes and see where the sound is coming from, then close them again to listen now that she knows the location.

   d. You should play too; you may be surprised how hard it can be to localize sounds.

**Purpose:** To give children practice in listening and deriving meaning from

---

[9] Television game shows such as this, "Concentration," and others make good source material to develop activities for children.

sounds. A large amount of the information we must process every day comes to us through the auditory channel. These kinds of games can help children learn to pay attention to sounds and to "know" things and actions in their world by the sounds they make. They help children learn to sort out figure and ground. This is an essential skill that we, as adults, take for granted. But if we couldn't "select" which of the many noises in our world to listen to at different times, we'd have great difficulty learning and even coping.

In infancy, one of the baby's major learning tasks was to integrate various ways of knowing an object into a whole—coming to understand, for example, that Mommy's face, touch, smell, and so on all went together to make up one whole person. At this stage of their learning about their world, one of children's main tasks is to "take the world apart" again, finding out about the elements that go into making up a whole object or event, looking at, comparing, and contrasting things in terms of their different characteristics and dimensions—how they appear (color, texture, size, configuration), how they feel, how they sound, and so on. This type of game and others like it which focus on other senses, alone and in combination with each other, help children in this developmental task.

**Variation:**   Record classroom sounds for about fifteen minutes. Play back the recording and see if the children can identify what's happening, who's talking, who's laughing, and so on.

## WHAT IS A FRIEND?

**Participants:**   Four- to five-year-old children and parents. The principles stated here can be applied at any age level.

**Explanation:**   Children are in the process of developing friendships with others outside the family environment now. The model you give your children will greatly influence the kind of friend they will be to others. Following are some of the qualities that should characterize your relationship with your child in order to help him learn the meaning of friendship.

1. Friends are able to share joy and sadness, words and feelings, thoughts and emotions. They stick by each other through thick and thin, and each is always there when the other needs him. Friends care about each other's needs, and they respect each other's thoughts and feelings. They stand up for one another, and they take joy in each other's joy. Friends want for each other what the other most wants for himself.

2. Friends take pride in each other's successes, and they offer comfort and understanding when it is needed. They expect the best of each other, but they are accepting of the other as he is. Friends are able to reach out to one another in both directions—not only to offer help to the other, but also to ask for help themselves. They are able both to give and to receive. They are trusting and trustworthy, cooperative and caring. And through their caring, they enable the other to grow as they grow themselves.

3. In order for your child to learn to be this kind of friend to others, he must first have experienced this kind of friendship with another. You must lead the way through being such a friend to him, and he will learn from your model to be such a friend to you and others—and most importantly, to his own children, your grandchildren, when he becomes a parent.

**Purpose:** To promote the development and maintaining of a deep caring and friendship between you and your children as an essential element of your relationship. To the extent that you are able consistently to treat your children in a way that reflects this sort of caring relationship with them, they will be capable of developing such relationships with others in the future.

At the same time, of course, through the experience of caring for another in this way, you will reap the rewards of loving, human parenthood—you will grow increasingly more human yourself. And the human relationship you have experienced with your children will enable you, like them, to relate more humanly to others as well and thus to have them relate back to you in a similar manner.

# 7

# Five to Six Years: Help Me Not To Be Afraid

The period from five to six years is another period of transition for children, similar in ways to that which they experienced from two to three years. At five, most children seem well in control. They can care for many of their own needs; they identify themselves with more competent adults and older children; they use language articulately and meaningfully; they are in control of their body movements, and so on. But, following the typical course of development, this period of self-containment and relative competence in coping with the world is followed by one of apparent disintegration. Six-year-olds are, in fact, more competent than five-year-olds, but they may seem less so. Whereas at five they seemed to accept their role in life, by six many children are not at peace with themselves and others. They may be argumentative, subject to abrupt mood swings and changes of mind and opinion, and so on.

What has happened between five and six years to produce this kind of change is a growth in children's social intelligence which, until they work out the problems that this new awareness brings them, is more a liability than an asset. At the beginning of the year, most children are not consciously concerned about defining themselves as persons; they just accept themselves without too much question. Through the year, children typically become increasingly sensitive to their role in relation to other people.

243

In the same way as when they were two to three, new demands are being put on children from five to six, and the demands may be more than they can handle comfortably. Thus, at a time when they are becoming more consciously aware of themselves as persons, children see themselves as incompetent in comparison with adults, and they are realistically so. But their inability to always cope with the demands of adults reinforces their feelings of incompetence. In defense of their own position and in fear of progressing into the increasingly demanding adult world, children may behave in a way that might seem less mature than before.

This change in behavior that occurs in the sixth year is not serious except for the moment. Children have simply become increasingly self-conscious and therefore overly harsh on themselves. They may have internalized too well the discipline they have received, punishing themselves now for the smallest error or even for one in thought but not in action. If children are treated with concern and understanding and demands are lessened to a comfortable level, if they are not forced to do things which cause them pain, fear, or anxiety, this stage will pass and most children will be able again to function competently, at their own level, and happily.

Children are once again in the process of reorganizing their thought processes. Language is becoming more distinct from the things, actions, and events it is used to describe. It is becoming more of a reality in itself rather than the inseparable part of what it describes that it was for the younger child. When the child first began to learn words, they were more to her than a way of representing experience; they *were* the things they described. That's why the child had trouble understanding how someone else could have *her* name or how the same thing could have two names (e.g., coat and jacket).

From five to six years, children are becoming less literal about both their understanding and use of language. A reflection of this is the name-calling behavior of many children in this stage and the retort "Sticks and stones can break my bones, but words will never hurt me." In general, the child at this stage is very good in using language. By the end of this year, most children are using all types of sentences and kinds of words found in the language of their culture. They can use language to describe things, to argue, to tease and joke, to lie and make believe.

Through their experience with objects, children learn to compare sizes, shapes, colors, and textures. They learn concepts of numbers and the relations of parts and wholes by such activities as working with puzzles and blocks. They learn about volume and conservation through such experiences as play with sand and pails and with water and containers. They continue to practice classification of objects through what they can do with them, what they look like, and so on. In line with their developing flexibility with language, children's classification skills are becoming both more consistent and more flexible; they can begin to order things along more than one dimension (e.g., according to both color and size), but still one after the other, not at the same time.

The knowledge of order children have at five to six years is greater than that of younger children. They can tell what part of something is missing; they can compare things; they can begin to use what they have learned about order so that they can take something apart and remember how to put it together again correctly. (Before, they could take things apart and put things together, but not necessarily the same things.) Five- to six-year-olds are able to organize their own thoughts, too, so that they can tell long stories, correct their own errors, and begin to reason with ideas based on past experience, rather than having to try everything out with real objects.

Children's growing knowledge of order is also illustrated by the fact that they become more able, between five and six years, to play games with simple rules. In their own behavior, they are beginning to follow the rules of their cultures; so, for example, girls and boys are beginning to separate in their play choices into more "socially approved" role behavior. But though they may be more aware of the rules of the adult world than before, by six, children may rebel against adult rules if they don't coincide with their own ideas about the way things should be. There is a tendency, in this period, for children to become increasingly concerned about their relationships with other children and more rejecting of adult control.

In summary, five- to six-year-olds are continuing to expand their learning and development of skills. But because they are on the threshold of a new role in life, because more demands are being put on them, and because physiologically they are in a period of change, their behavior may seem to be becoming less organized throughout the year. But this is a period of transition. By seven, most children should once again be in a stage of equilibrium and integration.

## WHAT WOULD YOU DO IF . . . ?

**Participants:** Small group of five- to six-year-old children and an adult. Some younger children whose verbal skills are highly developed may also benefit from this activity.

**Explanation:** The following activity can give children practice imagining problem situations, then imagining and trying out solutions to them. This can be helpful to children this age not only in developing the cognitive skills involved in problem-solving, but also in enabling them to feel more secure about their ability to cope successfully in such situations.

1. Present the children with a problem situation, e.g., "What would you do if you got lost?" Listen to their answers, making sure each child gets a chance to contribute. If children have stories to share about when such a thing really did happen to them, encourage them to tell about it as well as to answer questions about how they felt and what they did.

2. Using examples that have first been discussed among the children, you and the children should take turns role-playing the situation. In the example given, one child could play the lost child and others could play roles such as a policeperson, a woman who offers to drive the child home, a man who offers to take the child to the police station, and so on. After role-playing, discuss the situation further with the children in terms of any new alternative solutions that might have been brought up.

3. Proceed, in your choice of "problems," from ones that are likely to be familiar to the children and within their potential range of experience to ones they might encounter in the future, and finally to probably unfamiliar situations which nevertheless contain enough similar elements that the children, with your help, can learn to apply familiar problem-solving strategies to their solution.

4. Other examples of the first class of problems would include: "What would you do if another child took away your toy?" and "What would you do if you broke another child's toy?" An example of the second kind of problem is "What would you do if you went to the store to buy something for your mother and found out you didn't have enough money?" An example of the third type is "What would you do if you bought a popsicle at the store, and the salesperson gave you back too much money?" or ". . . too little money?"

5. Let the children propose problems they'd like to discuss—ones they've had or possible ones that present some anxiety for them. You should take part, too, offering not advice on what they should do, but rather—like the children—an explanation of what you would do in a situation or what you did, as a child or as an adult, when you did encounter such a problem.

**Purpose:** To help children (and you) develop problem-solving and evaluative skills through talking about and role-playing problem situations. By confronting and rehearsing problems in this way, the children get an opportunity to explore different solutions they and others might apply to the situation. Hearing and seeing others' solutions to the proposed problems helps the children understand that other people may see things differently than they do.

The activity gives the children practice dealing with problems in the context of a safe game, thus giving them preparation for dealing with such situations more calmly and confidently if they actually occur. They also gain problem-solving skills and strategies that can be applied to the solving of other, different problems they will encounter in the future. Finally, the activity gives the children valuable practice in language skills as they discuss and role-play the problem situations.

In addition to benefits you will gain from joining the children in their discussions and role-playing of problem situations relevant to them (and perhaps shared by you in your own childhood, if not now), you may learn even more through adapting the technique to rehearsing, with other adults who share them, problems that are particularly pertinent to you as an adult.

## WHO WOULD YOU LIKE TO BE . . . ?

**Participants:** A small group of children, five to six years and older, and an adult. Some younger children whose command of spoken language is very good may also enjoy participating.

**Explanation:** Just as the younger child defined who she was through observing others and "trying on" their roles, the child this age continues to gather material for her own definition of self through comparing and matching herself up against others. The following are examples of some ways to make this process more accessible to the child's awareness so that she can become better able to consciously evaluate, in terms of her growing ideas about who she is, those behaviors she might otherwise tend to adopt unconsciously as habits.

1. Sit down on the floor in a circle with a small group of children. Ask them all to think about people they know, have heard about, seen on TV or in a movie, or read about. Then ask them who, among all the people in the world they know or know of, they would most like to change places with if they could. After you've given them a chance to think, ask the children, one at a time, to give you their answers to this question.

2. As the children answer, try to get them to explore their reasons—what it is about the people they chose that they like enough to want to trade lives and identities with them. Help the children really to carry their ideas out as far as they can. Help them fill in the gaps about their choices, trying to define what they would gain and what they would

have to give up. Guide them to consider the advantages as well as the disadvantages of becoming the person with whom they say they'd like to exchange places. Wait until all the children have had their turn, and then tell them who you would like to be. Let them ask you questions like those you asked them, and be honest (with yourself and them) in your responses.

3. Ask the children who they would dress up like for a "Come as you'd like to be" party. Again, help the children, through leading questions (but not ones that are biased in a particular direction), to look at the reasons for their choices. If a child, on any of these activities, says that she doesn't want to trade with or be anybody else, that's fine, too; just explore with her the reasons for that decision. When the children have finished their explanations, share with them your choice and your reasons.

4. Ask the children who they would want to be if they were all alone (1) in a spaceship to another world, (2) on the desert, (3) in a ship at sea, (4) in the woods, and so on. You and the children can think up many more possibilities of places you could be stranded by yourself. Ask them also, after this series of questions, who they'd most like to have with them in these situations. As with the other activities, encourage the children to explain *why* they made the choices they did. And remember to take your turn too.

**Purpose:**   To give children (and adults) the opportunity to explore, in their minds, the idea of being someone other than who they are, thus beginning to clarify what qualities they most admire in others and why. In some cases, this can be used to help the child adopt for herself (or recognize, already existent, in herself) some of the behaviors she would like to have. In others, it will be helpful for the children to look realistically and thoroughly at their own and others' roles in life.

Many adults spend time wishing they were someone else or envying others' lives without ever taking the time to explore that idea completely. They never think about what that person's *whole* life, from the inside out, might really be like, and what they'd have to give up in order to be someone other than themselves. If you can guide children at this age to begin to look thoughtfully at their fantasies, you can help them learn to use them productively. You can help them integrate aspects of their fantasies into their own real lives rather than simply retaining them as idle, unexplored dreams of what might be.

Further, this kind of activity helps stimulate children's imaginations and creative thinking. For example, deciding who you would want to be and why if you were alone in a spaceship to another world compared to your choice if you were alone on the desert, and so on, requires the children to give serious thought to what characteristics and skills might be useful in each of those situations.

Finally, these activities give you and the children practice in making and justifying choices, two essential human skills. The failure to make choices or making them by default (by just accepting things as they are without question) is at least partially responsible for many adults' failure to grow and for many of their inhuman behaviors. Making choices is very hard for children this age and can cause behavior problems when quick or definite decisions are required. This activity is a fun, neutral arena in which the children can practice making choices *if* you are patient, accepting, and don't rush them.

**Variation:**   In addition to activities such as these which stimulate its participants to explore what it might be like to be someone else, try a game whose focus is helping the players examine their own ideal images of themselves.

Ask the children to pretend they are grown up and to imagine what they're like—what things are most important to them, how they behave toward others, what their favorite activities are, what kinds of people they most like to be with, what kind of work they do, and so on. Try the game once with you and the children describing how you imagine you *will* be in twenty years. Then, try it again imagining yourselves in twenty years as you'd most like to be, as if you were everything you could hope to be.

Try, also, both kinds of self-analysis in terms of the present time: Ask the children to describe themselves as they think they are now. Then, later, ask them to describe themselves as they wish they were.

Help the children, in your discussions, to explore (1) the accuracy of their self-perceptions, and (2) the influence, on their ideal self-image, of other people's expectations of them. You'll set the tone for sharing openly and exploring these important aspects of self-concept by your own full and honest participation in the discussions.

## THIS IS HOW I FEEL TODAY

**Participants:**   A five- to six-year-old or older child, and an adult to help in preparation of materials.

**Materials:**   Cardboard or oaktag, posterboard, scissors, magic marker, brass fasteners, clear contact paper, scotch tape, a wall hook, pencil, string, and a ruler.

**Explanation:**   Children this age, especially as the year wears on, seem to become increasingly subject to abrupt mood swings. In addition to helping your child understand his low moods better through talking and otherwise enabling him to express the way he feels (See "What Can You Do When You're Feeling Low?" Four to Five Years, page 224), it might be helpful for him to have some mechanism through which he could let people know how he's feeling so they can adjust their expectations of and responses to him accordingly. Following are suggestions for making such a device.

1. Suggest to your child that you think it might be a good idea for him to have a picture to put on his door that would let you know how he's feeling (i.e., if he's feeling happy, sad, tired, or angry). If he seems receptive to the idea, offer to help him make it.

2. On a piece of plain paper, show your child how to draw a cartoon-like face whose emotional expression you can change by varying the smile, eyebrows, or eyelids (see the faces on the "Feelings Chart").[1] Then give him some paper and a crayon or magic marker, and suggest that he try for a few days drawing you pictures to let you know how he feels. Give him some scotch tape, also, to put his pictures up on his door or somewhere else that you'll see them.

[1] To learn how to draw cartoon faces, people, objects, and scenes in easy, systematic steps, see Dan O'Neill, Marian O'Neill, and Hugh O'Neill Jr., *The Big Yellow Drawing Book* (Nevada City, Calif.: Hugh O'Neill & Associates, 1974).

3. If the idea catches on, and your child seems to respond well to it, offer to help him make a picture that would be more permanent—a kind of chart with choices of different faces on which he could indicate which face portrays his mood. If he thinks that's a good idea, offer to help him.

4. Show your child how to make a compass with a pencil and a piece of string that he can use to draw circles. Show him how to use a ruler to measure off about nine inches of string for a big circle to make the chart with. Once he's set up his compass, have him practice using it to draw circles on paper. When he's got the knack of it, then have him draw his big circle on a piece of cardboard or posterboard and cut it out.[2]

5. Next, have your child decide which emotional expressions he wants on his chart and, on that basis, determine how many and what size small circles to make for faces. Then, either using a shorter piece on your makeshift compass or by tracing around a cup or some other round object, help your child draw and cut out of oaktag small circles for the faces. Suggest to him that he draw the faces first in pencil to make sure they're what he wants, and then to go over them in magic marker.

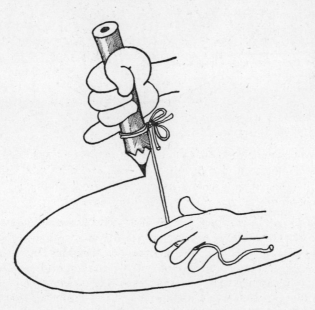

[2] At any stage along the way, if your child asks you to do something for him, do so; otherwise, let him do it himself. The project doesn't have to be finished in one sitting; it can be extended over as long a period of time as it takes to complete it.

6. Now it's time to put the chart together. Help your child decide first what he wants to write at the top. Suggest "This is how I feel today," but accept whatever he decides upon since it's going to be *his* chart. Next, help him arrange the faces around the big circle so that there's enough room for all of them and they're evenly spaced. Help him use the ruler to check on the spacing. Show him how to trace around each face lightly with a pencil so that he'll know where to paste it down. Then, have him paste them all onto the large circle and print his title at the top. You can help with that, if necessary, by sketching out the words lightly in pencil for him to fill in with magic marker himself.

7. Once that part is done, and the paste has dried, help your child measure and cut out a large enough piece of clear contact paper to cover both sides of his chart. Then help him with the contact paper, making sure it doesn't get wrinkles or bubbles when you put it on. Have him use scissors to trim off the excess around the big circle.

8. Help your child use the ruler to measure how big an arrow he needs; it should be long enough to reach from the center of the big circle to the edges of the faces. Then show him how to draw it, and help him, if necessary, to cut the arrow head. cover the arrow with clear contact paper, make a hole in the middle of the big circle and the end of the arrow (*You* do it, with an awl or an icepick.), and insert the brass fastener to connect the arrow to the circle. Your child now has a feelings chart.

9. Punch another hole at the top, and hang the chart up with a wall hook on his door or somewhere else that he chooses, putting it at such a height that he can move the arrow with ease.

**Purpose:** To give your child a mechanism through which he can communicate quickly and graphically how he's feeling. This can be used to enable others to gear their behavior toward him accordingly, learning to understand, for example, that if he gets very upset over some small thing, it probably is more closely related to his general mood than to the particular thing he's focusing on. This, in turn, can help you and other family members not to take his occasionally unreasonable behaviors personally and thus keep you from feeding his acting-out behavior by becoming emotionally tied up in it.

It can also help you to know when he's most accessible to talking about issues that have been creating problems for him and others. It's rarely productive to talk about emotionally-charged issues when a child is feeling the anger or unhappiness. If you wait until you see a happy face, you'll find a far more receptive child, and you'll be able to get through to him so you can help him learn to handle and reduce his low moods.

Further, this kind of technique can be very useful in helping your child become more aware of his moods, the first step toward dealing effectively with them. Finally, the process of making the feeling chart can be a lesson, not only in learning to express feelings through drawings that others can interpret, but also in measurement, counting, and writing.

## WORKING TOGETHER

**Participants:** Pairs of children five to six years old and an adult to explain the games and help with the materials. This type of activity is good for older children in the first grades of school also.

**Materials:** Wooden beads of different colors and shapes; paper and different-color pencils, crayons, and felt-tip markers; pieces of felt to put together as faces—large round pieces, eyes of different colors and shapes, different kinds of ears (e.g., cat ears, dog ears, rabbit ears, people ears), mouths with different expressions, etc.; wooden blocks of different colors; parquetry blocks; Potato Head dolls; cardboard, pictures and photographs of people and animals, glue, scissors.

**Explanation:** Young children, especially those whose language background has been chiefly with people who share their experience and with whom they can thus use a kind of verbal shorthand, have a tendency to use a lot of vague and nonspecific words (e.g., "Put this one here and that one there."). They need to learn to use more specific words with which they can communicate effectively to another person about things that are not present and which do not assume that the listener has the same information as they have. Following are a few exercises to help children develop this skill:

1. Set up an area for the pairs of children to work in so that one member cannot see the other's work. Small portable study carrels can be purchased through most school supply distributors, or the children can simply sit, back to back, at separate tables. You should participate in the game, too, pairing up with one of the children.

2. Stringing beads.
   a. Give each child a long shoelace and a set of beads, including the same number of each color and shape, e.g., six round beads for each child, one red, one orange, one yellow, one green, one blue, and one purple; six square beads the same colors; and six oblong beads, the same colors. Make sure both children can describe each shape and color accurately; remove any beads that either child cannot identify and name.

b. Explain to the children that you want one of them to string her beads and, as she does, to tell the other one how to string his in the same way. When they're both done, they should compare their bead strings to see if they're both the same. Suggest to them that they begin with just a few and then get more complex as they practice.

c. Also, let them try having one child put together her entire set first and *then* tell the other how to put his together. Another way to play the game is for you to make up patterns on cards (see picture for examples) for one child to use in making her own string of beads and instructing the other. The children should take turns being leader and follower. Don't forget to play yourself.

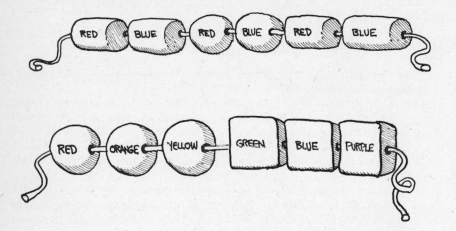

3. You and the children can play a similar game using parquetry and regular square colored blocks. This is harder than using the beads because you must attend to the positions of the blocks (next to, on top of, below, on the left side, on the right side, in the middle). In this game, also, suggest that the children start with simple patterns such as a row of blocks; you might make up some patterns on cards to get them started.

4. Drawing pictures.
   a. Give each child, and take yourself, several pieces of paper and several different-colored felt-tip markers, pencils, and crayons. The task this time is for one person to lead the other in drawing a similar picture. Here, there's need for specific language telling your partner whether to use a crayon, a pen, or a pencil, and what color, as well as what shape or figure to draw.
   b. Through trial and error on this game, the children should learn that

they have to be very specific in their drawing instructions. It's not enough, for example, to say "Draw a cat," since each child's cat is likely to be different. Try, in this activity, too, drawing some patterns on cards (see pictures for examples) for the children to use in addition to making up their own pictures.

5. Making faces.
   a. Give each participant a set of felt pieces with which she can make different kinds of faces, e.g., several different-shaped faces; several pairs of eyes, different shapes and colors; several different kinds of eyebrows; several different kinds of noses; different kinds of ears; different kinds of mouths. (See the pictures on page 256 for examples.)
   b. The goal of this activity is for the two participants to end up with the same face. This one promotes a great deal of specific vocabulary use. For example, the "leader" can start off by telling her partner what they're going to make: "We're going to make a bear. You need a large brown circle for the face." Then she must use specific words to describe body parts, their color, size, shape, and in some cases, expression (e.g., the smiling mouth, the angry eyebrows). The children (and you) can construct animal faces, people faces, or silly faces.

6. An activity similar to the one just described using felt pieces can be played using commercially produced Potato Head dolls or a similar toy using styrofoam for heads and plastic pieces for eyes, ears, mouth, and other features.

7. Mix and match "puzzles."
   a. You can buy or make[3] various kinds of three-piece puzzles consisting

---

[3] You can make such puzzles by mounting full-length pictures of people, about 2″ × 3½″, on cardboard and covering them with clear contact paper. Cut them into three pieces, top, middle, and bottom. The top should correspond to the head, the middle to the shoulders, arm, waist, and hips, and the bottom to the legs.

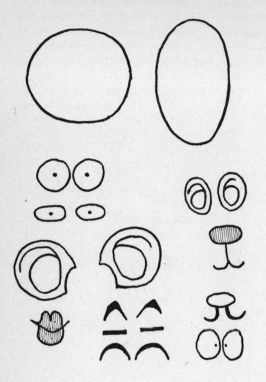

of top, middle, and bottom pieces. They may be of people dressed in different occupational uniforms (e.g., doctor, nurse, mailperson, policeperson). Be sure that they're evenly and fairly assigned to males and females, not all males and a female nurse and teacher, for example. They may be different kinds of animals dressed in silly costumes; full-length pictures of the children, themselves; or any other subject.

b. Give each pair of participants (including you and your partner) duplicate sets of one of the topics and a long piece of cardboard each, on which to set out their puzzle pictures (see illustration on page 257). Have the numbers one to ten written on top to give the children a guide to where to put together each picture. The leader must then instruct her partner to put together ten pictures in the same way she does.

c. The children can put the puzzle pieces together in a silly way, e.g., a giraffe head, an elephant body, and duck feet, or so that all the pieces match, e.g., the top, middle, and bottom pieces for a carpenter. Whichever the child decides upon, she should give specific instructions to her partner about the top, middle, and bottom pieces so that he can come out with the same combinations she has.

**Purpose:** To give children (and adults) practice working together, both directing another and following another's direction. For the "instructor," this requires the use of very specific language, helping her—through the feedback of the results of the other's work—to learn to step outside herself and realize that the other person does *not* automatically know what she's talking about.

In addition, it's an opportunity for children to increase their functional vocabulary, words they can use along with their activities. Further, each activity provides opportunities for cognitive learnings about spatial relationships; classification according to size, shape, and color; body image; people and professions; and so on.

## ATTENDING EXERCISES

**Participants:** Five- to six-year-old or older children, and adults.

**Materials:** Bright-colored masking or mending tape; paper and pencil; a bell, triangle, drum, or piano; any kind of food; a fragrant flower, perfume, and other things with strong odors.

**Explanation:** One of the characteristics of many children approaching six is a tendency to be very unfocused and easily distracted. This is accompanied by an increase in level of tension and difficulty maintaining emotional balance. The following "attending exercises" can help children this age learn to focus and relax. They also should be helpful to adults who have to live with children through this stage, providing some tools which can be used to retain composure in the face of their children's unpredictable mood swings.

1. Using bright-colored masking or mending tape, make a large circle on the floor. Walk this circular line, slowly, heel to toe, in front of your child, trying to concentrate all your attention on maintaining a smooth, regular rhythm and balance in your movement. Explain this to your child as the goal of the activity, and invite him to join you. Sometimes put on some slow, calming music to walk by. Continue until you can feel a noticeable slowing down and relaxing of your body.

2. Sit down in a comfortable place with your back straight, but not stiff, and your hands lying loosely in your lap, palms up. Breathe out through your nose, as slowly as you can, and count (one kangaroo, two

kangaroos, and so on) how long it takes you to exhale completely. Show your child how to do the same. Then, both of you should breathe in as slowly as possible, counting to see how many seconds it takes to inhale completely. After inhaling, hold your breath in as long as you can do so comfortably, and time yourself.

3. Make a note on a piece of paper what your and your child's baseline is. Then try, each time you do this activity, to increase slightly the amount of time you take to exhale, inhale, and hold in your breath. Take it at a comfortable pace, and don't strain yourselves. The purpose of the activity is to relax physically and psychologically through slowing down your breathing and increasing your intake of oxygen. Any strain would interfere with this.

4. Have your child practice writing his name. If he needs help, sketch it out dot-to-dot fashion for him to fill in (see "I Can Write," page 264, for ideas to help your child with this skill). When he's practiced for a few minutes or when he's ready to stop, ask your child to close his eyes and try to picture printing the letters of his name, one by one, in his mind. You might help by slowly spelling out his name as he tries to visualize the letters. Try it yourself with your own name.

5. Look at an object with your child, perhaps a favorite toy of his. Then, both of you close your eyes and try to picture that toy in your "mind's eye." Practice this regularly, a few minutes at a time, until you can visualize an object with ease. Can you or your child "see" colors in your mind? Try picturing a red circle, then yellow, then blue, then white, then black. After you and your child have been somewhere together, sit down and close your eyes, try to picture the place you've been, and describe it to each other. See how many details you can recall.

6. Go on a magic journey in your mind. Close your eyes, and have your child close his. Tell him a story such as the following while the two of you "enact" it inside your heads.
   a. Picture yourself in the middle of a forest. It's spring, and the weather is cool, but not cold. Everything is lush green. Under your feet there is soft moss, like a beautiful green carpet. The trees tower so tall, you can barely see their tops when you look straight up. The sun is shining brightly above the tree tops, but because the forest is so dense, the light inside is filtered. There are patches of bright sunlight dancing on the forest floor where it is able to find a space in the trees.
   b. The sounds all around you are wonderful. If you listen carefully, you can hear the songs of at least five different birds. Pause to

"listen." There are frogs chirping and croaking, insects buzzing, and little animals making the sticks and pine needles rustle under their feet as they move along the forest floor. The wind is blowing softly through the trees, and there's a faint sound of rushing water from a far-off stream.

c. There's a strong, enveloping smell of pine all around you. There are also some more delicate smells. There's a flower bed almost under your feet. Bend down, and smell the flowers. There's a fresh, spring smell, and the smell and feel of water nearby. And, if you try very hard, you can sense the smell of the animals, too, rabbits, deer, raccoons, maybe even a bear.

d. You start to walk, and you see a slight clearing in the woods. There's a little house. Look at it carefully. How big is it? What is it made of? What color is it? How many windows does it have? Walk up to the door, and knock. No answer. Look inside one of the windows. What do you see? Take turns with your child describing your house in the woods and imagining who might live there.

e. It's time to leave the forest. Take your child part way out, describing the sights, sounds, smells, and feelings around you. Then let him take you the rest of the way out and home. Then take each other to dinner. You must be very hungry after your day in the forest. Describe and imagine what you'll have to eat. Can you taste it?

f. You can make up endless "mind excursions" like this with your child, you doing some and him doing some. Try to include as many different kinds of sensory experiences as you can, to really get into and "live" the experience. And always add some parts for which each of you has to think of your own details (e.g., a surprise box, a secret room), and then tell each other what you see. As you lead each other on your "journey," go very slowly, pausing often, so that you have time to really experience what the words say, not just listen to words.[4]

7. Close your eyes and have your child close his. Tell him to think about a place that makes him feel very happy and peaceful. It can be a real place he likes (e.g., the seashore, a forest, a park, a special hiding place) or a make-believe place (e.g., floating on a cloud). You can offer some suggestions, but he should decide on his own special place. Do the same yourself. Then, tell your child to pretend that he's in that place, and he feels very happy and relaxed. Everything there is just the way he wants it to be. Imagine yourself somewhere that makes you

---

[4] This is an excellent small group activity, also. Let each child have a turn to contribute to a story you begin as well as to initiate his own.

feel that way. Explain to your child that sometimes when he's feeling upset, it may help to take a pretend "vacation" to his special place. Try it yourself; it can be very calming and therapeutic.

8. Listen to a sound with your child, e.g., a bell, a note on the piano, a tone on a triangle, a beat on a drum, and then try to continue "hearing" that sound inside your head. We do this involuntarily when commercial jingles or phrases from popular tunes we've heard keep going through our mind. *Trying* to do it requires focused attention

9. Choose one note, and "hum" that note through your nose as you exhale your breath completely. Concentrate on the sound and the vibrations in your head as you hum. Try high and low notes. Which makes you feel more relaxed? When you're feeling nervous, this is a good one to try: You may be surprised how hard it is to emit a smooth, strong, uninterrupted sound when you're physically or emotionally tense, and how it can relax you to work until you are able to do so.

10. Share some food with your child, e.g., a piece of fruit or cheese. Chew each bit very slowly, paying careful attention to how it tastes, how it feels inside your mouth, how it smells, how it feels to swallow, and so on. When you've each finished a bite, stop, close your eyes, and try to recall the experience—to "feel," "taste," and "smell" the food inside your mind. Then, eat another bite, and try again.

11. Smell a flower. Really breathe in deeply and concentrate on how it smells. Then move away from it, and try to recall its odor. Repeat this until you can begin to do so. Try other things with different kinds of odors—perfume, mustard, garlic, pine needles, leather, and so on.

**Purpose:** To give your children and yourself practice learning to focus your attention completely on one thing. This is a hard thing to do: You, perhaps even more than your child, may find all sorts of stray thoughts popping into your head when you're trying to concentrate on one of these exercises. That's to be expected, but through repeated practice, you'll both learn to focus for longer periods of time. And as you do, you'll not only be calmer and more relaxed while you're doing the exercise (because focusing causes the mind and body to relax), but each of you also should find one or more favorites that you can adapt to times when you need to calm yourself down (e.g., deep breathing, visualizing a relaxing scene).

These "attending exercises" do more than help you learn to focus your mind so you can be more relaxed. Learning to focus is an important skill in making most effective use of your energies in whatever you do. Further, many of the exercises provide practice using the part of your brain that is too often neglected in more "traditional" learning activities that concentrate on verbal ideas, logical relationships, and correct answers.

With these kinds of activities, you gain practice in "imaging"—forming sight, sound, smell, touch, taste, and movement images inside your head. It's like making conscious what you do routinely when you dream. And, especially in an activity such as "the magic journey," you are able to integrate the more structured, verbal part of your brain's functioning with the less structured, more imaginative, nonverbal part. Developing both kinds of functions, separately and in combination with one another, is important to your and your children's developing your minds to their fullest capacity.

**Variation for Adults:** In addition to these special activities, you should try to make everything you do into an "attending activity." Try to get your whole self, body and mind, in the same place at the same time. This may sould silly to you, but notice for the rest of today how often your mind wanders from what you're doing at the time. Sometimes, such as when you're washing dishes, this is a welcome release from a task that otherwise is rather boring. But, in many tasks, you can get much more done in less time and with more pleasure if you are able to concentrate all your energy on that task while you're involved in it.

You may also find that you are much calmer if you don't divide your time and energy by always doing one thing and wishing you were doing something else or being one place and wishing you were somewhere else (and in your mind, therefore, being there instead of here). If something keeps popping into your mind, make a mental note of it, and "assign" yourself some time just to attend to that subject, thus carrying the thought through and reducing its intrusive effect on your other thoughts.

## THE THING THAT SCARES ME THE MOST IS . . .

**Participants:** A small group of five- to six-year-old and older children and an adult. Some children as young as four years also may be interested in this activity.

**Explanation:** The following are a series of incomplete statements that can be used to get children talking about how they feel about people and things, fears and joys, beliefs, hopes, and so on.

1. Sit in a comfortable place with the children, and explain to them that you are going to say part of a sentence and then you want each of them to finish the sentence in *her own* way. If, at first, the children all seem to

be copying what the first child said, remind them that you want to know what each one feels, not what she feels; you already heard what she feels. Otherwise, be accepting of whatever a child says.[5]

2. After all the children have completed a sentence, spend some time talking with them about their reasons for their answers and giving them a chance to share their similarities and differences in feelings. How many of these incomplete statements you'll deal with in any one sitting will depend on the children's interest in and enjoyment of the activity and how long they spend on each statement. Follow their lead, and let them spend as long or as short a time on a particular statement as their involvement indicates.

3. The following are examples of the kinds of unfinished statements that are useful in this kind of activity:
   a. The person I like best in the world is . . .
   b. The thing that makes me happiest is . . .
   c. I wish . . .
   d. My Mommy . . .
   e. I get very mad when . . .
   f. The thing that scares me the most is . . .
   g. My Daddy . . .
   h. The thing that makes me sad is . . .
   i. My brother . . .
   j. My sister . . .
   k. My _____ got mad when . . .
   l. God . . .
   m. Sometimes I feel like . . .
   n. When I'm alone, I . . .
   o. People should . . .
   p. I don't like it when . . .
   q. When I grow up, I . . .
   r. My secret is . . .
   s. If I could have anything I wanted, I . . .
   t. Teachers . . .
   u. It makes me smile when . . .
   v. The world . . .

4. You probably can think of many more unfinished statements to use that will be specifically appropriate for you and your children. Don't forget to play yourself: The children will be interested in your feelings, and you will set the tone of sharing honestly.

[5] Be particularly patient and understanding of the child who is painfully shy, self-conscious, and reluctant to speak for herself. It will take a while for this kind of child to trust enough to really open up.

5. The only "rule" that should be followed here as in any activity is that no one should say anything in their statements or in the discussion that will hurt someone else and discourage him from feeling comfortable in freely participating in the game.

**Purpose:** To give you and the children an opportunity to explore some of your feelings about people and things through open-ended, incomplete statements that can be finished in any way a person wishes. Because the statements are so unstructured in the kind of response they ask for, they can be particularly good at bringing out each person's thoughts and feelings.

If you were playing this "game" with adults, you'd probably be inhibited by fears that your statements would be interpreted in ways you didn't mean. Young children tend, even at this somewhat inhibited and self-conscious age, to be more spontaneous and less judgmental, so you should also enjoy the opportunity to listen to your own as well as their responses to these open statements.

In addition, the activity provides the children with further language practice as they compose sensible sentences out of incomplete phrases. And most important, it enables them to put their feelings into words, good practice for us "civilized" beings who seem too often to keep the two widely separated.

## I CAN WRITE

**Participants:** Five- to six-year-old children, and an adult to help prepare materials and give initial guidance. The materials for these activities and guidance in them should also be available to children at any age who indicate an interest in learning to make letters. Some children as young as three are ready to learn; others still won't be ready at six.

**Materials:** Paper, primary pencils, cardboard, posterboard, sandpaper or sand and glue, clear contact paper, grease pencils, magic markers, white paste, pieces of celluloid the thickness of lightweight cardboard (the kind used with overhead projectors), a blackboard and chalk, cardboard or plastic alphabet and number stencils, mimeograph machine, plastic "envelopes" like those used in photograph albums, an experience chart, a hole puncher and string for "binding" homemade books.

**Explanation:** The fine motor skills required to control and coordinate a pencil to make legible marks on paper must wait until children's neuromuscular systems are ready. When that occurs varies greatly among children, and your best clue to when to help children learn to write is the children themselves.

Following are some devices you can make with and for children who have indicated, through their own crude efforts to form what they refer to as "letters," that they're ready to learn, at their own pace, to write. These devices and techniques cover a wide range of skill in writing and, for any individual child, probably a fairly long period of time and practice with each one. Every child's own rate of progress is your best clue to when to proceed to a new technique. Let him try several to begin with to determine which is best for him, and then let him practice until he's fairly skilled with that technique.

1. Initials first.
   a. For children just learning to write, start off by helping them learn to print their initials. Sit down at a table with the child to your right (or to your left if you're left-handed). Print his initials in very large capital letters[6] at the top of a big piece of paper, and note the direction in which you write the letters.
   b. Then, under the child's first initial, make a big dot and have the child place his pencil on the dot. (Start children out with fat "primary pencils," not with skinny ones like yours.) Next, going in the same direction as you do in printing the letter, make another dot for the child to join with the first one by a straight line (or curved if it's a curved letter such as an O).
   c. Do this, dot by dot, until the child has drawn the whole letter. Then do the same with his final initial. Continue to practice with the child as long as he's interested. You can also make up a sheet for the child to continue practicing on his own what he learned with your help.
   d. Using generous spacing so that the final product will be letters three to four inches high, make up an $8\frac{1}{2}'' \times 11''$ piece of plain paper with four to six dot-to-dot pictures of the child's initials. On the first one, draw arrows indicating in which direction the child should go. All those dots together on one page may be confusing to the child at first, so try enclosing each set of initials in a box by itself. Also, fill in the outlines of the letters very lightly so that it's clear which dots go together. (See illustration on page 266.)
   e. Expand your dot-to-dot technique with the child to include his whole name, his first and then his last. After you've taught him the movements for each new component, make up dot-to-dot sheets for him to do on his own that include the new element. As his coordination improves, you can try giving the child smaller-sized

---

[6] Capital letters are easier for young children to form than are small letters.

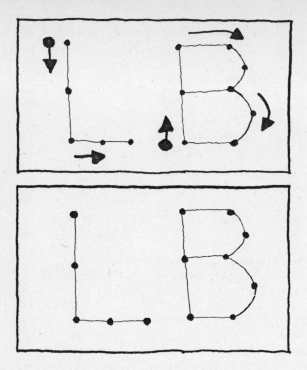

letters, but large letters requiring large movements are easier in the beginning than small ones.

2. Sandpaper letters.
   a. Buy some rough sandpaper, and cut it into large capital letters (3 to 4 inches high; see picture). Also cut out letters of heavy cardboard, and mount the sandpaper letters on them with glue. Another way of making this kind of "textured alphabet" is to cut the letters out of cardboard, cover the pieces of cardboard with glue, and cover the wet glue with sand. When the glue has dried, shake off the excess sand, and your alphabet is ready. The children can help you with the latter parts of this process.
   b. Starting with the initials of his name, guide the child's fingers (of his dominant hand) over each letter in the way he would move them in printing the letter. When he has finished feeling a letter, let the child try to print it. If he likes this activity, extend it to include his whole first name, then his last name, and later, the whole alphabet.

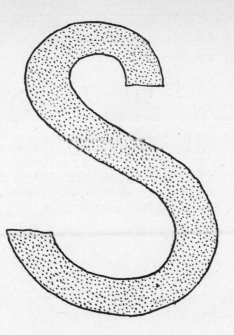

3. Groovy letters.
   a. Make a device for each child with his name etched into a piece of cardboard in large capital letters: Cut the outlines of letters into a thick piece of cardboard or cut the letters out of a thin piece of cardboard and glue it to another one. Draw arrows on each letter to show the direction in which to write.
   b. Show the children how to move their pencils within the grooves for the letters. Make sure they do it in the right direction. Talk to each child about what he's doing as he does it so that he gains a verbal memory of each letter as well as a visual and a haptic (the way the movement feels) memory. For example, *M* would be up-down-up-down.
   c. Make up several sets of these "groovy letters" of the entire alphabet, also. Do a few with the whole alphabet on one piece of cardboard and a few with each letter on a separate piece of cardboard by itself: The latter kind also can be put together by the children to make words they want to practice writing.

4. Name-writing plaque.
   a. Make up a special name-writing plaque for each child who has come this far in the writing process: Divide a heavy piece of

cardboard, about $8\frac{1}{2}'' \times 11''$ (or longer, if the child has a very long name), into two sections, each $4\frac{1}{4}'' \times 11''$. Draw a line with black magic marker between the two sections. In the bottom section, draw a dot-to-dot picture of the child's first and last names, with the individual letter outlines each about $1\frac{1}{2}''$ high. Now cover the piece of cardboard with clear contact paper.

b. Cut, out of sandpaper or some kind of textured material such as burlap, velvet, or corduroy, the letters of the child's first and last names; make them the same size as the dot-to-dot outline. Glue them on the upper portion of the plaque in a similar configuration to the outline on the bottom part. Punch a hole in the bottom left-hand side of the plaque, and tie onto it a piece of string just slightly longer than from the hole to the right-hand side of the cardboard. On the free end of the string, attach a felt-tip marker.

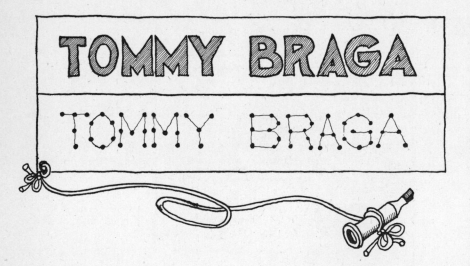

c. When the child's not using his "name plaque," show him how to hook the pen onto the side. When he wants to use it, show him how to trace over the textured letters with his fingers, and then to use the felt-tip marker to print his name by following the dots. When he's done, he can use a tissue to wipe off the ink, and he can try printing his name free-hand on a piece of paper.

5. Stencils.
   a. You can buy plastic or lightweight cardboard stencils with capital letters and numbers in most dimestores. The plastic ones will be more durable, but the cardboard ones are fine. Get enough sets that you can cut out and tape together the letters for each child's name. Give it to him to practice with and to use, until he's learned to write it free-hand, to put his name on his projects.
   b. Leave a few of the stencils whole for the children to use when they wish to practice "writing" the alphabet, and cut up a few into individual letters for them to use to write words on projects, for example, to describe what's in a picture.

6. Make up picture-and-word cards for the children to use for practicing writing the names of familiar objects and events. On top of the card, draw or paste a picture. Underneath the picture, draw a dot-to-dot or stencil version of the name of the object or activity portrayed in the picture. Cover the card with clear contact paper. Then, the children can use them to write on with a felt-tip pen or grease pencil and can wipe the card clean when they're done.

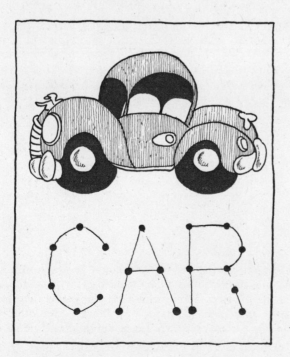

7. On pieces of celluloid, paint words in which the children have indicated interest in learning to write. Attach pictures above the words to remind the children what the word says. As in the activity above, they can use a grease pencil to write over the painted words and then wipe their writing off with a tissue when they're done.

8. Mimeographed sheets.
   a. If you have access to a mimeograph machine, you can prepare some mimeographed sheets for the children to use on their own for practicing writing. Make one for each child who is learning to write. Put on it his first and last name, and a few favorite words with accompanying pictures: Do all the words in dot-to-dot fashion so that the child can fill them in. Remember to pencil in, very lightly, between the dots so that the child can distinguish letters from each other.
   b. Make multiple copies of each child's own sheet so that he can practice with them whenever he wishes. Some children may enjoy trading sheets with each other, too. In addition, do some sheets for all the children with the alphabet and the numbers one to twenty in dot-to-dot form.

9. Blackboard games.
   a. Blackboard activities can be used to give children practice writing, also. With a small group of children who know the alphabet, play a game in which you write a partial alphabet on the board, leaving blanks for letters you've omitted. Let the children take turns coming to the board and filling in the missing letters.
   b. Another game is to start the alphabet by writing A. Then, have each child add a letter. When they're practiced at doing it this way, try starting in the middle of the alphabet and working backward as well as forward.
   c. Use the blackboard, also, to give the children practice copying words: Ask them to give you a word: Write it on the board, and ask for a volunteer to come up and copy it.

10. Children's books.
    a. Help children write their own stories before they can do so free hand: Transcribe, word-for-word, stories they tell you, and write them out in dot-to-dot fashion for them to fill in. Do some stories with a group of children, then mimeograph copies for everyone, and do some for individual children.
    b. As you collect more stories, make books out of them with the names of the contributors included, and cover the "pages" with the kind

of plastic sheets used in photo albums. Then, the children can practice *writing* their own story, on the plastic, filling in the dot-to-dot letters with a grease pencil and wiping it off when they're done.

c. Observe the children in play or on field trips, also, and take notes of conversations between them (word for word). Then, make up "workbooks" for them that picture them (in photographs or drawings) doing whatever they were doing at the time and with balloons from their heads containing their conversations, as in a cartoon or a fumente.

d. Write their conversations in dot-to-dot style on mimeographed sheets, and bind them in a book like that just described with the sheets inside plastic "envelopes" that the children can write on. Make up a master, perhaps on an experience chart or as a mural done with the children that they can consult as a model.

e. Scrapbook projects done by the children can contain one word, a phrase, or a short sentence about the picture written underneath in dot-to-dot fashion for the children to fill in, or with a space for letters underneath your model for the children to copy freehand.

**Purpose:** To give children who indicate interest in (and therefore readiness for) writing, some tools and devices that they can use to gain practice and skill in the fine motor control and coordination needed to manage a pencil and form letters.

Some children will be eager to learn to write as young as three years, and they should be helped to do so. Others may show no interest at all any time in the preschool years; their judgment also should be respected. Writing, like all other skills, should be learned as an exciting and self-chosen, self-directed activity, never as a task that causes problems, frustrations, and feelings of failure.

**Variation:** Practicing the movements to form letters is easier (and more fun) using substances such as sand, sugar, clay, peanut butter, or honey to write in than it is to write on paper. These substances provide just the right amount of resistance to the child's movements that he can control them; sand, sugar, and salt offer less than the others, so start off with clay, peanut butter, or honey. Fill shallow cake or cookie tins each with one of these substances, and show the children how to form letters with their forefingers and then with a stick the size of a primary pencil (holding the stick like a pencil).

## *WHOM DO YOU BELIEVE?*

**Participants:** A small group of five- to six-year-old children and an adult. This game can be played also with older children.

**Explanation:** This is a critical stage in children's development of strength of conviction in their own ideas—learning to say what they mean, mean what they say, and stand by it. Because of their increased self-consciousness at this time, many children this age become more hesitant to assert themselves and more reliant on others' opinions. The following activity can give them practice in sticking by their own ideas.

1. Sit in a circle with a small group of children. Explain to them that you would like one of them to volunteer to answer some simple questions. Explain, further, that when the other children hear you ask the question, you want them to yell out answers to "help" the child who is it (as the audiences do on some TV game shows). If you point your thumb up, you want them to yell out the right answer and tell the child she's right when she gives that answer. If you point your thumb down, they should yell out anything but the right answer and tell the child she's wrong even if she does give the right answer.

2. Have the child who has volunteered to be "it" stand in front of you facing the other children so she can't see your thumb signals. Ask her a question such as "What color is an apple?" or "How many feet does a dog have?" If the child answers correctly, give a thumb-down signal to the group and see if she changes her answer. Repeat the process with a few more questions, alternating between having the group yell out right or wrong answers in such a way that the child won't be able to predict it.

3. Have the child sit down with the rest of the group. Talk with all of them about how they feel when their opinion is different from others—do they change their mind or stick to it? Does it depend on the situation? Do they get confused? What about the child who was "it?" How did she respond to people telling her she was right or wrong, to their yelling out answers?

4. Repeat the exercise until all the children have gotten a chance to be "it." Ask for a volunteer to be the teacher while you play "it," too. Make the questions harder as the children gain more practice at the

game, and let the children take turns asking as well as answering questions. Take time after each child's turn to talk about how the other children's behavior affected her response.

5. Once the children understand the game and have learned to stick to their own answers, vary the game somewhat: Change the nature of the questions so that there really is not a clear-cut right or wrong answer. In particular, include questions that are likely to provoke differing opinions and beliefs from the children, e.g., "Who's smarter, girls or boys?" Don't coach the children now with thumb signals; just tell them to agree or disagree with the child who's "it" in terms of their own beliefs.

6. Now that the "rules" are changed, you need to guide the children to be flexible in shifting gears to a slightly different strategy when they're playing "it." With these kinds of questions, the child who is "it" should be encouraged to listen to others and weigh their opinions against her own before reaching a conclusion since there is no right or wrong answer, per se.

7. You should be able to bring this out through discussions with the children following the question-and-answer sessions. You might open the discussion by asking "What was different about this question?" "Did you have more or less trouble sticking to your own answers?" and so on.

**Purpose:** To help children develop intrinsic motivation—an "inner supreme court" that guides their behavior and decision-making. It is necessary and important that we all be concerned about one another's opinions, beliefs, and feelings and that we learn cooperative methods for solving mutual problems. But the competitive orientation that pervades our society (and is reflected in and reinforced by an advertising establishment which is continuously selling us, from an early age, things we don't need with promises that they'll make us popular with others) actually works against our having a *healthy* concern for others. And worse, it discourages the development of personal conviction that can withstand pressure to be acceptable to others, so essential in making moral choices.

Children need to learn early to listen to others' input thoughtfully, but always to be their own final judge of what is right for them (as long as it does harm to no one else). This is an artificial game that can be used to bring some of these issues into the open, and you may be surprised at how insightful young children are about these issues when you're open to discussing them. But, in addition to this kind of game, it is important that you encourage the children in day-to-day experiences to learn to rely on their own inner supreme court to guide them in making decisions and sticking by them.

Don't forget the importance of your model to the children in encouraging them to give careful consideration to others' opinions, but to develop a sense of confidence in their own judgment after having considered alternative interpretations of issues and questions. Your participation with them in the game plus your general orientation to decision-making in relation to routine matters in the classroom (or home) will have a strong influence on their behavior in this area.

## WHERE DO YOU STAND?

**Participants:** A small group of five- to six-year-old children and an adult. This activity will continue to be useful for older children in the early grades in school.

**Explanation:** The previous activity, "Whom Do You Believe?" is an exercise to help children this age learn to formulate and stick by their own answers to questions they or others raise. This activity goes a little further in giving children practice taking a stand and defending it, having first thoroughly investigated and considered the alternative answers to the question before making a commitment to one consistent with their own inner valuing system.

1. Sit in a semicircle with the children, and have one person at a time (you included) take a turn sitting in a chair or on the floor facing the others. Each person must choose, when it is his turn to be "it," an issue of importance to him that he wishes to "take a stand" on. The other members of the group each are allowed to ask him several questions intended to explore or challenge the stand he's taking.

2. You might explain the game best by being the first "it." Some ideas for issues that might appeal to you and the children are: Should they be allowed to go to the bathroom without being accompanied by an adult? Who should decide what activities they will engage in or toys they should play with each day? What kind of punishment should be given for hitting another child? Should they take a nap every day? Should boys and girls be treated differently? You can probably think of many more that are specifically relevant to you and your children. Let the children take the lead in deciding what issues they'd like to consider.

3. Help the children see, through your example when you are "it," that the person who is "it" shouldn't just decide an answer and then stick with it, no matter what. Through listening and responding to the others' questions and comments, it's possible and advisable to change or

adjust your stand if your argument does not appear to you to have been well thought out before and if the discussion has helped you examine it more thoughtfully. But, then, once you have considered all the various points of view and decided upon one that seems right to you, *then* you should stick by it, defend it, and behave in accordance with it.

4. You may need to give the children a little coaching at first on the kinds of questions to ask the person who's "it" in order to get him to clarify where he stands on the issue. For example, it sometimes works better to ask "What is your reason , , , ?" than to ask "Why . . . ?" A question such as "What would you do if somebody hit you?" coupled with another asking "What do you think the teacher should do if you hit another child?" can help a child look at the issue from different angles.

**Purpose:**   To give the children and you practice in developing effective valuing skills—the process of gathering as much information as possible on all sides of an issue and weighing it until you arrive at a conclusion that you can feel confidence in and commitment to, that you will be willing to stand by and support with behavior that reflects that commitment.

**Variation:**   Once the children understand how the game works, you can begin to have them try taking controversial stands on world issues: Sometimes they can take a stand consistent with their own beliefs, and sometimes they can take a stand different from what they themselves actually believe to be true in order to try to put themselves in another's shoes by looking at it through the other's "eyeglasses." You might also try having a small group of children divide into two groups and "debate" an issue between them in the same way.

## LET'S PRETEND

**Participants:**   Five- to six-year-old children and an adult. Some children as young as three years may enjoy the simpler parts of the activity.

**Explanation:**   "Pretending" to be someone or something else is a good release for children in this overly self-conscious stage, and it provides food for the imagination as well. This activity has unlimited possibilities; you can pretend to be anything, animate or inanimate, and it's something you should do with the children often.

1. Getting into the mood.
   a. Clear an indoor space large enough that each child can sit or lie down on the floor without bumping into the next child. Have the children stand to begin with. Tell them to pretend they are rag dolls. Use a Raggedy Ann or Andy or another kind of rag doll to show the children how floppy a rag doll looks.
   b. Using a slow, soothing, relaxing tone and tempo of voice, "talk" the children into relaxation until they are hanging loosely and limply from their waists, e.g., "Your whole body is loose and limp. Your arms and legs, your neck, even your waist, are all floppy. Your body feels completely relaxed, just like a rag doll."
   c. Some of the children will be able to do this exercise easily with no more direction than this, and by this stage they will be so relaxed and floppy that they may end up in a pile on the floor. Others still will remain standing very stiffly. Help those children by having them relax one limb at a time until, for example, when you pick up their arms and let go of them, they flop to the side.
   d. These children may be able to relax best by lying down. Show them how to "talk" to each part of their body, telling it to relax ("Relax toes; feet relax, etc."), and waiting a few seconds while they feel that part of their body start to release its tension. Start them off, then let them finish, and you can come back and check to see how they're doing. This relaxation exercise becomes increasingly more effective the more you practice until you really can feel each separate part of your body noticeably relax as you "talk" to it. Try it yourself: You can do it standing up too, any time you're in a tense situation, to calm yourself down.

2. When all the children seem loose and relaxed, you're ready to proceed with the activity.
   a. Say to the children: "Pretend you're a tiny, tiny seed in the ground. Make yourself as little as you can." Continue this with verbal coaching while you take part, too, until you and all the children have "made yourselves tiny."
   b. Then, say "Now you are growing. You are a green leaf sprouting from the ground." . . . "You are a flower. You are reaching up to the sun, and now you're taking a bath in the rain. You are blowing in the wind." "Show me how you can grow." . . . "Now you're getting bigger. The years are passing, and you're becoming a tree." . . . "You are a wise old tree. Your trunk is strong, and your branches reach to the sky. The wind blows through your leaves, but you stand firm and strong."
   c. Go very slowly, pausing between the "stages of growth," to give yourself and the children a chance to really "grow" and to

"become" a leaf, a flower, a tree. There is no right or wrong way to do these exercises. Each child should do it as she feels it.

d. If the children are watching and copying you, encourage them to concentrate on really "being" what they're portraying; you'll do it the way *you* feel it, and they each should do it the way *they* feel it. If there are any children who still are particularly stiff or self-conscious, you might help by holding their hands, talking just to them, and helping them to "grow."

3. Another example.

a. Say to the children: "Pretend you are a caterpillar, moving along a twig." [7] . . . "You are hungry for a leaf." . . . "Now you have found a leaf and you are eating. You're a very noisy eater." . . . "Now it's time for you to build your house for the winter. There are silk threads coming from your mouth. Use them to build a cocoon around yourself; then go to sleep." . . . "Winter's over. It's time for you to come out of your cocoon. Are you a butterfly or a moth? Fly away."

b. Go slowly with your words, giving yourself and the children a chance to fully act out each stage. You don't have to use these exact words; just tell a good story the children can become involved with. Never criticize or correct a child's portrayal of whatever she's pretending to be. And if you're giving out praise, be sure to have a kind word to say to each child, not just to a few. At this insecure age, especially, lack of praise when others are receiving it can be viewed as silent criticism.

**Purpose:** To give the children (and yourself) a chance to practice developing concepts about the world through the use of active fantasy—using dramatic play to "become" different things and events in their world.

Make-believe is one of the ways children represent ideas. It is a powerful source of learning because it involves the whole child, from the inside out, unlike language (the adult's most prevalent system of representing experience), which is known more from the outside in. This activity also helps, however, to build vocabulary as the children learn to connect new words and their own bodily actions that go with those words (e.g., a "slithering" worm, a "sprouting" leaf).

Further, it serves as an excellent release and escape valve, especially needed by children in this age group, for whom the pressures of the "real world" are sometimes overwhelming. It can take their minds off mundane

[7] Clearly, it would be helpful for the children to have the opportunity to observe whatever they're pretending to be to get some idea of what that thing is like. Filmstrips and movies can be used, too, especially to show something like the transformation of a caterpillar into a butterfly or moth.

anxieties about themselves, their relationship to others, and their place in the world, helping them to relax and become less painfully self-conscious.

## Variations:

1. Suggest pantomime ideas to the children based on animal communica tions, e.g., bees "telling" other bees about a new patch of flowers, a chameleon telling another chameleon to stay out of his territory, a mommy and daddy bird teaching a baby bird to fly.

2. Have the children watch *Sesame Street*, animal shows, and other information-giving TV programs as sources of pretend activity ideas.

3. Try using some of the children's favorite stories as material for pantomime.

4. Have one child pretend to be some object in the room and let the others try to guess what she is.

5. Encourage the children to work together in groups, each pretending to be one part of a mechanical object such as an electric can opener or a toaster.

6. Let the children take turns directing the others in pretend activities.

7. Always give the children a chance to just pretend to be anything they wish. Although at this age, they often are reassured by some structure from outside, once they've practiced enough that they have the idea, they may then prefer to choose for themselves what they want to pretend to be.

# To the Reader

Thank you for your participation in the activities we've offered in this book. We would like to invite your further involvement. We'd like to hear from you about your experiences doing the activities—which ones worked well for you, what directions you took them in as a result of your own and your children's spontaneous responses, ways in which you improvised new activities using the ones in the book as springboards for your own ideas, surprising things you found out about yourself and your children, and so on.

We'd particularly appreciate your sharing any activities you've invented or adapted which you think others could benefit from. Send us your comments, ideas, and favorite activities, and we'll send you a rainbow for your pocket made by The Rainbowman, Thom Klika, the artist responsible for this book's cover.

We hope that the insights gained from participation in the activities with your children may help you not only to guide them in their growth, but also to continue your own growth as a human being.

*Joe and Laurie Braga*

Department of Psychiatry
University of Miami Medical School
Miami, Florida 33152

**279**

# Resources

# Resources

The activities in *Children and Adults* emphasize children and adults learning and growing together, particularly in the area of social and emotional development. There are many good resources available which feature or include activities for preschool children in areas such as pre-reading skills, arts and crafts, pre-math skills, dramatic play, and the like. The following annotated list includes books, journals, magazines, pamphlets, and news-letters which are sources of activities for you and your children. Many, in addition to providing suggestions of games and activities, also supply instructions, patterns, or "recipes" for making equipment and materials for children's play. Some of the resources are intended particularly for children with special learning problems, though their activities are also appropriate for normal children. An asterisk next to a resource indicates that it is one that has been of particular use to parents and teachers with whom we've worked.

## BOOKS

APPALACHIAN REGIONAL COMMISSION, *Programs for Infants and Young Children, Part IV: Facilities and Equipment.* Washington, D.C.: Appalachian Regional Commission (1966 Connecticut Ave., N.W.), 1970.

Notes practical and educational considerations in designing space and purchasing equipment and materials to furnish programs for infants, toddlers, or preschoolers. Includes checklist for indoor and outdoor equipment and supplies for every program aspect, and gives patterns for making equipment.

AHR, A. EDWARD AND BENITA SIMONS. *Parent Handbook: Developing Your Child's Skills and Abilities at Home*, 1968. Priority Innovations, Inc., P.O. Box 792, Skokie, Ill. 60076.
Activities for parents to do at home and on excursions with their children to help them develop language, motor, and conceptual skills.

ARNOLD, ARNOLD, *The World Book of Children's Games.* Greenwich, Conn.: Fawcett Publications, Inc., 1972.
Hundreds of indoor and outdoor games for children from preschool through elementary school age, adapted from age-old children's games from all over the world.

ASCHEIM, SKIP, *Materials for the Open Classroom.* New York: Dell, 1973.
A catalog of games and materials; gives supplies, equipment, and ideas for using them, all in a context of promoting children's own self-directed learning. For kindergarten through the elementary school years.

* BECK, JOAN, *How to Raise a Brighter Child.* New York: Trident Press, 1967.
Explains ways parents can stimulate their children's intellectual development (from birth to six years), while presenting learning opportunities in a way that shows respect for children's interests, attention span, and emotional reactions. Includes section on teaching children to read.

BIBER, BARBARA, EDNA SHAPIRO, AND DAVID WICKENS, *Promoting Cognitive Growth: A Developmental-Interaction Point of View*, 1971.
Available from the Publications Dept., National Association of Young Children, 1834 Connecticut Ave., N.W., Washington, D.C. 20009. (Ask for a list of their other publications, also.) Explains educational goals for the preschool years, general approaches to meeting those goals, and specific elements of classroom structure, teacher attitude, selection of materials, and the like.

BLAKE, MARY ELIZABETH, *Day Care Aides: A Guide for In-Service Training* (2nd ed.), 1972. National Federation of Settlements and Neighborhood Centers, 232 Madison Ave., N.Y., N.Y. 10016.
Gives pointers on how to approach the training of day care aides as well as ideas, materials, and resources to help aides learn about children's socio-emotional and learning needs. Includes many suggestions of quiet and active games, art and music activities, finger plays, and other things to do with children. Particularly useful are short anecdotes of typical problem situations and alternative ways of handling them.

* BLAND, JANE COOPER, *Art of the Young Child.* New York: The Museum of Modern Art, 1968.
Describes stages children three to five years go through in developing their creative potential, and explains how adults can help, including what kinds of materials, spaces, and opportunities they should provide for children.

* BRAGA, JOSEPH, AND LAURIE BRAGA, *Child Development and Early Childhood Education: A Guide for Parents and Teachers.* Chicago: Office of the Mayor and Model Cities/CCUO, 1973. Available from Model Cities Public Information Service, 640 N. LaSalle, Chicago, Ill. 60610.
Describes the characteristics of infants (birth to two years) and young children (two to five years) and suggests activities to help them develop. Includes appendices to guide selection of toys and materials for different-age children and to lead the reader to further resources relating to children.

* BRAGA, JOSEPH, AND LAURIE BRAGA, *Growing with Children*. Englewood Cliffs, N.J.: Prentice-Hall, Inc., 1974.
A guide to the growth of self-concept in the early childhood years. Explains how children develop, what they need at different stages from birth to six years, and how adults can best meet those needs while growing, themselves, through the understandings and insights they gain about human development from participation in children's growth.

* BRAGA, LAURIE, AND JOSEPH BRAGA, *Learning and Growing: A Guide to Child Development*. Englewood Cliffs, N.J.: Prentice-Hall, Inc., 1975.
Explains how to recognize the specific capabilities and limitations of children at each stage of growth from birth to age five. Detailed developmental information is integrated with suggestions of activities to stimulate growth in the areas of motor, language, cognitive, and socio-emotional development. An extensive resource chapter is included.

BYRNE, MARGARET, *The Child Speaks: A Speech Improvement Program for Kindergarten and First Grade*. New York: Harper & Row, Publishers, 1965.
Stories and games, organized according to difficulty level in producing different sounds, to use in giving children practice with different speech sounds.

COLE, ANN, CAROLYN HAAS, FAITH BUSHNELL, AND BETTY WEINBERGER, *I Saw a Purple Cow and 100 Other Recipes for Learning*. Boston: Little, Brown, and Company, 1972.
Activities and games for preschool and older children using common household materials and everyday experiences; includes things to make and things to do; simple, easy-to-read format with lots of illustrations.

CANEY, STEVEN, *Toy Book*. New York: Workman Publishing Company, 1972.
Contains instructions for making toys for and with children three years and up; emphasis is on toys which promote and enable discovery and creativity. Other activities books published by Workman: *Steven Caney's Playbook*, 1975, *Snips and Snails and Walnut Whales*, 1975, and *Growing Up Green,* 1973. Write for their catalog.

COPELAND, RICHARD, *How Children Learn Mathematics: Teaching Implications of Piaget's Research*. New York: The Macmillan Company, 1970.
Explains how young children, preschool and school age, learn mathematical concepts and operations in relation to their developmental level at different stages. Relates this to what can be presented and how to enable children to learn in ways that are consistent with the way their mind works at the time.

* CRATTY, BRYANT, *Active Learning: Games to Enhance Academic Abilities*. Englewood Cliffs, N.J.: Prentice-Hall, Inc., 1971.
Over 100 active movement activities to teach reading, writing, memory, and math skills. For normal children from three to six years old or older mentally retarded children; gives age guidelines and special instructions for physically handicapped children. Includes exercises to help hyperactive children relax and learn greater self-control of their movements and moods.

* CROFT, DOREEN, AND ROBERT HESS, *An Activities Handbook for Teachers of Young Children*. Boston: Houghton Mifflin Company, 1972.
Hundreds of very creative, easy-to-follow activities for preschool children in such areas as language, prescience, art, music, dramatic play, creative movement, premath, and cooking. Companion volume by Hess and Croft, *Teachers of Young Children*, a basic introductory text in early childhood education, gives a context for the activities; but the activities book easily stands by itself.

DODSON, FITZHUGH, *How to Parent*. New York: New American Library, 1971.
Describes the first five years of life and suggests activities for different stages. Section on discipline contains practical and humane suggestions. Appendices explain how to choose

toys, materials, books, and records for children and give annotated lists of books about children.

DUMAS, ENOCH, *Math Activities for Child Involvement.* Boston: Allyn & Bacon, Inc., 1971.
Activities for making math fun and meaningful to children in kindergarten through the elementary school years. Includes notes of things parents can do at home. Stresses making math a part of children's lives, using everyday experiences to develop math activities.

EDUCATIONAL FACILITIES LABORATORIES, INC. *Found Spaces and Equipment.* New York: EFL (477 Madison Ave.), 1972.
Shows how various early childhood education programs have transformed discarded, overlooked, and inexpensive spaces and objects into useful places and things for learning.

* ENGEL, ROSE, WILLIAM REID, AND DONALD RUCKER, *Language Development Experiences for Young Children.* Los Angeles, Calif.: Dept. of Exceptional Children, School of Education, Univ. of So. Calif., 1966.
Hundreds of activities of all types for normal and handicapped preschool children. Includes summaries of developmental characteristics of children at different ages, and notes special considerations for children with different kinds of special problems (e.g., hard of hearing, blind, physically handicapped).

GARMAN, CHARLOTTE, *Pennsylvania Kindergarten Guide.* Harrisburg, Pa.: Pennsylvania Dept. of Education (Box 911), 1969.
A guide to setting up and running a kindergarten class, including explanations of the role of teachers, types and areas of experience needed by children, materials, and simple activities.

* GESELL, ARNOLD, AND FRANCES ILG, *Infant and Child in the Culture of Today* (rev. ed.). New York: Harper & Row Publishers, 1974.
Reviews the developmental characteristics of children from birth to five years, giving a behavior profile and outlining a typical day. Sections from 18 months to 4 years include cultural and creative activities, nursery behavior, and nursery techniques.

* GOODWIN, MARY, AND G. POLLEN, *Creative Food Experiences for Children,* 1974. Available from the Center for Science in the Public Interest, 1779 Church St., Washington, D.C. 20036.
Filled with nutrition facts and activities to help preschool children learn about eating, preparing foods, health, their bodies, and other topics related, in the broadest sense, to food.

* GORDON, IRA, *Baby Learning Through Baby Play: A Parent's Guide for the First Two Years.* New York: St. Martin's Press, 1970. Also, with BARRY GUINAGH and R. EMILE JESTER, *Child Learning Through Child Play: Learning Activities for Two- and Three-Year-Olds.* New York: St. Martin's Press, 1972.
Easy-to-do, fun learning games for babies and young children, using common household materials and everyday experiences as a basis for the activities. Includes simple explanations of children's developmental needs at different stages, with special consideration to the development of a healthy self-concept through experiencing success and enjoyment in the activities and other interactions with their caregivers.

* GRAND, CAROLE, AND RAHLA GOLD, *Guiding the Learning Process: A Manual for Teachers of Young Children.* New York: Harper & Row, Publishers, 1973.
Takes the beginning teacher of preschool children from the point of planning for the children's arrival through setting up a classroom and engaging in various activities with children. Includes general suggestions as well as specific games and activities related to music, dramatic play, language arts, and so on. Good section on discipline and guidance and one on relationships with parents.

\* GREGG, ELIZABETH, and members of the staff of the Boston Children's Medical Center, *What to Do When "There's Nothing to Do."* New York: Dell Publishing Co., Inc., 1968.
601 easy-to-do, imaginative play ideas for babies, toddlers, and two- to six-year-olds, using ordinary household items such as milk cartons, corks, cereal boxes, pots and pans, and paper bags. Fun things to do with children or for them to do on their own, with special suggestions of which things to do when parent or child is feeling "out of sorts."

GRIFFIN, L., *Books in Preschool: A Guide to Selecting, Purchasing, and Using Children's Books,* 1970. Also, *Multi-Ethnic Books for Young Children,* 1970. Available from NAEYC, 1629 Twenty-first St., N.W., Washington, D.C. 20009
Booklets to help parents and preschool teachers find books to suit individual children and groups. The latter lists and annotates children's books with an accent on different cultures such as American Indians and Eskimos, Appalachia and the Southern Mountains, and Afro-Americans. The former explains the function of reading in the preschool and gives techniques for reading to children, instructions to help children make their own books, and an extensive list of resources related to children's books.

HENDRICKS, GAY AND RUSSEL WILLS, *The Centering Book: Awareness Activities for Children, Parents, and Teachers.* Englewood Cliffs, N.J.: Prentice-Hall, Inc., 1975.
Contains activities to help children and adults focus, relax, develop skill in visual imagery, and the like, stressing development of aspects of the mind and body ordinarily given little or no attention in traditional educational programs.

\* HARTLEY, RUTH E., AND ROBERT GOLDENSON, *The Complete Book of Children's Play* (rev. ed.). New York: Thomas Y. Crowell Company, 1963.
Describes the function and form of play at different stages in children's lives from birth through the teen-age years. Includes descriptions of characteristic behaviors and suggests activities to enhance children's development at each stage. Instructions and illustrations for making different kinds of play materials and equipment are given.

HEFTER, RICHARD, AND MARTIN MOSKOF. *A Shufflebook.* U.S.A.: Western Publishing Company, Inc., 1970.
104 durable, wipe-clean two-sided cards, each side with an illustration and a word, phrase, or number (e.g., "and the fireman," "screamed," "and the chicken," "ate"). To be put together in any combination, creating an unlimited number of stories to use in developing reading skills and vocabulary.

\* HODGEN, LAUREL, JUDITH KOETTER, BEVERLY LaFORSE, SUE McCORD, AND DAISY SCHRAM, *School Before Six: A Diagnostic Approach.* Ithaca, N.Y.: Cornell University (Dept. of Human Development and Family Studies, N.Y. State College of Human Ecology), 1970.
Contains diagnostic games to assess children's level of skill in the areas of large motor, small motor, perceptual motor, language, socio-emotional, and conceptual development, accompanied by discussions of how to interpret children's responses and suggestions for helping children in areas of deficit. Describes hundreds of interesting and stimulating activities with notes as to their use in developing these different areas of skill. Also includes section called "Trash to Treasures" on using "junk" to make materials for an early education program.

HOLLANDER, CORNELIA. *Portable Workshop for Preschool Teachers.* Garden City, N.Y.: Doubleday & Company, Inc., 1966.
Ten booklets in a slip-case to give teachers of young children ideas for activities in art, language, dramatic play, music, and other areas.

\* HOPKINS, TOM, AND MARIANA JESSEN, *A Kindergarten Curriculum Guide for Indian Children: A Bilingual-Bicultural Approach.* Dallas, Texas: Jarvis Press, 1970.
Explains the types of experiences young children need and describes materials needed for

these experiences. Includes patterns for making materials and equipment for indoor and outdoor activities. Although oriented to young Indian children, it can help people working with young children of every cultural origin. Insights gained about ways of orienting daily activities to make them meaningful for Indian children should alert teachers to considerations they should make about all their children.

* HUNTINGTON, DOROTHY, SALLY PROVENCE, and RONALD PARKER (eds.), *Day Care: Serving Infants.* Washington, D.C.: Superintendent of Documents, U.S. Government Printing Office, 1971.
Includes a discussion of babies' needs in relation to adults; explains considerations in setting up a day care program for infants, with particular emphasis on relationships with parents; and provides activities for children from birth to three years in the areas of language, thinking, gross motor, fine motor, self-awareness, and social responsiveness and mastery. Includes lists of materials needed to set up an infant-toddler center plus ones that can be homemade.

ISAACS, SUSAN, *The Nursery Years: The Mind of the Child from Birth to Six Years.* New York: Schocken Books, 1968.
Sensitive and humane review of how children develop, why they behave as they do at different stages, and what the best response of a parent is. Playthings and activities are discussed in a separate section as well as in relation to developmental changes.

* JOHNSON, DORIS and HELMER MYKLEBUST, *Learning Disabilities: Educational Principles and Practice.* New York: Grune & Stratton, 1967.
Explains the various kinds of learning disabilities and suggests activities for remediation, in preschool and school-age children. Many of the activities can be used for normal children also.

KAPLAN, SANDRA, JO ANN KAPLAN, SHEILA MADSEN, and BETTE TAYLOR, *Change for Children: Ideas and Activities for Individualized Learning.* Pacific Palisades, Calif.: Goodyear Publishing Company, Inc., 1973.
Well-illustrated ideas for structuring a classroom into different kinds of functional activity areas. Though written for school-age open classroom experiences, might stimulate similar ideas for the preschool teacher. Some of the activity ideas, also, can be adapted for younger children.

KING, EDITH. *Educating Young Children . . . Sociological Interpretations.* Dubuque, Iowa: Wm. C. Brown Company Publishers, 1973.
Explains the "hidden curriculum" of preschool situations, the nature of the interactions between teacher and children and among the children; proposes a focus on worldmindedness in early childhood education settings and recommends resources appropriate for developing such a program.

LAVATELLI, CELIA (ed.), *Language Training in Early Childhood Education.* Urbana, Ill.: University of Illinois Press, 1971.
Includes discussions of theoretical issues related to language learning, some examples of training procedures that work, and some methods that preschool teachers can use to evaluate children's level of language comprehension and usage in order to help guide their language learning better.

LEWIS, WANDA, AMY BURGE, and WALTER HODGES. *Learning Activities Manual.* Atlanta, Ga.: Georgia State University, Dept. of Early Childhood Education, 1971.
Intended for use in the Parent Supported Follow Through Program (a program designed to help children in the early primary grades build on a foundation provided by a full-year Head Start or similar preschool program), it can be used in either the home or the classroom. Many of the ideas are applicable to preschool children. Includes section explaining how to develop and write learning activities.

* LORTON, MARY, *Workjobs: Activity-Centered Learning for Early Childhood Education.* Menlo Park, Calif.: Addison-Wesley Publishing Company, 1972.
Activities to develop language and math skills, using mostly inexpensive and "throw-away" items. Designed for children in the early elementary grades, most of the activities are appropriate for kindergarteners. Each activity is pictured with a child playing it and includes a description of skills to be learned and an explanation of getting started, doing the activity, following it up, and materials needed to put it together.

LOWELL, EDGAR, and MARGUERITE STONER, *Play It by Ear.* Wolfer Publishing Company, 1960. Compiled by the John Tracy Clinic (806 W. Adam Blvd., Los Angeles, Calif. 90007).
Auditory training games to help deaf and hard-of-hearing children learn to listen to and make sense out of sounds, to the extent that their hearing makes this possible. Many of the activities can be used or adapted for young children who can hear, to help them make maximum use of their hearing capacity. Techniques and instructions to make materials for motivating and rewarding children's responses can be particularly useful for working with children with learning and attention problems.

* MONTESSORI, MARIA, *Dr. Montessori's Own Handbook.* New York: Schocken Books, 1965.
Describes, systematically and with accompanying photographs, the key elements of the Montessori method and materials for early childhood education. Another which does this, but more in the context of the philosophical foundations of the approach, is *The Discovery of the Child* (New York: Ballantine Books, 1967).

MORRIS, EARL (ed.), *Early Childhood Education in Illinois: Focus on Kindergarten.* State of Illinois: Division of Instruction, Office of the Superintendent of Public Instruction, 1970.
Contains guidelines for developing a kindergarten curriculum, including discussion of the various kinds of activities and materials needed. Also covers administrative and planning issues.

* NIMNICHT, GLEN, ORALIE MCAFEE, and JOHN MEIER, *The New Nursery School.* New York: General Learning Corporation, 1969.
Includes six Learning Activities Booklets with activities related to developing a positive self-image, the senses and perceptual acuity, language development, concept formation, and problem-solving. Also includes a good section on classroom management and control and a description of various toys and materials to use in teaching young children. Especially interesting is a section on the use of O. K. Moore's "autotelic, responsive environment booths"—areas with electric typewriters adapted to enable pre-school children to teach themselves, at their own pace, to read and write on the typewriter.

* NORMAN, SARALIE (ed.), *Coordinated Helps in Language Development (CHILD).* Portland, Oregon: Northwest Regional Educational Laboratory, 1970.
Series of simple, easily-followed activities classified according to instructional goals to "expand language power" and "link language and thought." The goals are: hears and imitates sound of language, increases vocabulary, extends meanings, expands language patterns, expresses feelings, conveys imagination, classifies things, solves problems, expresses abstract reasoning. Includes sample letters to parents explaining school activities and giving suggestions for follow-up at home.

NUFFIELD MATHEMATICS PROJECT, *Environmental Geometry.* New York: John Wiley and Sons, Inc., 1969.
Ideas to help children five to thirteen learn principles of geometry as they relate to the things around us; activities actively involve children in constructing, drawing, measuring, and the like to discover how the shape of things influences their relation to other things,

and so on. There is an entire series of books describing the theory and practice of the Nuffield math project in addition to this one, including *I Do and I Understand, Beginnings, Your Child and Mathematics, Shape and Size,* and others.

OSMON, FRED, *Patterns for Designing Children's Centers.* New York: Educational Facilities Laboratories, Inc. (477 Madison Ave.), 1971.
Contains patterns for such things as the organization of a children's center, a place for parents and children to part or meet, and special activity areas. Suggests interesting ideas for the use of space, and includes drawings.

PITCHER, EVELYN, MIRIAM LASHER, SYLVIA FEINBURG, and NANCY HAMMOND, *Helping Young Children Learn.* Columbus, Ohio: Charles E. Merrill Publishing Company, 1966.
Creative activities in the areas of art, music, literature, science, cooking, carpentry, waterplay, and various academic preliminaries. Instructions for activities reflect a concern for children's being allowed to develop at their own pace in their own creative directions through sensitive and informed teacher guidance.

ROSENAU, FRED, and BETTY TUCK, *The Parent/Child Toy-Lending Library.* Washington, D.C.: Superintendent of Documents, U.S. Government Printing Office, 1972.
"The Toy Library program actively involves parents in educational activities with their own 3- to 5-year-old children. Both during and after a short 8-session training program, each parent is able to use a variety of toys and games at home to stimulate the growth of her preschool child's intellectual skills and to enhance his self-concept." Explains how to develop such a program, including finding funds for it. Toys basic to the program are pictured and described, including instructions on how to make some of them.

RUDOLPH, NANCY, *Workyards—Playgrounds Planned for Adventure.* New York: Teachers College Press, 1974.
Describes and provides illustrations of playgrounds which recognize children's need to work and be productive and constructive in their play. These "workyards" are easier and less expensive to put together than complex, concrete, adult-designed and adult-oriented playgrounds, and this book should provide many ideas for starting one.

SCHAEFFER, CHARLES, *Becoming Somebody: Creative Activities for Preschool Children.* Buffalo, N.Y.: D.O.K. Publishers, Inc., 1973.
Simple, imaginative activities to develop children's innate creativity. Send for their catalog for other activities books for preschool and school-age children.

SHAKESBY, PAUL. *Child's Work: A Learning Guide to Joyful Play.* Philadelphia, Penn.: Running Press, 1974.
Montessori-based activities with instructions for making toys and materials, using common household materials, to use in the games.

SMITH, CARTER and SARA STEIN, *Games to Grow On.* Open Family Press, 40 E. 23rd St., N.Y., N.Y.
Two kits, one for babies and toddlers, the other for preschoolers, containing toys, materials, activity cards, and cards explaining how, when, and why to use the activities. Also from the Open Family Press, a series of books to help parents open up communication with their children about such potentially anxiety-producing life situations as going to the hospital, and dying.

\* STANT, MARGARET, *The Young Child: His Activities and Materials.* Englewood Cliffs, N.J.: Prentice-Hall, Inc., 1972.
Full of ideas for activities for young children, two to five years, in all the various nursery school areas—two- and three-dimensional arts and crafts, music, stories, dramatic play, science, oral language, math, social studies. Instructions for making all sorts of materials for games as well as large indoor and outdoor equipment.

STEED, FREIDA R. *A Special Picture Cookbook*, 1974. Available from H & H Enterprises, Inc., Box 3342, Lawrence, Kansas 66044.
Written for use in teaching retarded children and adults to cook, this book can be used with normal preschool children to guide them in learning to cook before they can read the words for recipes.

\* TILTON, JAMES, DONNA LISKA, and JACK BOURLAND (eds.), *Guide to Early Developmental Training*. Lafayette, Indiana: Wabash Center for the Mentally Retarded, Inc., 1972.
Contains motor, cognitive, and language development norms and activities coordinated with those norms to enable a teacher to guide a child step by step from wherever he is (in terms of self-care skills, number concepts, motor, cognitive, and language development) to the next stage in development. Especially useful are hundreds of pages of simple, fun motor activities to develop balance and posture, perceptual-motor, locomotion, and body image skills. Written for use with mentally retarded children, the activities can be used for any child.

UPCHURCH, BEVERLY, *Easy-to-Do Toys and Activities for Infants and Toddlers*. Greensboro, North Carolina: The Infant Care Project (University of North Carolina), 1971. (Send for their complete catalog of materials for those who work with infants and toddlers.)
Attractively illustrated booklet about making toys for young children; instructions for simple toys for infants, toddlers, and two-year-olds. Suggestions for activities, ideas for wall decorations, hints to the adult for collecting and storing materials.

USLANDER, ARLENE, and CAROLINE WEISS, *Helping Kids Understand Sex*. Palo Alto, Calif.: Learning Handbooks (530 University Ave.), 1975.
". . . provides practical and specific answers to questions of kindergarten through junior high children and a classroom-tested approach to presenting sex education in a relaxed, non-threatening way. It contains detailed descriptions for a number of lessons. This humanistic approach to sex education will help you deal with children's questions, misconceptions, fears, and anxieties about sex, their own sexuality, and growing up."

UTZINGER, ROBERT, *Some European Nursery Schools and Playgrounds*. New York: Educational Facilities Laboratories, Inc., 1970.
Describes and shows photographs of interesting indoor and outdoor play spaces for young children in various European countries. Persons involved in designing such spaces will find many stimulating ideas from the pictures and from the section on Conclusions and Recommendations.

WEIKART, DAVID, *The Cognitive Curriculum*. Ypsilanti, Michigan: High-Scope Educational Research Foundation (125 N. Huron), 1970.
Describes the theoretical framework and methodology of the Ypsilanti Preschool Curriculum Demonstration Project, a program based on Piaget's theory of how children's thinking develops. Includes explanations of classroom structure, daily schedule, typical activities, and purpose and function of each of the different activity areas (e.g., science, music) in terms of Piagetian constructs.

## OTHER PUBLICATIONS

"A Multicultural Bibliography for Preschool through Second Grade—Black, Spanish-Speaking, Asian-American, and Native American Cultures," 1972. Available from Multicultural Resources, P.O. Box 2945, Stanford, Calif. 94305

\* ARNOLD, LEONA, "Ideas for Putting a Day Care Classroom Together and Things to Make and Do with Children," The Bank Street College of Education, 610 W. 112th St., N.Y. 10025. (Request that they send a list of available resources.)
Mimeographed booklet containing lots of ideas for collecting, making, and using materials and equipment for early childhood education programs. Good, simple illustrations accompany descriptions of equipment and materials to make as well as activities.

BLAKESLEE, ALTON, and BRIAN SULLIVAN, *Your Child's Health.* The Associated Press, 1974.
Practical information on the care of children's physical and mental health needs. Answers many questions parents have on these subjects.

*Childhood Education.* Association for Childhood Education International. 3615 Wisconsin Ave. N.W., Washington, D.C. 20016. Ask for a list of their other publications.
Journal "for those concerned with children from infancy through early adolescense." Includes articles dealing with early childhood education practices and techniques.

\* *Children Today.* Available from the Superintendent of Documents, U.S. Government Printing Office, Washington, D.C. 20402. Journal of the U.S. Department of Health, Education, and Welfare, Office of Child Development, Children's Bureau.
Articles about children's programs across the country; occasionally includes ones related specifically to activities for young children.

"Closer Look Report," National Information Center for the Handicapped, Box 1492, Washington, D.C. 20013.
Newsletter for the national information center concerned with handicapped children and adults. Write to *Closer Look* to have your name added to the mailing list to receive materials, free of charge, including a guide to finding services for handicapped children, information packets, information about rights of handicapped children to public education under state laws, information about how to organize parent groups, and the newsletter.

"Criteria for Selecting Play Equipment for Early Childhood Education," free from Community Playthings, Dept. 2, Rifton, N.Y. 12471.
A pamphlet outlining and describing the characteristics of good toys and materials for young children and including a chart of toys which will be enjoyed by children at different ages from three to five in their play in different areas (e.g., block and dramatic play, creative arts, and books).

\* *Day Care and Early Education.* 72 Fifth Ave., New York, N.Y. 10011.
"Magazine of the child growth movement," includes features designed to inform people involved in early childhood education about programs, resources, legislation, and other shared concerns. Regular features relating to activities and materials include "Learning Set-Ups" (a series of simple activities for infants, toddlers, and preschoolers), "Material Things" (a column that reviews available materials for preschool education), and "Recipes for Fun."

Early Childhood Education Study, "A Useful List of Classroom Items That Can Be Scrounged or Purchased." Newton, Mass.: Educational Development Center (55 Chapel St.)
Mimeographed paper, notes kinds of businesses, shops, and factories that can be asked for discarded materials to use in the preschool and elementary school classroom; free and inexpensive materials to use in different areas of the educational program (e.g., playground, house corner, dramatic play, shops, math); supplies to purchased, with note of manufacturers.

*Early Years.* Box 1223, Darien, Conn. 06820.
"A magazine for teachers of preschool through grade 3," filled with ideas for activities and materials to use with young children.

\* *ERIC/ECE Newsletter.* University of Illinois at Urbana-Champaign, 805 W. Pennsylvania Ave., Urbana, Ill. 61801.
The newsletter of the national clearinghouse for resources and information in early childhood education, it contains notification of resources available through the clearinghouse, information and resources in the field that have been brought to the attention of people responsible for publishing the newsletter, and activity ideas that can be put to use by teachers in early childhood education. It's a forum for the exchange of information, resources, and ideas in the field.

EVANS, BRENT, *Instant Play and Learn Games,* free from The Quaker Oats Company, Chicago, Illinois 60654 (Include a self-addressed envelope and four stamps).
Ten pages of games from the Life Cereal Learning Program, including activities to stimulate visual alertness and curiosity, laterality and directionality, visual motor and small muscle control, and other skills in preschool and school age children.

\* FEITSHANS, SANDY and MANA TRAUB (eds.), *SWAP,* free from Herman M. Adler Center School, P.O. Box 1048, Champaign, Illinois 61820.
"Booklet designed for teachers of regular classrooms who are daily confronted with problem children," includes simple and fun activities for preschool and school age exceptional children. Ideas are very useful for normal children too.

"Fun in the Making." Washington, D.C.: Dept. of Health, Education, and Welfare, Office of Child Development, 1973. Order from the Superintendent of Documents, U.S. Government Printing Office, Washington, D.C. 20402.
Booklet of ideas for making children's toys and games from throw-away materials usually found in the home (e.g., egg cartons, paper towel rolls, milk cartons, shoeboxes).

\* GOLICK, MARGARET, *A Parents' Guide to Learning Problems.* Montreal, Canada: Quebec Association for Children with Learning Disabilities, 4820 Van Horne Ave., Montreal, Quebec, Canada H3W 1J3, 1970.
Easily understood short explanation of problems that interfere with learning in preschool and school age children plus fun activities parents can do at home to help their learning disabled children. Activities are appropriate for normal preschool children also.

HUCKLESBY, SYLVIA, "Opening Up the Classroom: A Walk Around the School," ERIC Clearinghouse on Early Childhood Education, 1971. Available from the College of Education Curriculum Library, University of Illinois, 1210 W. Springfield Ave., Urbana, Ill. 61801.
Paper with ideas to help elementary school teachers open up their classrooms, using the children's spontaneous interest as a stimulus for many different kinds of learning activities. Many of its ideas are applicable to or can be adapted for preschool children.

\* *Learning: The Magazine for Creative Teaching.* Education Today Company, Inc., 530 University Ave., Palo Alto, Calif. 94301.
Features articles dealing with innovations, strategies, and opinions related to creative teaching. Of most interest to preschool teachers probably will be the section called "The Learning Center," which contains specific teaching ideas, information related to learning materials, and related items.

MAZYCK, AURELIA. "Suggested Equipment and Supplies for Infant-Toddler Center." Greensboro, N.C.: Infant Care Project (University of North Carolina), 1969.
Includes list of furnishings, linens and supplies, toys, books, and records with manufacturers

and price at the time of purchase of items bought for a program of all-day care for 15 infants and 10 to 12 toddlers. Also included is a list of household items used for toys with their purpose in different kinds of activities.

OJEMANN, RALPH, et al. *What Can We Do Today, Mommy? A Parents' Manual of Preschool Home Experiences.* Available from the Psychology Dept., Educational Research Council of America, Rockefeller Bldg., Cleveland, Ohio 44113.
Booklet for parents suggesting simple-to-do activities utilizing everyday experiences and household materials.

*Preschool Equipment for a Multi-Use Center* and *Children's Things.* Available from Stone Mountain, 60 Broad St., Westfield, Mass. 01085.
Booklets giving instructions for making inexpensive indoor and outdoor play equipment.

\* *Preschool Quarterly.* Cooperative Extension Service, 33 Stanley Hall, University of Missouri, Columbia, Mo. 65201.
An excellent small magazine for early childhood teachers. Contains lots of useful ideas about young children, programs, and activities. Also available from the same address: *Focus on Early Childhood Education*, a book with activities for three- to six-year olds.

RAMOS, SUZANNE, "Buying Toys for Babies," 1974. Free from Toy Manufacturers of America, Inc., 200 Fifth Ave., New York, N.Y. Ask also for "Choosing Toys for Children of All Ages."
Pamphlets describing the kinds of activities babies and young children engage in at different stages and what sorts of toys they may enjoy.

RASMUSSEN, MARGARET (ed.), "Creating with Materials for Work and Play." Washington, D.C.: Association for Childhood Education International (3615 Wisconsin Ave., N.W.), 1957. Ask them to send a list of other publications also.
A folder with twelve separate leaflets, each covering a different area (e.g., drawing and painting materials, puppetry, simple instruments). Each contains a short discussion of the importance of the area to children's development, descriptions of materials recommended (and, where appropriate, how to make them), how they might be used by young children, and a reference list.

SAUNDERS, MINTA, and MARY ELIZABETH KEISTER. *Curriculum for the Infant and Toddler.* Greensboro, N.C.: Infant Care Project (University of North Carolina), 1971.
"This slide series and script make the point that day-to-day caregiving and play are full of opportunities for learning by babies, toddlers, and their caregivers. It is designed to help those who care for very young children develop awareness of the many learnings infants and toddlers are achieving every waking moment of every day."

SCHNEIDER, MARLENE, "A Turtle Manual." Department of Psychology, Point of the Woods Laboratory School, Stony Brook, N.Y. 11794.
Written by a teacher of school-age children with behavioral problems to help them cope with their frustrations and become more in control of their own behavior, the techniques can be adapted for preschool children also.

Selected U.S. Government Publications, Issued by the Superintendent of Documents, U.S. Government Printing Office, Washington, D.C.
Brochure describing new books and pamphlets published by the government, including ones related to living and learning with children. Ask to be put on their mailing list and to receive a copy of back-listed books available through the Supt. of Documents.

The Children's Museum, "Teacher Shop Catalog." The Jamaicaway, Boston, Mass. 02130.
A catalog of materials available from this self-service, try-it-yourself, shop, containing ideas about how to use them plus how to make things and get other things not carried by the Teacher Shop.

* *Teaching Exceptional Children.* 1920 Association Drive, Reston, Va. 22091.
  Journal containing ideas for working with children with all sorts of different special learning problems, needs, and challenges. An excellent resource for any special education teacher as well as for teachers of normal children, especially at this time when there is a growing trend to include children with special learning needs in regular classrooms. The "Teacher Idea Exchange" is a feature that should prove especially useful to teachers looking for interesting activities.

The Friends of Perry Nursery School, *The Scrap Book.* Available from Perry Nursery School, 1541 Washtenaw Ave., Ann Arbor, Mich. 48104.
  A pamphlet describing ways to use household scraps to provide activities for 3–5 year olds.

* VAN TASSEL, JEAN, *Pots and Pans: Activities for Parent and Child.* Free from Charmaine Young, Department of Exceptional Children, 907 West Nevada, Urbana, Illinois 61801.
  70 activities for parents to do at home with their young handicapped child, using everyday situations and common household items as teaching materials. These enjoyable learning games are appropriate, also, for normal preschool children, at home or in preschool situations.

*Voice for Children.* Day Care and Child Development Council of America, Inc. 1012 14th St., N.W., Washington, D.C. 20005.
  Newsletter including interesting articles about current events in day care program development, legislation, and so on. In addition, some issues feature articles about making equipment and inventing activities. DCCDCA also distributes and publishes materials and resources related to various aspects of child care including activities. Write for a copy of "Resources for Child Care."

WARNER, DIANE, and JEANNE QUILL, *Beautiful Junk.* Project Head Start, Office of Child Development, U.S. Dept. of Health, Education, and Welfare, Washington, D.C. 20201.
  Booklet including an annotated list of sources (e.g., grocery stores, telephone co.) of materials which could be obtained by a preschool or head start teacher for very little money or free to use in making equipment and materials for classroom activities. In addition, there are almost 50 illustrated ideas of ways to use "beautiful junk." Other Head Start booklets that might be useful for preschool teachers in planning activities and the play environment include: *Daily Program I, II, and III* (by Minnie Perrin Berson), *Equipment and Supplies,* and *Designing the Child Development Center* (by Ronald Haase).

* *Young Children.* National Association for the Education of Young Children (NAEYC), 1834 Connecticut Ave., N.W., Washington, D.C. 20009. The Journal of the National Association for the Education of Young Children.
  Full of articles with information and ideas about children and activities to engage in with them.

* "Young'uns," Free from Child Development Division, Governor's Office of Education and Training, Suite 182, Universities Center, 3825 Ridgewood Rd., Jackson, Miss. 39211.
  Newsletter of the Mississippi Child Development Council, includes information about and activities for preschool children.

# Index

# Index

Hide and Seek, 79–81
Say What I Say, 125–26
Who Was That?, 150–51
More Memory Games, 171
Getting Ready to Read, 198–99
Read Me a Story, 207–10
Tell Me a Story, 223–24
Be Very Quiet, 231–33
What's That Sound?, 237–41
attention span (*see* Attention span)
identifying voices, 69, 150–51
sound identification, 198–99
sound localization, 240

**B**

Baby-talk, 36
Ball play:
 activities:
  Play Ball, 101–102
  Feed the Bear, 140–42
  Kickball, 156–58
Behavior management, 26–29, 97–98, 98–101
 activities:
  Wait Is a Better Word than No, 97–98
  How Do You Say No to a Baby?, 98–101
  How Do You Feel about Me?, 129–32
  Remember and Do, 132–34
  Cleaning Up, 158–60
  Acting It Out, 205–207
  Be Very Quiet, 231–33
 and learning, 27
 methods
  attention, 26, 28, 99–100
  consistency, 5, 29, 56
  distraction, 99
  eye control, 100
  Golden Rule, 4
  humor, 100

modification of expectations, 99
No!, 100
prevention, 98–99
reinforcement and punishment, 26–29, 99–100
rules, 4
severe punishment, 27, 100
time-out, 28
Wait!, 97–98
 purpose, 27
Body image:
 activities:
  Touch and Name, 71
  Mirror Games, 74–75
  This Is Me, 109–11
  Do As I Do, Do As I Say, 115–17
  Happy Face, Sad Face, 121–22
  Getting Dressed, 135–38
  More Mirror Games, 184–85
  How Can You Move?, 220–23
  Working Together, 253–58

**C**

Children's growth records:
 activities:
  The Baby Book, 62–63
  This Is Me, 109–11
Classification skills, 138–40, 147–50, 158–60, 215–20, 229–31, 253–58
Cognitive development, 54–55, 92, 129, 174, 214–15, 244–45
 activities:
  Take a Walk with Baby, 68
  The Name Game, 69
  Touch and Feel, 70–71
  Fun in the Bathtub, 72–73
  Baby's First Book, 76–79
  Hide and Seek, 79–81
  The Toy behind the Screen, 81–83